A USER GUIDE
TO THE

SYSTEM

A USER GUIDE
TO THE
UNIX™
SYSTEM

Rebecca Thomas PhD
Jean Yates

OSBORNE/McGraw-Hill
Berkeley, California

Disclaimer of Warranties
and Limitation of Liabilities

UNIX is a trademark of Bell Laboratories. *A User Guide to the UNIX
System* is not sponsored or approved or connected with Bell
Laboratories. All references to UNIX in the text of this book are to the
trademark of Bell Laboratories.

CP/M is a registered trademark of Digital Research.

Othello is a registered trademark of Gabriel Industries Inc.

UNIQUE is a trademark of InfoPro Systems.

Portions of information appearing in Chapter 7, "The UNIX System
Resources," have been reprinted with permission of InfoPro Systems
from the InfoPro Systems newsletter, "UNIQUE™" (formerly "The
UNIX Software List").

Published by
Osborne/McGraw-Hill
2600 Tenth Street
Berkeley, California 94710
U.S.A.

For information on translations and book distributors outside of the U.S.A., please write
Osborne/McGraw-Hill at the above address.

A USER GUIDE TO THE UNIX™ SYSTEM

Cover design by KLT van Genderen
Editor for this book was Denise E.M. Penrose.
Technical reviews were completed by Eugene Dronek and Robert Greenberg.

ACKNOWLEDGMENTS

THERE ARE SO MANY PEOPLE TO THANK, it is impossible to name them all. Some stand out in our minds and are mentioned here.

First and foremost, we would like to thank Denise E.M. Penrose for her editing and management assistance. Also Joanne Clapp, who logged countless late night hours at the terminal to get the manuscript just right. Thanks to Eugene Dronek for an excellent edit and many useful suggestions, and Robert Greenberg for his editorial comments. We appreciate the assistance given by John W. Fisher, of the legal department at Western Electric, in naming this book. We also thank Armando Stettner and Karen Shannon of DEC for catching some errors in the first printing.

We appreciate Gnostic Concepts and MicroPro's understanding and support in getting out this book, and the perseverance of all our friends who listened to nothing but discussions related to the UNIX system for the last year. Thanks are also due to the University of California at Berkeley for access to the system — it made this book possible.

We thank those who have offered suggestions for this book and welcome more. Our address is Box 22411, San Francisco, CA 94122.

And last but not least, we acknowledge the excellent work performed as paperweights, paper shredders, and cheerleaders by our four cats, Pestilence, Bobo, Beetle, and Nub.

Thanks also to Uni-ops for many of the items in our resources chapter, and for the use of their annotated bibliography, which forms the heart of our own.

R.T.
J.Y.

CONTENTS

INTRODUCTION

A COMPUTER IS NOT A SINGLE ENTITY; it is an interrelated system of hardware devices and software programs. The traffic director that keeps these components running together smoothly is the operating system program. Today the UNIX system is one of the most powerful operating systems available for mainframe computers, minicomputers, and microcomputers.

Bell Laboratories scientists designed the UNIX system to be changed easily. They did not develop the system for a single research project or a specific computer, or as a commercial product. As a machine-independent operating system, the UNIX system has the potential for broad applications in educational, industrial, and commercial environments.

An *operating system* is a set of programs that controls and organizes the activities of a computer. The UNIX operating system directs the activities of the components, simultaneously manages multiple users, allows those users to perform several tasks at once, and manages the system's files without user participation or supervision. The simple interaction between users and the system, the versatility of the system, and the elegant system design explain the increasing popularity of the UNIX system.

The power and capabilities of the UNIX system can overwhelm beginners, but you can learn to use it with little previous computer experience. Bell Laboratories has thoroughly documented the UNIX system, but the material was written by and for internal programmers and research scientists, and is often too technical for many users. Furthermore, the UNIX system is large and general, and the Bell Laboratories documentation thoroughly describes the entire system, including almost 200 commands. This book covers a subset of the total system, the most frequently used commands. We focus on this essential material to present a solid foundation to beginners, and to isolate the core information everyone needs to use the UNIX system successfully.

If this is your first experience with the UNIX system, or even with computers, this book has been written for you. We define and examine the system's basic concepts and terms and provide computer-side tutorials for immediate, practical fluency.

If you are already familiar with the UNIX system, you will find this book an excellent reference to the most frequently used commands and to a wealth of consumer information about UNIX system software. If you are considering using the UNIX system, this book can help you evaluate it for your specific application.

This book was written on the UNIX system adapted for the University of California at Berkeley by their computer science department. As closely as possible, we have presented "plain vanilla" Version 7 of the UNIX system. However, even with this version there are different ways to set up the system. If you are working in a multi-user environment on DEC PDP-11 or VAX equipment with Version 7, this book will largely conform to your system. Many commercial installations use Version 6, which is generally compatible with the discussion in this book. Recently, System III was introduced by Bell. This book is compatible with System III with some minor exceptions.

Microcomputer systems based on Bell Laboratories' UNIX operating system, such as Zilog's System 8000 and Onyx's 8002 computer, have made discernible additions to the total system, rather than changes to the basic commands we present. If you are using a microcomputer, review the documentation supplied by the vendor to determine any differences between versions. Systems like the UNIX system, as listed in Appendix A, differ significantly from the UNIX system, and this book's tutorials and command summaries may not apply.

Chapter 1 briefly chronicles the development of the UNIX system by Bell Laboratories, highlighting the evolution of the C language and introducing contemporary applications.

Chapter 2 illustrates single-user and multi-user computer systems, describes the functions of hardware components, examines the software system, and introduces the UNIX operating system for multi-user systems.

In Chapter 3 you begin work. Several computer-aided tutorials focus on your first interactions with the UNIX system. Screen displays accompany the sessions for readers without access to a terminal. These tutorials introduce fundamental concepts and will prepare you for the commands described in Chapter 4.

The basic UNIX system commands are treated in Chapter 4. Each command description is accompanied by examples, screen displays, error messages, and optional input.

Chapter 5 describes how the UNIX system functions in business environments. Text editing, text processing, accounting systems, data base management, and other functions are considered as constituent elements of an automated office system network.

To help you evaluate the UNIX system for your current and future computing needs, Chapter 6 describes how the system functions in specific applications. This chapter explains how to gain access to UNIX software and examines time-sharing and educational opportunities.

Chapter 7 lists related UNIX system resources, including hardware suppliers, software vendors, time-sharing systems, university facilities, newsletters, and user groups.

Appendices include several tables used in programming and text processing, a complete summary of all 200 commands in the UNIX system, and a glossary. If an italicized term is not explained in the text, you will find it in the glossary.

The annotated bibliography provides an excellent reference to a broad range of sources, from introductory material to specific technical papers describing the UNIX system.

Appendix F summarizes basic information about the UNIX system. We recommend you use the appendix frequently as you interact with the UNIX system. We also strongly recommend you read this book while seated in front of the computer. Beginning with the tutorials, enter each example and try each command; do not merely read about them. You will become familiar with the UNIX system much sooner than you expected.

A HISTORY OF THE UNIX SYSTEM

Chapter 1

1

A HISTORY OF THE UNIX SYSTEM

Bell Laboratories was established in 1925. Owned jointly by Western Electric and AT&T, Bell Laboratories is one of the largest research groups in the world. It employs more than 23,000 people, owns patents on more than 18,000 products, and puts together thousands of technical publications and seminars each year. More than 60 scientific and engineering awards, including seven Nobel Prizes, have been awarded to Bell Laboratories scientists.

The corporate headquarters and one of several research facilities of Bell Laboratories are pictured in Figure 1-1.

Bell Laboratories serves several dynamic functions in the Bell System. As a basic research organization, Bell Laboratories investigates scientific fields relevant to communications, including mathematics and the physical sciences. At the forefront of applied research in communications technologies, it also designs and develops products, and provides systems engineering. All of the Bell System's facilities, as well as many independent telephone companies, use the UNIX system internally.

For a brief period in 1969, the Computing Science Research Department of Bell Laboratories used a General Electric 645 mainframe computer with an operating system called "Multics." Multics was an early multi-user interactive operating system. A *multi-user system* permits several users to run several programs simultaneously on the same computer. *Interactive* refers to the computer's almost immediate response to a typed-in command.

Previously, only batch-oriented operating systems were available. These systems required an intermediary process. To convey data or to

FIGURE 1-1: Bell Laboratories in Murray Hill, New Jersey

request information from the computer, you first "typed" coded punch cards which were subsequently processed (read) by the computer in large batches. Several minutes to several hours later, you received the printed results confirming your entry or fulfilling your request. This method was too slow for programmers who needed an immediate response from the system.

Although interactive, Multics still lacked capabilities which were essential to programmers. It retained certain batch mode characteristics that once preserved the privacy and security of each user's data, but now served to isolate the programmer's work. In 1969, Ken Thompson originated an operating system that would support coordinated teams of programmers in the development of products, and would simplify the dialog between human and machine, thus making computers more accessible to beginners and programmers alike. The result, the UNIX system, was not written all at once. It evolved in response to the programming requirements of specific projects, and continues to evolve today.

The Development of the System

One such project was a program Ken Thompson developed called "Space Travel." It simulated the movement of the major celestial bodies in the solar system. Finding the cost of single-user interaction with a mainframe computer to be prohibitive, Thompson rewrote "Space Travel" for a lower-cost minicomputer, a Digital Equipment Corporation (DEC) PDP-7. In Figure 1-2, Thompson operates a similar machine, the DEC PDP-11.

PHOTO COURTESY OF BELL LABORATORIES

FIGURE 1-2: Bell Laboratories scientist Ken Thompson, who helped develop the UNIX system

Minicomputers were the first systems inexpensive enough for a single university department or small company, and small enough for single-user interaction. However, there was limited software available for the PDP-7; it did not have the memory capability to store the source program for continuous development. Programs had to be written with the GE mainframe, then compiled, and then stored on paper tape. The object program on paper tape was then loaded to run on the PDP-7. While it was less expensive to run "Space Travel" on the minicomputer, any program changes had to be written on the GE mainframe before execution by the PDP-7. Continuous loading of the paper tape was a slow and vulnerable process. To both write and run programs on the minicomputer required developing the necessary software. Thompson wrote an operating system, a PDP-7 assembler, and several utility programs, all in assembly language specific to the PDP-7. The operating system was christened the UNIX system, a reference to the unified, team-programming environment it would serve.

The Evolution of the C Language

An operating system based on assembly language is "machine dependent." The program runs on one particular type or brand of computer and cannot be easily "transported" to a different computer. For this reason, Thompson developed the transportable language, B. The B language was modified by Dennis Ritchie, who developed the C language, and then rewrote UNIX software in C. The UNIX system, based on Multics and written in assembly language for the PDP-7, was now rewritten in C and could be moved to virtually any computer.

The C language has been used by software developers to write utility, operating system, and application programs for research and business uses. UNIX software includes many C programs. Some are incorporated as new system commands for users or system managers, while others perform specific functions in the system. For example, one program updates a data base describing the condition of industrial machinery, while another provides text editing functions. University professors and students have written numerous C programs compatible with UNIX software. Consequently, Western Electric sells licenses for the UNIX system with approximately 200 programs.

With the increasing power and decreasing cost of minicomputers, the

UNIX operating system rapidly became popular. These machines were quickly employed to control laboratory experiments, support machine-aided design, supervise telecommunications networks, and perform business functions. Developing software to fulfill these specific applications presented programmers with a new challenge, and the UNIX system offered effective tools to meet it. By 1978, more than 600 UNIX system installations were running in universities, government facilities, and the Bell System.

The System Today: The Programs

The UNIX system programs are functionally categorized as follows:

• The *kernel* schedules tasks and manages data storage.

• The *shell* is a program that connects and interprets the commands typed by a system user. It interprets user requests, calls programs from memory, and executes them one at a time or in a series called a "pipe."

• *Utility programs* perform a variety of routine and special system maintenance functions.

The UNIX system can be supplemented or modified by anyone who has licensed access to the source code. A large community of programmers has enhanced the system, including individuals with the University of California at Berkeley, Harvard University, and the Rand Corporation. The version of the UNIX system used at the University of California at Berkeley now includes Berkeley's vi and ex text editors, and other programs are being developed, including an engineering calculation program developed at California Institute of Technology that performs symbolic as well as numerical mathematics. These new programs will be joined by many more, adding to the library of available UNIX software.

Most operating systems include commands for moving and storing files, programming, and maintaining the system. Separate application programs are required for additional functions. The UNIX system utility programs include additional commands to edit text, create spelling dictionaries, imitate a desk calculator, prepare tables, and send electronic mail. Some UNIX system programs and their general applications are listed in Table 1-1.

TABLE 1-1: Programs in the UNIX System

Application	Program and/or Data File on UNIX System
Spelling dictionary	spell, /usr/dict/words
Desk calculator	dc, bc
Text editing	ed, [ex and vi (University of California, Berkeley)]
Text print formatting	ROFF, NROFF
Typesetting	TROFF
Accounting and invoicing system users	ac, sa, accton
Electronic mail	mail
Computer-aided instruction	learn
On-line manual for UNIX system	man
Formatting	tbl
Typeset mathematical equations	eqn
Interactive program debugger	adb
Assembler	as
Pattern scanning and processing language	awk
BASIC language interpreter	bas
Reminder service	calendar
C language compiler	cc, pcc
FORTRAN compiler (compatible with C)	f77
Relocating program loader	ld
Line printer spooler	lpr
Maintain program groups	make
Structured FORTRAN preprocessor	ratfor
Find and insert literature references in documents	refer, lookbib
Stream editor	sed
Command processing	sh, [csh (University of California, Berkeley)]
UNIX intersystem communication	uucp, unlog, uux
On-line communication	write, wall
Compiler generators	lex, yacc
File management	ar, cat, cd, chgrp, chmod, chown, cmp, comm, cp, diff, find, ln, ls, mkdir, mv, pr, rm, rmdir, tail, tar, touch
System status information	date, du, file, ps, pwd, stty, tty, who
System maintenance	clri, dcheck, df, dump, icheck, iostat, mkfs, mknod, mount, ncheck, quot, restore, sa, umount
Running program support	at, cron, echo, expr, kill, nice, sleep, tee, wait
Text processing (not including editors)	crypt, grep, look, sort, uniq, wc

The System Today: The Users

Educators, administrators, researchers, managers, and program developers adapt and employ UNIX systems to fulfill their specific needs, which might include

- Text preparation and printing
- Document storage and manipulation
- Programming
- Electronic mail.

Text preparation encompasses clerical, editorial, and production functions. The UNIX system has equation, table, and text preparation software that supports total in-house production of journals and books.

By creating functionally defined directories and invoking commands to manipulate them, you can create an "electronic filing cabinet" without procuring additional software.

Since the UNIX system was designed by and for programmers, it offers several major program development features. For many applications, programs can be written without a programming language. Users select and link together system commands to create specific programs within the shell program, called *shellscripts*.

Electronic mail is an integral part of the UNIX system. You can send messages to yourself, to other users in the same computer system, to users of other computers networked into your computer, or, by modem, to computers at distant locations. In many UNIX system installations, daily phone messages, departmental memos, reports, and accounting data are sent from person to person via their desk-top terminals. These desk-top units can be conventional CRT monitors, or they can be more powerful microcomputers.

The UNIX system is supplied to educational nonprofit organizations at a very low cost. Approximately 90% of university computer science departments license the UNIX system, and many advanced programmers and computer science majors learn to use the UNIX system and to program in the C language. It has been improved and continuously modified by several generations of computer science students and professors.

In universities, the system runs computers used for teaching and research projects. Programs calculate statistical results of experiments in biology, chemistry, computer science research, and other fields. Numerous data bases are developed and maintained on UNIX systems. At the University of California at Berkeley, one data base tracks the cancer-causing properties of common products, and correlates it to trends in populations consuming those products.

University administrative offices use UNIX software to speed office tasks. Letters and papers are typed using the **ed** command and other text editing programs, and the UNIX system's TROFF typesets many university publications. The system not only bills system users, but also handles the general accounting needs of the university. Throughout campuses accessing UNIX systems, departments develop separate mailing lists and data bases and prepare documents using the system programs.

Research institutions use UNIX systems for many of the same functions universities do. Bell Laboratories designers use the system to accelerate and simplify complex circuit design. In Figure 1-3 an engineer uses a computer-controlled wire-wrap machine to build a prototype

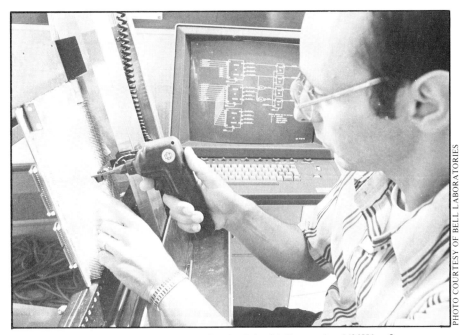

PHOTO COURTESY OF BELL LABORATORIES

FIGURE 1-3: Bell Laboratories scientist John Vollaro using UNIX software
to design circuits and control machines

electrical circuit. An experimental set of UNIX system programs allows him to design the circuit on a graphics display terminal and to control the wire-wrap machine. He uses the system to remember complex processes, and to alter these processes quickly. The computer displays results, and allows the scientist to "preview" the consequences of an action.

In Figure 1-4, a UNIX system program controls an experiment that tests the qualities of metals. It monitors and processes data as an instrument collects it, then evaluates the data and calculates the results of an experiment. Calculations that take several days to do by hand are performed almost instantly by the computer.

In 1979, Bell Laboratories introduced the UNIX system Seventh Edition and dramatically decreased the single-user binary license fee. This permitted computer manufacturers to economically develop UNIX software for use with licensed UNIX systems, and small businesses to license the UNIX system for their personal computers. In November of 1981, Bell released System III as the first "commercial" UNIX system. It has spurred great interest and costs less than Version Seven.

There are two ways to license UNIX software: *source licenses* and user, or *binary, licenses*. A computer manufacturer that wants to alter the UNIX system for its own product obtains an expensive source license from Western Electric. This source license provides the information required to change and rewrite UNIX software. A user, perhaps a small business, will obtain a much cheaper binary license from a company that owns a source license. To ensure compatibility, a user would generally obtain both the computer system and the UNIX system from the same source-licensed company.

The year 1980 marked a major change in the use of the UNIX system. It began to migrate from the academic and research environment of mainframes and minicomputers into the commercial world of microcomputers. A growing number of companies worked on or introduced products based on the UNIX system during 1981, and more are anticipated in 1982.

The UNIX system lacks some essential features for business applications. For example, the command names are obscure; **grep**, **pwd**, and **cat** do not convey a command function. With some commands it is easy to destroy files, and if you type a space in the wrong place you can erase everything you have stored in the system.

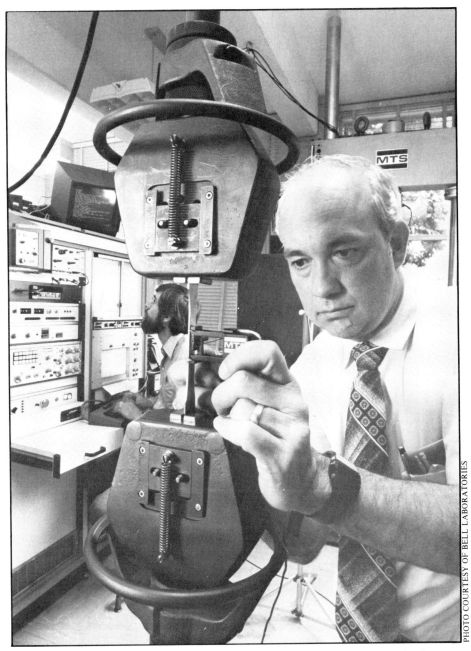

PHOTO COURTESY OF BELL LABORATORIES

FIGURE 1-4: Bell Laboratories engineers P. Leland Key and Bud C. Wonsiewicz
using the UNIX system to control metallurgical experiments

It often seems as if the system thinks "no news is good news." It prompts you only when you have made a mistake. No prompts, options, menus, or questions indicate you've done something *right*.

Users must remember a lot of commands: a reference card is essential. The card in common use at Bell Laboratories is 14 pages long. Many users won't need to learn the function of each level of command structure available in the system, yet moving from simple to complex levels is a necessary step for all users, and is initially quite confusing.

Computer manufacturers offering the UNIX system on their systems are adding help features to improve system/user interaction. Many large installations have added prompts and helpful on-screen aids to using the system.

COMPUTER SYSTEMS AND OPERATING SYSTEMS

Chapter 2

COMPUTER SYSTEMS AND OPERATING SYSTEMS

PEOPLE WHO USE COMPUTERS HAVE A vocabulary all their own. The tutorials in the next chapter assume you understand basic computer terms and concepts. In this chapter we will explain the role of hardware and software components in a single-user system, introduce multi-user systems, and describe the general functions of an operating system. If you are already familiar with computer systems you may wish to skip this chapter and begin working with the UNIX system in Chapter 3.

In general, *mainframe computers* are the largest and most sophisticated machines, *minicomputers* are intermediate, and *microcomputers* are the smallest. Yet the most powerful microcomputers offer greater capability than the least powerful minicomputers, and the most powerful minicomputers offer greater capability than the least powerful mainframes.

Comparisons of the power of these systems are based on the range of possible applications, the volume of data being processed, the speed of the processing, the way in which data is manipulated, the ability to accommodate multiple users and perform multiple tasks, and the number and variety of peripheral devices comprising the system.

Computer Systems: The Essential Elements

All computer systems share essential elements. It is the degree of complexity and power of one or more elements which differentiates computers. We will consider the following computer system elements:

- Central processing unit (CPU)
- Main memory
- Memory storage devices
- Data input devices
- Data output devices
- Software.

CPU

The central processing unit interprets and executes the instructions which comprise a computer program. A CPU can be a single microprocessor chip, a set of chips, or a box of boards of transistors, chips, wires, and connectors.

Differences in CPUs distinguish mainframe, mini- and microcomputers. Semiconductor manufacturing technology developed through the early 1970s, and in 1972 the first microprocessor (a complete processing unit on a single chip) was released.

Consider the size of the microprocessor shown in Figures 2-1 and 2-2. The microprocessor CPU is magnified to show detail in Figure 2-1, and lies in the square in the center of the package in Figure 2-2. In contrast, the CPU of a mainframe computer is shown in Figure 2-3. Notice the greater size and degree of complexity of the mainframe CPU. It consists of many chips like the microprocessor, connected together on several boards.

Main Memory

Memory stores information by recording electronic impulses as on or off states. Two types of electronic memory exist in all computers. *Read/write memory* (RAM) can be read from and written to; it changes as data and programs are moved into and out of memory by the computer. *Read-only memory* (ROM) can only be read from; it typically contains programs or data that are used continuously. Read-only memory is designed to stay the same; it cannot be modified, except with special hardware, because it cannot be written to.

Main memory contains the programs the CPU is executing and the

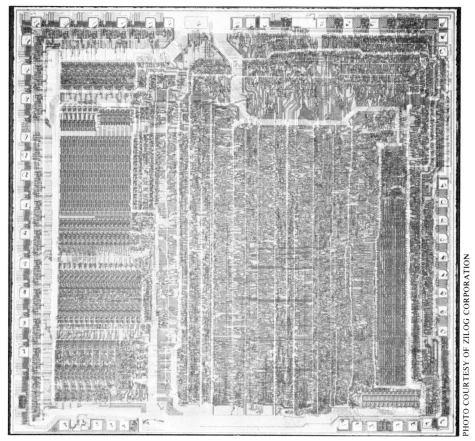

PHOTO COURTESY OF ZILOG CORPORATION

FIGURE 2-1: Detail of Z8000 microprocessor

data the programs affect. The contents of main memory continually change as programs are executed and results are stored. In multi-user systems, memory is shared among users. The CPU manages each program, bringing into memory only those portions of the programs currently being executed. When another portion of the program is needed, the CPU transfers it from storage to main memory.

Memory Storage Devices

Diskettes (or floppy disks), hard disks, and magnetic tapes store files of data, text, and programs. The magnetic surfaces used to store informa-

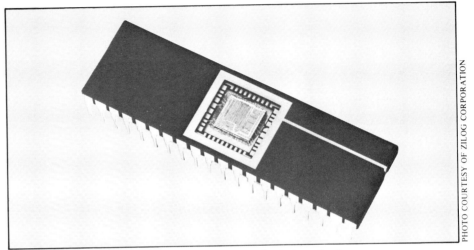

PHOTO COURTESY OF ZILOG CORPORATION

FIGURE 2-2: Microprocessors in their packaging

PHOTO COURTESY OF AMDAHL CORPORATION

FIGURE 2-3: Central processing unit of a mainframe computer

tion for computer systems are placed in units which read information from or write information to the magnetic surface. You may store data, text and programs in a library of magnetic surfaces.

Floppy disks, so named because they are made of a flexible material, store information as sequences of magnetic pulses on the surface of the disk. This information can be written onto the disk, or read from it, by means of a magnetic read/write head. This head can be compared to a phonograph stylus, in that it can be moved to different positions on the disk to access recorded information.

In all but the simplest single-user systems, a floppy disk will not hold enough information for business needs, and it will access information relatively slowly. Table 2-1 lists typical disk storage capacities.

Larger computer systems store data on *hard disks.* A hard disk is an aluminum plate, coated with a magnetic recording emulsion. As with floppy disks, information can be written to or read from the disk by a head located in the disk drive.

TABLE 2-1: Typical Storage Capacity of Various Devices

Device	Approximate Capacity in Bytes	Typical OEM Price-Drive Only
Optical disk	10^9 to 10^{11}	6,000
Mass storage system tape	10^8 to 10^{10}	28,000
½-inch tape	10^7 to 10^8	3,900
¼-inch cartridge	10^7 to 10^8	635
Data cassette	10^5 to 10^6	330
8-inch floppy disk	10^6 to 10^7	330
5¼-inch floppy disk	10^5 to 10^6	270
Minidata cassette	10^4 to 10^5	90
14-inch Winchester disk	10^7 to 10^9	2,900
8-inch Winchester disk	10^7 to 10^8	1,700
5¼-inch Winchester disk	10^6 to 10^7	900

Multi-user business applications need the greater speed and storage capabilities provided by hard disks. Hard disks can access any part of the disk in thousandths of a second. Information can be written onto the disk, or read from it, at approximately 1 million characters per second.

There are two types of hard disk drives: removable cartridge disk drives and Winchester disk drives (see Figures 2-4 and 2-5). Removable cartridge disk drives, as the name implies, house the hard disk in a container which can be removed from the disk drive. You can store information on a series of cartridge disks, which is similar to using a series of floppy disks or cassette tapes. The disks are stacked in a large box. Winchester disk drives have a rigid disk permanently sealed inside the drive. You cannot remove the disk, and you cannot store information on a series of disks. You are limited to the capacity of a single disk, but Winchester disk drives are the least expensive storage device available

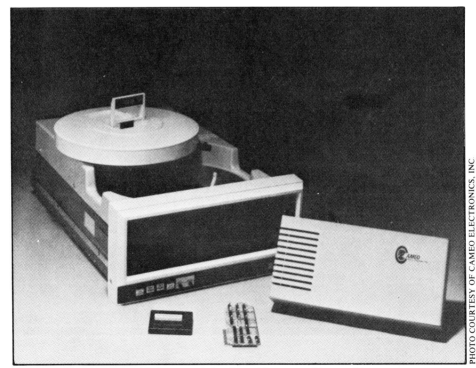

FIGURE 2-4: Hard disk drive with removable cartridge

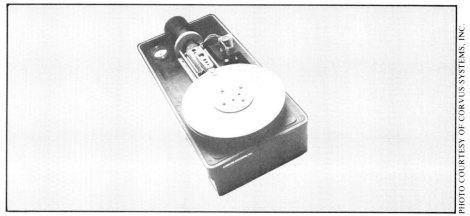

PHOTO COURTESY OF CORVUS SYSTEMS, INC.

FIGURE 2-5: Winchester drive

for the volume of data they access. They are faster and less expensive than cartridges, and less susceptible to damage. Floppy disks may be used to supplement data storage when the Winchester disks fill up.

Data Input Devices: Keyboards and Displays

Information is usually entered into a computer by typing characters on a keyboard. Almost all computer keyboards have the standard typewriter layout; a few extra keys denote special operations. Many keyboards offer an additional ten-key numeric pad on the right-hand side. The video display terminal, illustrated in Figure 2-6, is the most widely used device for communicating with a computer.

All terminals consist of the following four basic parts:

· The monitor, to display the characters
· The keyboard, to enter characters
· The control unit, to manipulate the display
· Communications, to connect the terminal to the computer.

All modern microcomputer systems include a monitor or screen to display both the dialogue between user and system and the information stored. Some specialized terminals display graphic images. Some have special keys for text editing, as shown in Figure 2-7.

PHOTO COURTESY OF INTERACTIVE SYSTEMS

Figure 2-6: Video display terminal and keyboard

Data Output Devices: Printers

Three common varieties of printers are shown in Figures 2-8, 2-9, and
2-10. They include

- Matrix printers that generate characters by printing dot patterns;
- Daisy-wheel printers that work like typewriters, and generate
  letter-quality printout; and
- Fast line printers that produce solid letter-quality characters, but
  use more expensive print mechanisms to print entire lines at
  once.

PHOTO COURTESY OF INTERACTIVE SYSTEMS

FIGURE 2-7: Specialized keyboard

Matrix printers offer the best value for your money if you do not need letter-quality printout. Matrix printers can print special characters or graphic symbols, since every character is generated as a series of dots. Most matrix printers generate characters using a 63-dot rectangle (seven dots wide and nine dots high). By stretching a single character across many character spaces, a matrix printer can generate large letters suitable for headings, labels, etc. Matrix printers can print 150 characters per second, and are generally quite reliable.

Typewriter-quality printers use a *daisy-wheel* print element. The element has 96 "petals," each with a character embossed on the tip. The element rotates until the required character petal is in front of a hammer, which then fires. In this fashion, lines are printed one character at a time. Daisy-wheel printers are reliable, but in computer terms they are quite slow, printing between 30 and 60 characters per second.

Most expensive *line printers* use a drum on which the characters are embossed. As the drum spins, the paper moves, and numerous hammers strike the characters, permitting the high-speed printing of entire lines of text. Line printers are fast and reliable; some can print 1,000 lines per minute.

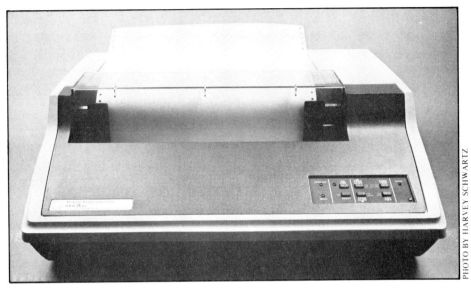

FIGURE 2-8: Matrix printer

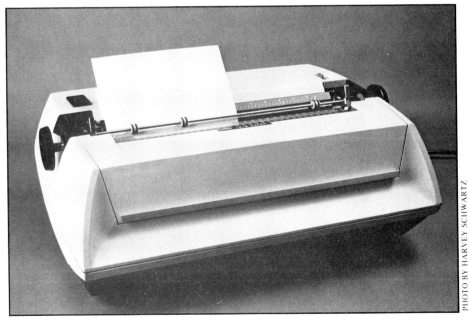

FIGURE 2-9: Typewriter-quality printer

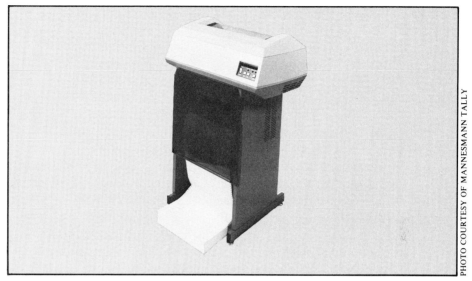

PHOTO COURTESY OF MANNESMANN TALLY

FIGURE 2-10: Line printer

Software

Everything that happens within a computer system is controlled by the CPU. The CPU, in turn, is controlled by a sequence of binary instructions. A binary digit can have one of two values: 0 or 1. These digits are transmitted to the computer as electronic impulses which represent one value when on, and the other when off. Just as the decimal digits 0 through 9 can be combined to create numbers greater than 9, binary digits can be combined to represent numbers of any magnitude.

A sequence of binary instructions is called a *computer program.* Every program instructs the computer to perform specific tasks in a given order. A program may instruct the computer to perform simple calculations or complex data processing. It may instruct the system's devices to display, print, or store information. *Application programs* perform specific tasks, such as accounting, word processing, or communications. *System programs,* or operating system programs, perform the routine tasks required by the computer's hardware. System programs provide the interface between the computer hardware and the application program.

Computer Languages

Programs must be written in a language the computer will understand. There are several levels of computer languages. At the core of programming are *machine instructions*. These are the binary ones and zeros that are interpreted by the CPU. Each different pattern of ones and zeros causes the CPU to perform a unique task. Each CPU has a particular set of instructions it understands. To program a computer at this level you need a way of entering the machine instructions.

A machine instruction is composed of one or more computer words made up of eight binary digits. These are called *bytes*. The sequence of binary zeros and ones looks to us like like numeric hieroglyphics, although this is the only form of instruction that the CPU can understand. A machine instruction (such as 11000011) bears no resemblance to the operation which the computer performs in response to it. While the ones and zeros represent various on and off states to the computer, they mean nothing to the computer user. In order to program a computer, an intermediary translation is necessary.

Assembly language moves one step away from the computer, providing an English-like mnemonic, such as PUSH, INC, DEC, or LD, to describe the action of each machine instruction. Assembly language is translated into machine language by a program called an *assembler*.

Assembly language mnemonics are certainly more understandable than machine instructions, but they might not mean much to a novice computer user. *Comments* may be added to a program to describe what the instructions in that program do. A comment might say "Save character on stack," or "Load data word into accumulator." Comments are ignored by the assembler, so they do not take up space in the computer's memory.

One step further removed from machine instructions are *high-level languages,* which can be interpreted by the computer. Here assembly language instructions are combined into larger building blocks. For example, a program to print the letter "A" on a piece of paper in a printer would be written as follows:

PRINT "A"

The concept of what the program does is now evident. PRINT "A" may actually trigger the execution of several (or even several hundred) machine instructions, but by PRINT "A" we immediately understand the function of the program. As we get closer to understanding the task the computer accomplishes, we get further from the machine instructions the CPU actually executes. The first high-level language compilers were created using the next most sophisticated method — in this case, assembly language. The first assembly language level programs were actually written as machine instructions.

Operating System Programs

An operating system program controls the low-level processes of a computer and mediates between the application program and the computer hardware. The operating system schedules and controls the use of the system's hardware resources. These hardware resources may include memory, disk drives, printers, and CRTs (terminals).

The goal of a good operating system is to simplify the use of the computer by providing a common set of practical, easy-to-use commands that bridge the gap between application programs and the physical processing of the computer. The commands typed into the UNIX system set into motion a complex series of events, many of which are not obvious to the user.

An operating system also directs data flow. It tells streams of data, generated from the keyboard of the terminal, to move to different places at different times. It operates as an elaborate traffic cop, making sure that the right information goes to the right places.

Operating systems fall into two major classifications: batch and interactive. A *batch system* executes a single program at a time, irrespective of size. Typical batch environments include university computing centers used in research, and commercial payroll departments. Batch systems frequently require long turnaround time for a given job, since you must wait in line with everyone else for your program's turn to be run.

In contrast, an *interactive operating system* almost immediately responds to user-provided stimulus. Typical applications for an interactive operating system include computer-aided instruction (CAI), industrial-process control, telecommunications, and real-time process simulation. The UNIX system is an interactive operating system.

An application program interacts directly with the operating system. The operating system receives specific requests to activate printers and disk drives, or to perform other hardware-related tasks. The operating system translates these orders into directives for the computer hardware.

Consider the following word processing program example. You type a brief command and hit the return key. The request is sent to the central processor where it is evaluated; the disk is searched, the word processing program is retrieved and put into memory, and the screen display tells you the program is ready to run.

Generally, when you use a computer to perform a task such as word processing, you are interacting with a high-level application program. For instance, you might command the program to print a business letter you have stored on disk. The word processing program breaks this high-level request down into a number of specific tasks for the operating system to perform. In this example, it might tell the operating system to move a particular file from the disk into main memory, then send each character of the file from main memory to the printer. The operating system receives these directives, translates them into several low-level steps, and directs the hardware to perform the print operation you requested.

Comparing the Systems

We have reviewed the essential elements of computer systems to accelerate your working knowledge with any system you might use. An understanding of these elements permits you to compare mainframe, minicomputer, and microcomputer systems, as well as distinguish single-user and multi-user systems.

A microcomputer system consists of a microprocessor chip, memory, and other circuits packaged in a box with the necessary lights, switches, and power supplies, and a CRT terminal. A microcomputer system is shown in Figure 2-11. It consists of a microprocessor CPU, disk drives, a printer, and software on floppy disks.

Many microcomputer systems are *single-user systems;* only one person can use the system at a time, and most single-user systems can handle only one task at a time. For example, in a single-user system you cannot write letters with a text-processing program while the computer is processing payroll checks. Newer microcomputers, like minicomputers and

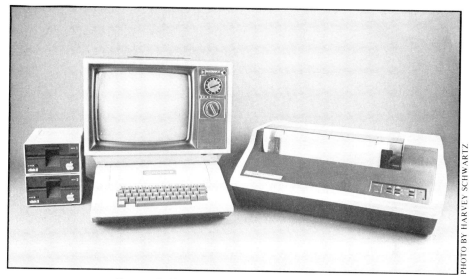

FIGURE 2-11: A typical microcomputer system

mainframe systems, can serve several users simultaneously.

In *multi-user systems,* several terminals are connected to the computer, and each person using the system can simultaneously use several programs in the system. Consider the following simultaneous, yet separate, system users in a manufacturing company:

- Clerks enter orders
- Shipping clerks update inventory
- Secretaries type correspondence
- Clerks process invoices
- Production manager estimates manufacturing costs.

When the computer can be applied to several different tasks at once, computing power becomes practical for business. Large volumes of common information, called data bases, cross-reference and maintain information which each user may need.

The UNIX system can simultaneously accommodate multiple users from several computer systems which in turn link to a single, larger system. At the University of California at Berkeley, more than seven computers are linked together, and each computer has as many as 20 users at a time.

Minicomputers were developed in the late 1960s. The introduction of DEC's PDP-8 system in 1965 for about $18,000 provided lower cost computing power suited to individual departments of a company or research institution. These computers were much smaller than mainframes. They fit on a desk, in the corner of a room, or on a rack. Minicomputers were inexpensive enough to be dedicated to specific projects. They could control or test telescopes, microscopes, and airplane engines for scientific and industrial research. New companies developed hardware and software products for measurement, data control, manufacturing, process control, and business applications. Advances in programming languages and packaged software accelerated, and prices dropped as performance increased. Minicomputers today range in size from desk-top units to large systems that support

PHOTO COURTESY OF DIGITAL EQUIPMENT CORPORATION

FIGURE 2-12: A minicomputer system

PHOTO COURTESY OF AMDAHL CORPORATION

FIGURE 2-13: A mainframe computer

many users. In comparing minicomputers, the computer's processing unit (CPU) is essentially similar — it is the amount of memory and the number and type of devices attached to the central processor that determine the capabilities of the system. A DEC PDP-11, the most common computer running the UNIX system today, is shown in Figure 2-12.

Mainframe computers have dramatically increased in power over the last decade, and continue to provide complex and massive data handling. A mainframe system is shown in Figure 2-13. Mainframe systems can contain hundreds of thousands of records, allow many users on a system, and manage massive data files such as charge card and bank account records. Mainframe computers are owned by large corporations and government agencies which devote entire buildings to their computing divisions. Today, large companies with mainframe systems are moving specific jobs off the central system onto mini- and microcomputers. Only the largest, most complicated data handling jobs need be left to the expensive mainframes.

Consider these comparisons: mainframe computers can regularly process 500,000 active receivable files, minicomputers can process 20,000 files, and microcomputers can process 2,000 files. The difference in capacity to manipulate and process data reflects both the computing power and storage capacity of the computer system.

Comparisons of power, capacity, and other quantifiers are only valuable when they measure a computer system's ability to serve specific applications. The decreasing cost of smaller systems has broadened the use of computers and created applications in new areas. The traditional dividing line between the users and functions of mainframe, minicomputer, and microcomputer systems disappears in this application-based situation. This is further reflected in the successful combination of different types of systems within a single facility. Since the UNIX operating system supports mainframes, minicomputers, and microcomputers, single-user and multi-user systems, it supports the creation of multiple and compatible application-driven systems.

TUTORIALS

Chapter 3

TUTORIALS

THE BEST WAY TO LEARN ABOUT THE UNIX system is to use it. In the following pages, we will present a series of tutorials designed to teach you to use the operating system. We will introduce several commands and explain basic UNIX system concepts. If you have access to a computer with UNIX software, study this chapter while seated at the terminal. Enter the examples and compare the screen displays on your terminal with the illustrations in this book. If you don't have access to a system, study the screen examples as you read the text.

The results displayed on your terminal may differ somewhat from our examples. UNIX software is often modified for specific purposes, and your displays may reflect such changes. If this seems to be the case, check your documentation to identify major changes.

Throughout the tutorials we have consistently used the symbols and procedures outlined below.

• The "$" character indicates the UNIX system *shell prompt*. The shell program prints this character on an otherwise empty line to signal its readiness to accept your next command.

• A UNIX system *command* is a program which performs some desired function. For instance, **date** is a utility command that displays the current date and time of day. These commands are shown in **boldface** type.

• A *command line* includes all the characters you type following the shell prompt ($) until you press the carriage return to terminate this line.

• A command line consists of one or more distinct *elements*. Each element is a sequence of non-blank characters, separated from other elements by one or more spaces.

• The first element, which is placed immediately after the $ prompt, is always the name of the command (or program). For a simple command (such as **date** or **who**) you type the command, then immediately terminate the command line with the carriage return.

• For a more complex command, you type the command name then one or more spaces (blanks), followed by one or more elements which specify additional information. These additional elements, called *arguments* or *parameters*, are numbered from left to right. For example, in the command line "cp temp /usr/your-name", "cp" is the command name "temp" is the first and "/usr/your-name" is the second argument. Arguments generally specify what piece or pieces of data the command is to operate on.

• A special class of arguments is called *options*. In the UNIX system, options look like arguments. They usually appear immediately after the command name and consist of a leading dash (-) which is usually followed by one or more letters and numbers. Each option (letter) specifies a modification to the normal command operation. Commands may have several possible options.

• Additional arguments may be present. A space separates arguments from the preceding command name, from option letters, or from each other. These arguments are generally directory or file names which the command operates on.

We will show all elements in the command line (such as the command name) which are entered exactly as indicated in **boldface** type, and generic elements (such as *filename*) italicized.

We use the following conventions to denote commands and keystrokes:

• *Press* means press a single key.

• *Type* means press a sequence of keys.

• <CR> indicates a *carriage return*. A typical example is:

ls<CR>

This means type the letters "l" and "s" and then press the carriage return key. The carriage return key on your keyboard may be labeled

RETURN, CARR RET, ENTER, NEWLINE, or some other abbreviation. Terminate all command lines with a <CR>.

Consider this complex command:

$ **ls -tr file1 file2**<CR>

Here, "$" is the shell prompt, "ls" is the command name, "-tr" are the options, "file1" and "file2" are additional arguments referring to two particular files named **file1** and **file2**, and "<CR>" represents the carriage return.

• A *command format* specifies a command line in general terms. For instance, in the above example, the specific command has the following general format:

$ *command options arg1 arg2*

In the UNIX system, several possible options exist for most commands. In describing how to enter a complete representative command line we use the command format.

• The command format can be generalized with the addition of brackets "[ ]" to indicate an argument that is optional, and ellipses ". . ." to indicate that the argument may be repeated. Consider the following command line:

$ *command option [arg . . .]*

The command *may* have an argument (denoted by "[*arg*]"), and may have more than one argument (denoted by ". . .").

Control characters are subject to special interpretation by the computer. Just as you hold down the shift key to type a capital letter on a typewriter, you hold down the control key to type a control character. ^ **D** means press and hold down the control key, type the letter D, then release the control key.

The control key is often abbreviated as CTRL or CTL; it is often found in the lower left-hand corner of the keyboard, usually near the shift key.

• Most commands in the UNIX operating system are entered in lower case. The UNIX system distinguishes between UPPER-CASE and lower-case letters. An upper-case character may be interpreted differently from the lower-case version. Unless otherwise specified,

always enter the commands in lower case to ensure correct interpretation.

• The space character, typed by pressing the space bar, is frequently
required when entering commands. Even though it appears to be
"nothing" or "blank space," it is just as important as any other
character. In fact, your computer and the UNIX operating system are
quite finicky about spaces. Be sure to imitate our examples correctly.

The following illustration shows commands entered incorrectly and
correctly.

Incorrect	Correct
$ ls -l	$ ls -l
$ diff -etemp1 temp2	$ diff -e temp1 temp2
$ rm -r i filename1	$ rm -ri filename1
$ cd/usr/your-friend	$ cd /usr/your-friend

We use the following conventions in the screen displays:

• Boldface type indicates user input. Your terminal displays both what
you type and the computer's response. We differentiate between output
from the computer and data typed at the keyboard: operator input
appears in **boldface type**, computer-generated characters do not.

```
$ ls
Letters        Manuscript temp
$ □
```

In this example, the computer places a prompt $ on the terminal screen.
You type "ls", followed by a carriage return. The computer replies with
"Letters," "Manuscript," and "temp" on the next line, and finally
another *prompt* on the following line. Note that the *cursor* □ is waiting
for your next input command. Your input will appear after the $ prompt.

Throughout the text, the command, file, and directory names appear in **boldface** type. When you are instructed to type material at your keyboard, what you should type will appear in quotes in the text. For example, "w<CR>" means press the "w" key, then the carriage return key.

On the sample screens, characters you type will appear in **boldface** type.

Tutorial Sessions

We assume you already have an established account and have been assigned a *login name* and *password.* Your login name is a one-word name that identifies you to the computer and anyone else using the system. On some systems you may need a password for accounting and security purposes.

Session 1

**How to Enter and Exit Your UNIX System;
Login; Password; Date; Logout**

How to Enter and Exit Your UNIX System

First, you must turn on the system. If you are working at one terminal in a multi-terminal system, the screen will light up when the power is on. If you are interacting with the UNIX system through a *modem* (telephone lines), refer to the modem instructions. If you are using a stand-alone system, refer to the manufacturer's instructions.

Login

To get the computer's attention, press the carriage return key (denoted by <CR> hereafter). You may need to press LINE FEED, BREAK, ESCAPE, or some similar key on your system. A UNIX system *banner line* may appear, telling you the system is running and ready to receive input. The banner line is followed by a request for your login name. Your login logo may appear as **:login:** or **login:**. Both prompt you to enter your login name.

```
YOUR UNIX SYSTEM BANNER
:login: □
```

Password

Type your login name and press <CR>. Remember to type in lower case. If you type in upper-case the system will use all upper-case letters until you log out and log in again. If you make a mistake, just press <CR> twice and try again. After the UNIX system reads your login name, it will usually prompt you for the password.

```
YOUR UNIX SYSTEM BANNER
:login: your-name
Password: □
```

Enter your password and press <CR>. For security reasons, your password does not appear on the screen. After the system accepts your password, you are officially logged in. The system may display the latest messages for users. You might learn the system's maintenance schedule or read a description of recently added features. The system indicates it is ready for your commands by displaying the *shell prompt* ($, %, or whatever).

```
YOUR UNIX SYSTEM BANNER
:login: your-name
Password:
(UNIX SYSTEM MESSAGES)
$ □
```

If you made a typing mistake or entered the wrong login name or password, the UNIX system will display "Login incorrect" or an equivalent message and ask for your login name again.

```
YOUR UNIX SYSTEM BANNER
:login: your-name
Password:
Login incorrect
:login: □
```

Enter your login name again and the system will ask you for your password again. You will be caught in an endless login loop until you type both your login name and password correctly.

Date

Now that you're logged into the system, type "date<CR>", and the system will respond with the current date and time. Note—the date command is *not* an essential part of the login procedure.

```
$ date
Mon Aug 31 09:23:10 PDT 1981
$ □
```

Note: To avoid confusion and redundancy, many of the screen displays that follow will show the results of just the last operation or two — not everything which has preceded it.

Try mistyping the word "date" (for example, type "datte<CR>") and the system will inform you that the command **datte** is invalid.

```
$ datte
datte: Command not found
$ □
```

The shell informed you it could not find the command **datte**, and prompted you to enter a valid command.

Logout

To conclude your first session, you must officially log out (sign off) of the UNIX system. You log out by typing a control-D (^D) after a $ prompt. Control-D is a non-printing character; it will not appear on your screen. You will know you have successfully logged out of the system when in a few seconds the screen displays a message to log in again.

```
$
YOUR UNIX SYSTEM BANNER
:login: ☐
```

Do not just turn off the terminal. You must log out, or else your terminal will remain on-line and your account will be charged for time you're not using. If you are connected by modem (telephone circuitry) the system may automatically log you off when you hang up. You should check with your system administrator to be sure.

Session 2

The Shell Prompt; The UNIX System Shell; Correcting Typing Errors; Changing Your Password; On-Line Documentation; Aborting Program Execution; Suspending Program Display; Sending Electronic Mail; Who is on the System; Type-Ahead Buffer; Sending Electronic Mail

---

The Shell Prompt

Log into your UNIX system as you did the first session. The system may report the last time you logged in, any messages of general interest to users of the system, and so forth. Ultimately the cursor appears to the right of the *shell prompt* symbol, which is usually a $ or %. This symbol comes from a program called the UNIX system shell. The $ prompt is characteristic of the Bell Labs Bourne shell and the % prompt of the U.C. Berkeley "C" shell and the older Version 6 Bell Labs systems.

The UNIX System Shell

The *shell* is a program that aids communication between you and the UNIX operating system. It reads the command lines you type on the keyboard and interprets them as requests to run or execute programs.

The shell finds the program requested by your command, brings it into memory, and executes it. The shell searches one or more particular directories to find the command. Normally, after searching your directory it will try to find the programs in **/bin** and **/usr/bin** (two standard directories where programs are located). After exhausting all possible directories it will display a message and another prompt. (Directories are explained in detail later in this chapter.)

```
command not found
$ □
```

After the command is executed, the prompt appears, indicating that the shell is ready for your next command.

Now type "date<CR>". When you press the carriage return to indicate that the command is complete, the shell will look for the program called **date** and will direct it to run, or *execute*. The result will be displayed immediately and the shell will issue another prompt for your next command.

```
$ date
Wed Sep   2 15:40:30 PDT 1981
$ □
```

Correcting Typing Errors

If you haven't yet pressed <CR> you can correct a typing mistake in the following two ways:

• You can correct the typing as you go by using the number character (#). It erases the last character typed, although the character remains on the screen. On many systems the character-erase code is a control-H, or the BACKSPACE key.

• You can start over, erasing all characters from the current input line by pressing the @ key. The cursor moves to the next line and waits for your input.

Note: The character- and line-erase codes may be different on your particular UNIX system implementation. In addition, you can customize your "environment" and reassign these erase codes to different characters. In particular, the character-erase code is often reassigned to a control-H (entered with the BACKSPACE key).

As an example, after the $ prompt type "datte". If you press <CR>, the shell responds with "command not found", as in the first session. To correct the entry, press one "#" for each character you wish to erase. Then type the correct characters. Now, when you press <CR> the shell will correctly interpret your command as **date**.

```
$ datte
datte: Command not found
$ datte # # e
Wed Sep 2 15:40:30 PDT 1981
$ □
```

Alternatively you can correct typing errors with the @ character. Press "@" to erase everything typed on the line so far. The cursor may jump to the next line. On that line, type the correct characters and then press <CR>.

```
$ datte @
date
Wed Sep 2 15:40:30 PDT 1981
$ □
```

Note: You must erase with # or @ before pressing <CR>, or the shell will consider your input as a valid request. If you press <CR> before correcting a command name, the shell simply informs you that a command with that name could not be found. Reenter the command name after the $ prompt.

Changing Your Password

You may wish to change your password from time to time in order to prevent unauthorized use of your account. Your new password should be at least four characters long if you use both upper- and lower-case letters and numbers, and at least six characters long if it is all lower or upper case. The longer the password, the harder it is to guess. You can enter a password up to eight characters long on most systems. You can use any characters but the typing-error correction codes (# or @) in your password.

We will change or define your password now. After the $ prompt, type "passwd" followed by < CR>.

```
$ passwd
Old password: □
```

Now type in your current password. It will not appear on the screen for security reasons. Remember to press <CR> after entering your password. The **passwd** program will now ask for your new password.

```
$ passwd
Old password:
New password: □
```

After you type your new password and press <CR> the system asks you to repeat the entry to minimize the chance of a typing error, since you can't see what you typed.

```
$ passwd
Old password:
New password:
Retype new password: □
```

If both new password entries match, the system login password file will be updated to reflect your new password.

Remember your password! You cannot log into the system without it. If you do forget it you will have to ask the person in charge of your system to delete your old password so that you can log in and reset it.

On-Line Documentation

Most UNIX system installations have Volume I of the *UNIX Pro-grammer's Manual* on-line. This volume describes features of the UNIX system that are available to users, and documents every shell command, although in a rather terse and technical manner.

Consider the command format for accessing on-line documentation:

$ **man** *title*

Title is the name of the desired command. Type "man date<CR>".

```
$ man date          UNIX Programmer's Manual          DATE(1)
DATE(1)

NAME
      date — print and set the date
SYNOPSIS
      date [ yymmddhhmm [ .ss ] ]

DESCRIPTION
      If no argument is given, the current date and
      time are printed. If an argument is given, the
      current date is set. yy are the last digits...

   ...
$ □
```

Your cursor may be "frozen" at the bottom of the screen. In this case, press the space bar or <CR> and continue reading. On some installations the entire manual section will be continuously displayed without freezing.

Aborting Program Execution

You can interrupt the execution of any program by pressing the delete key. This special purpose key may be labeled RUB (for rubout) or DEL (for delete). Interrupting most commands and programs will immediately terminate their execution. Some, however, interpret the interruption to mean something other than immediate termination. We will indicate an interrupt signal by [Interrupt] on the screen displays. You will not see anything on your screen when you press the interrupt character. After terminating a command, the UNIX system will respond with a new prompt ($), indicating that it is ready for your next command.

Suspending Program Display

You can also temporarily suspend the terminal display without aborting the command execution. Type "^S" and the display will halt. To restart the display, type "^Q". Other keys may be used on your system, so check your system's documentation if the keys just mentioned don't work. Freezing the display is especially useful when you want to read at a slower pace than the terminal normally displays. Always type "^Q" before giving up on a terminal; many "problems" are simply frozen displays.

Who Is on the System

To see who is currently logged into the system, use the **who** command. Consider the following responses to the **who** command.

```
$ who
veronica        bx066       Aug 27 13:28
rathomas        dz24        Aug 28 07:42
jlyates         tty5        Aug 28 07:39
$ □
```

The login names appear in the left-hand column, the terminal devices are listed in the next column, and the date and time of logging in appears in the last column.

In these tutorials the output of the **who** utility is sorted by the terminal field.

Type-Ahead Buffer

The system can read your next command while executing the last one. The characters you type at the keyboard are constantly being stored in a system buffer.

If you have a terminal with a slow display rate (1200 baud or less) then you can illustrate this point by typing in rapid succession "who<CR>" then "date<CR>".

```
$ who
veronica        bx066      Aug 27 13:28
rathomas        dzdate24   Aug 28 07:42
jlyates         tty5       Aug 28 07:39
Wed Sep 2 15:40:30 PDT 1981
$ ▢
```

To illustrate how the type-ahead buffer functions with a faster terminal, type a command which requires more time to execute, such as "sort -r/usr/dict/words<CR>" which sorts the on-line spelling dictionary in reverse, and enter **date** for the second command.

Sending Electronic Mail

You can send electronic mail to others on the system if you know their login names. The command form is the word "mail", followed by the login name of the addressee, followed by a <CR>. The cursor will be positioned on the next line, waiting for your input.

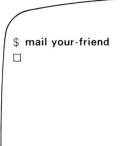

```
$ mail your-friend
▢
```

Now you can type your message. Remember to press the carriage return at the end of each line. You can terminate the message by typing either ^D or a period as the first and only character on the line, followed immediately by a <CR>.

```
$ mail your-friend
( YOUR MESSAGE )
.
$ □
```

Note: Since it is so easy to type too many ^D's and log out yourself, consider ending your messages with a period as a general rule.

You can send yourself mail. **Mail** is a convenient way to leave yourself a reminder. Type "mail", a space, then your own login name (indicated on the screen display by **your-name**) and end the command line with a <CR>. Then enter the following line: "This is a reminder to myself.<CR>". Type a period, and nothing else, on the next line to end the message.

```
$ mail your-name
This is a reminder to myself.
.
$ □
```

The next time you log in, the system will inform you that "You have mail." We will discuss how to read your mail in the next session. This is the end of the second session. Don't forget to log off: type "^D" after the shell prompt.

Session 3

Receiving Mail; Concept: File; Concept: Filename;
Ed Text Editor; Edit Buffer; Two Operating Modes;
Creating a File; Text Entry; Displaying the Text;
Saving the Text; Exiting the Editor

Receiving Mail

In the last session you mailed yourself a message before logging off.
When you log in this time, the UNIX system will announce that you
have mail.

```
YOUR UNIX SYSTEM BANNER
:login: your-name
Password:
( UNIX SYSTEM MESSAGES )

You have mail.
$ □
```

To read your mail, simply type "mail<CR>". The **mail** program will
first display the most recent message in your mailbox. After each
message, **mail** displays its own prompt, ?, and waits for you to direct the
disposition of the displayed messages.

```
YOUR UNIX SYSTEM BANNER
:login: your-name
Password:
( UNIX SYSTEM MESSAGES )
You have mail.
$ mail
From your-login name Mon Sep  7 09:00:34 1981
This is a reminder to myself.

? □
```

Note: Your UNIX system may display a different prompt character for the **mail** program, but one will appear.

Type "?<CR>" to display the list of commands on reading and disposing of messages. Display the previous message again with the "-" **mail** command. Next, save a copy of that message in your current directory by typing "s message<CR>" after the **mail** prompt (?).

```
? s message
$ □
```

You will clear your mailbox and exit **mail** after issuing this command, since only one message was in your mailbox. The shell prompt ($) will reappear. Note—the mail command may act somewhat differently for your particular UNIX implementation.

Concept: File

A *file* is a collection of information which is assigned a name and is stored on a secondary storage medium such as a disk or a magnetic tape. This information can be programs, data, or text.

Once you create a file, it stays in the system until you instruct the shell to remove it. Files can be created during any UNIX system session and can be accessed (if you have permission) at any time.

In the UNIX system, files have no internal structure; they are simply a finite sequence of arbitrary characters. A file contains from zero to 1 billion characters. The file size automatically increases to store more information.

Concept: Filename

The *filename* identifies files. To read or write file information, reference the filename in a command. The shell automatically locates the file, if it exists.

Filenames need not be unique to the physical file. The same physical file can have different filenames in the same directory, or the same filename in different directories.

Ed Text Editor

Before we discuss the UNIX system commands which manipulate files, you need to learn how to create files and enter text. If you have access to another, more sophisticated, editor on your system and wish to use it, do so. In any case, read the following discussion of **ed** to be sure you understand the concepts we cover.

The remainder of this session examines how the *text editor* creates, modifies, and displays a *text file*. **Ed**, available on all UNIX systems, allows you to manipulate text on a line-by-line basis. It is not *screen-oriented*; you cannot move the cursor randomly through a screenful of text in the file to create or modify text.

Edit Buffer

A *buffer* is an area in memory set aside for data. In text editing, a buffer serves as a temporary work space used during the editing session to create and change the text file. The **ed** editor allocates a transient work area in memory called the *edit buffer*. Text created with **ed** is first placed in this buffer. You can then modify and display the text in this buffer. The contents of the edit buffer are temporary; when you leave the editor program, any text remaining in the buffer is lost. If you wish to access that text in the future, you must make a copy of the buffer contents on disk before leaving **ed**.

Two Operating Modes

The **ed** editor operates in two modes: *command mode* and *text entry mode*. In command mode, the editor interprets your input as a command. In text entry mode, **ed** adds your input to the text located in the edit buffer area. When you first enter **ed** you are in command mode. The **append**, **insert**, or **change** commands are used to enter text entry mode. To terminate text entry mode, type a period as the first character on a line, followed immediately by a carriage return.

The text in the edit buffer is referenced by lines. Lines are separated by carriage returns, and are numbered consecutively. **Ed** renumbers text automatically as lines are added to or deleted from the buffer. At any one time the editor will be referencing one of the lines in the buffer, the *current line,* as shown in Figure 3-1.

Commands in **ed** have a simple and consistent structure: zero or more *addresses* followed by a single-character *command-letter,* optionally followed by *parameters* to the command. Entering one or more spaces between the address, command-letter, and parameters is optional, but improves readability. We frequently use one space in the illustrations. This command format can be represented as follows:

address range   command-letter   parameter . . .

You can construct **ed** commands in several forms. You can often shorten the address range by choosing the default case. Also, the **print** command-letter ''p'' can be omitted if the current line is to be displayed. In the examples which follow, you will see both the long form and several equivalent shorthand forms.

The address range of many commands is specified as one or two line-number prefixes (also referred to as *addresses*). The address range indicates which lines in the edit buffer a command will affect. One number refers to a single line only. Two numbers separated by a comma indicates an inclusive range of lines. If no line number is specified, a default command-line prefix, the current line, is assumed. For instance, entering the **print** command without a line-address prefix will display the current line.

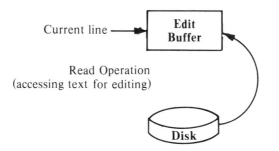

FIGURE 3-1: Accessing text from the edit buffer

Several special characters will address particular lines or parts of a line in the edit buffer. A period denotes the current line. A dollar sign indicates the final line in the buffer. Use these special characters as a shorthand when specifying **ed** commands. Other characters with special meanings will be discussed later.

Creating a File

Now that the preliminaries are out of the way, let's invoke **ed** to create some text. After the prompt ($) appears, type "ed", followed by one or more spaces, then the filename that you have selected. For your first example, type "ed temp<CR>".

```
$ ed temp
?temp
□
```

Ed responds with a "?" followed by the name **temp**. The question mark indicates that you have specified a file which does not yet exist in your current directory. This is normal; you will be creating **temp** in this session.

You are now in **ed** command mode. **Ed** doesn't provide any distinguishing prompt in either command mode or text entry mode. To learn which mode you are in, type a period on a line by itself and observe the response. If you type a period, a question mark appears because you just requested the current line to be displayed, but the edit buffer is still empty. **Ed**'s response indicates an error condition. When you do have some text in the edit buffer and press "." while in command mode, the current line will be displayed. If you are in text entry mode, you will harmlessly exit text entry mode and reenter command mode.

Text Entry

Recall that when you first invoke **ed** you are in command mode. To add text to the edit buffer you must be in text entry mode. Use the **append** command to do this. Type "a" followed by a <CR>.

```
$ ed temp
?temp
.
?
a
□
```

The cursor is positioned at the beginning of the next line. The text you type will be entered into the edit buffer. Type the text exactly as shown on the following screen (including the errors) and end each line with a <CR>. When typing the word "time" on the first line, misspell it as "timr", then correct it with the # erase character. Then misspell "citozens" on the second line. On the fourth line, after "fo their", press "@" and complete the text on the next line. Type a period as the first and only character on the next line to leave text entry mode. Consider the following display.

```
$ ed temp
?temp
.
?
a
Now is the timr#e
for all good citozens
to come to the aid
fo their@
of their country.
.
□
```

Are you back in command mode? To check, press the period as the first character of the line. If you see "of their country." displayed, you have returned to command mode. If not, you are still in text entry mode. Remember, to leave text entry mode type a single period as the first and only character on a line and immediately press the <CR>.

If you make a typing error before you press the <CR>, you can use one of the correction techniques (# for characters, @ for lines) discussed in Session 2. Your screen may be cluttered with # or @ characters, but they are not entered into the edit buffer, as you will see in a moment. How to correct mistakes noted on a completed line will be explained in a later session.

Displaying the Text

When you have returned to command mode you can display the text you just entered into the edit buffer with the **print** command. To display the entire buffer, type "1,$ p<CR>". Here, the numeral "1" denotes the first line of the buffer, the special character "$" denotes the last line, and the construction "1,$ p" means display the contents of the edit buffer from line 1 through the last line, inclusive.

```
1,$ p
Now is the time
for all good citozens
to come to the aid
of their country.
□
```

Note that neither the character-erase code (#) nor the line-erase code (@) was displayed, since they were not entered into the edit buffer.

Saving the Text

Before leaving the editor you must write the contents of the edit buffer to the disk with the **write** command.

To save the text, type "w<CR>"

```
w
75
□
```

Ed displays the number of characters just written to the file named
temp. The text in the edit buffer remains intact; a copy of it was saved.
You may continue to add or change the text in the edit buffer if you
wish; the contents of the file named **temp** on the disk will not be
changed further until you write to that disk file again. Figure 3-2 illustrates the write operation.

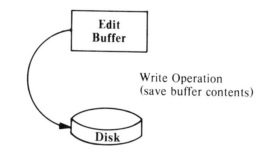

FIGURE 3-2: Saving the contents of the edit buffer

Exiting the Editor

To leave **ed**, simply type "q<CR>":

```
q
$ □
```

If you attempt to exit **ed** without performing a write operation since the last change to the edit buffer, **ed** responds with a "?" to indicate an error condition. In this case you either write the buffer to disk or you enter a second successive **quit** (q) command to leave **ed**, abandoning the text in the edit buffer.

A summary of this first **ed** session appears on the following screen.

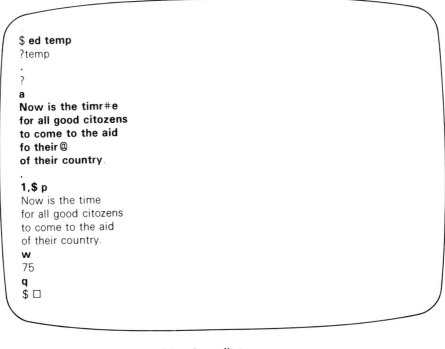

```
$ ed temp
?temp
.
?
a
Now is the timr#e
for all good citozens
to come to the aid
fo their @
of their country.
.
1,$ p
Now is the time
for all good citozens
to come to the aid
of their country.
w
75
q
$ □
```

$ ed temp	Invoke **ed** to edit **temp**
?temp	**Temp** not yet created
.	Press a period
?	No text in edit buffer
a	Enter append or text entry mode
Now is the timr#e	Enter text, correcting mistake here
for all good citozens	Enter text; leave "citozens" misspelled
to come to the aid	Enter more text
fo their@	Correct mistake with @
of their country.	Last line of text
.	Leave append mode
1,$ p	Display entire buffer
Now is the time	
for all good citozens	Contents of edit buffer
to come to the aid	
of their country.	

w	Write contents of buffer to disk
75	75 characters written
q	Quit (leave) **ed**
$ □	Shell prompt and cursor

For more practice, invoke your editor program with a different filename, **letter**. Add some text to the edit buffer: "This letter was created with ed.". Write the buffer to disk, and exit from the editor.

This tutorial does not cover all the details for operating **ed**. After you have mastered the tutorials on **ed**, read the documentation that comes with your system.

Session 4

Concept: Directory; Commands: Ls, Cat; Concept: Linking; Commands: Cp, Rm, Mv; Protecting Files

---

Now that you know how to use **ed** to create files, we will consider some of the basic UNIX system commands dealing with files and directories. First, we will explain directories.

Concept: Directory

A *directory* is a file containing a list of 16-character lines. Each line corresponds to one file in the directory. The first two characters of a line refer to a number that identifies a specific file. This is called the *i-number*. The next 14 characters are for the filename.

Ls: List Contents of a Directory

This tutorial session assumes that your current directory is your personal login directory. To be sure, type the command "cd<CR>".

Your login directory now includes the names of several files. To display those filenames, use the **ls** command. Type "ls<CR>" and an alphabetically ordered display appears.

```
$ ls
letter      message temp
$ □
```

Note: Our display of the format and contents of the directory may differ from your UNIX system implementation. This may be true for some of the other commands as well. For instance, your directory entries might be listed in a column, as follows.

```
$ ls
letter
message
temp
$ □
```

In either of the above screens, your directory contains at least three entries, named **letter**, **message**, and **temp**. Recall that you used **ed** to create the files named **letter** and **temp** and you used the **save** command from the **mail** program to create the file named **message**.

Cat: Concatenate and Print a File

Link has other UNIX meanings: **cat**, short for concatenate, means to connect together. **Cat** is most frequently used to display a file's contents. When you wish to display more than one file, the contents of the files are catenated together. Of course, you can display the contents of a file from **ed** (using 1,$ p) but if you are in the shell ($ prompt level), using **cat** will be more direct.

To display any of the files whose names are listed with **ls**, type "cat *filename*<CR>". Use the actual filename in place of *filename*. For example, consider the following file **temp**.

```
$ cat temp
Now is the time
for all good citozens
to come to the aid
of their country.
$ □
```

To concatenate the three files, type "cat temp message letter<CR>".

```
$ cat temp message letter
Now is the time
for all good citozens
to come to the aid
of their country.
From your-name Mon Sep 7 09:00:34 1981
This is a reminder to myself.

This letter was created with ed.
$ □
```

The contents of **temp**, **message**, and **letter** are displayed consecutively before returning to the shell $ level. If you mistype one of the filenames or request a file which isn't in your current directory, **cat** displays an error message. To illustrate, type "cat letters<CR>".

```
$ cat letters
cat: can't open letters
$ □
```

The filename **letters** (distinct from **letter**) doesn't exist in your directory.

Note: The "cat:" shown above means that the **cat** program issued the error message. If a command name doesn't precede the error message, then the shell has issued the error message. Of course, when you are in **ed** the error message comes from the editor.

Concept: Linking

Each entry in a directory associates an i-number (the physical file reference) with a filename. This connection is called a *link*. Two or more directory entries can have the same i-number, creating multiple links. Several filenames can be associated with the same physical file.

Type "ln temp testfile<CR>" to establish a second link, named **testfile**, to the file named **temp** in your login directory. Now list the directory with the **-i** option.

```
$ ln temp testfile
$ ls -i
413 letter        7975 message       23284 temp        23284 testfile
$ □
```

The actual i-numbers will probably be different on your screen, but both **temp** and **testfile** should have the same i-number. Display **testfile** and **temp** to verify that they are identical.

```
$ cat testfile
Now is the time
for all good citozens
to come to the aid
of their country.
$ cat temp
Now is the time
for all good citozens
to come to the aid
of their country.
$ □
```

If you use an editor to change the contents of **testfile**, you will change the contents of **temp**. The filenames are really aliases for the same physical file. To demonstrate, invoke **ed** to edit **testfile**. Delete the last line. Save the edit buffer. Exit the editor. Display **testfile** by typing the commands exactly as shown.

```
$ ed testfile
75
$d
w
57
q
$ cat testfile
Now is the time
for all good citozens
to come to the aid
$ □
```

To show that **temp** has also been changed, use **cat** again.

```
$ cat temp
Now is the time
for all good citozens
to come to the aid
$ □
```

To restore your practice file system, use the editor and append "of their country." to the file **temp**. After returning to the shell, remove **testfile** by typing "rm testfile<CR>".

In summary, UNIX system files do not have filenames intrinsically tied to the physical file reference (the i-number). The directories provide this association. The same file can have multiple filename aliases.

Cp: Copy a File

This command creates *backup* copies of files. It permits you to modify the original file without worrying that "all will be lost" if you make substantial errors. For instance, in a later tutorial session you will correct the typing errors you purposely made in **temp**. In case something goes wrong while you correct the errors, you can make a copy named **temp2** by typing "cp temp temp2<CR>". Use **cat** to verify that **temp** and **temp2** are identical.

```
$ cp temp temp2
$ cat temp
Now is the time
for all good citozens
to come to the aid
of their country.
$ cat temp2
Now is the time
for all good citozens
to come to the aid
of their country.
$ □
```

Temp2 was created by reading **temp** and writing a new file named **temp2**. To see that "temp" and "temp2" are names for two physically distinct files, list the directory with i-numbers.

```
$ ls -i
413 letters       7975 message       23284 temp       864 temp2
$ □
```

Your actual numbers will be different from those shown here, but your i-numbers for **temp** and **temp2** will have different values when you use **cp** to create **temp2** from **temp**.

If **temp** is destroyed, you now have another copy named **temp2**. This may be a trivial example, since a file as short as **temp** can be quickly produced with **ed**. But if you had a large file consisting of several pages of text and accidentally destroyed it, you would be grateful for the duplicate.

Rm: Remove a File

This command removes one or more files. The **rm** utility removes a file by unlinking and deleting its reference in the directory. In this way the link between that filename and the physical file is severed, so the file can no longer be accessed using that name. When the last or only name (or link) is removed for a given i-number file, all of the storage used to hold that file's information is automatically and irretrievably freed up.

Let's say that you don't yet need the backup copy of **temp** with the filename **temp2**. To remove it, type "rm temp2<CR>". To verify that you have removed the file, list your directory before and after removing this file.

```
$ ls
letter          message temp      temp2
$ rm temp2
$ ls
letter          message temp
$ □
```

Mv: Rename a File

The **mv** command changes a filename by linking a new name to a file and then removing the old link. A new directory entry establishes a link between the i-number (physical file pointer) and the new filename. The old directory entry is erased, breaking the link between the i-number and the old filename.

For example, to change the file named **temp** to one named **temp2**, type the command "mv temp temp2<CR>". A directory listing with **ls -i** before and after the move reveals that no new file has been created.

```
$ ls -i
   413 letter        7975 message       23284 temp
$ mv temp temp2
$ ls -i
   413 letter        7975 message       23284 temp2
$ □
```

Note: **temp2** is listed with the i-number which was formerly linked to **temp**, showing that the file denoted by i-number 23284 was renamed.

Compare this result with that from the file copy (**cp**) command.

```
$ ls -i
   413 letter        7975 message       23284 temp
$ cp temp temp2
$ ls -i
   413 letter        7975 message       23284 temp       864 temp2
$ □
```

Note: **temp2** refers to a file physically distinct from **temp** (the two files have different i-numbers).

To restore your file system, type "mv temp2 temp<CR>".

In contrast to the **mv** command, the **cp** command leaves the source file intact. The "move" operation is equivalent in effect to the two commands given in succession.

```
$ ln temp temp2
$ rm temp
$ □
```

Verify the last statement by listing the directory with **ls - i** before and after typing these two commands. Finally, type "mv temp2 temp <CR>" to restore your file system.

Protecting Files

It is possible to accidentally destroy your files. When you instruct an editor or a UNIX system command to write to a file which already exists, the system first removes the contents of that file.

Here are three common examples of how file contents are destroyed. If you write to a file which exists in a directory, the original contents of that file are destroyed. That file only contains the text which was written to it.

To begin with, make some backup copies of the file **letter** by typing the following commands.

```
$ cp letter letter2
$ cp letter letter3
$ cp letter letter4
$ □
```

Now verify by listing your directory.

```
$ ls
letter        letter2   letter3   letter4   message temp
$ □
```

For our first example, you will see how to overwrite a file by writing to it from an editor. The file **letter2** will contain the text "This letter was created with ed.". You can verify that fact with **cat**. Now invoke **ed** to edit **temp**. Then write the contents of the edit buffer, which now contains a copy of **temp**, to the file named **letter2**. After exiting the editor, use **cat** to display the contents of **letter2**.

```
$ cat letter2
This letter was created with ed.
$ ed temp
75
w letter2
75
q
$ cat letter2
Now is the time
for all good citozens
to come to the aid
of their country.
$ □
```

In our second example, we will destroy the contents of a file with the **cp** command. To illustrate, verify that **letter3** contains the text "This letter was created with ed.". Type the copy command, as shown in the following screen, and then print the contents of **letter3**.

```
$ cat letter3
This letter was created with ed.
$ cp temp letter3
$ cat letter3
Now is the time
for all good citozens
to come to the aid
of their country.
$ □
```

The contents of **letter** were overwritten with the contents of **temp**. Now the files named **temp** and **letter3** both contain the contents of **temp**, and the original contents of **letter3** are irrevocably lost.

In our final example, we use the **mv** command to destroy the contents of an existing file. As above, the file **letter4** will originally contain the text "This letter was created with ed.". Verify that with **cat**. Type the command "mv temp letter<CR>" and display the contents of **letter4**.

```
$ cat letter4
This letter was created with ed.
$ mv temp letter4
$ cat letter4
Now is the time
for all good citozens
to come to the aid
of their country.
□
```

Again you can see that the original contents of **letter4** are lost. **Letter4** now contains the former contents of the file **temp**. Note that the **mv** command also erases the directory entry for **temp**.

```
$ ls
letter      letter2   letter3   letter4   message
$ □
```

These examples demonstrate how easily you can inadvertently destroy a file. Considerations for file protection are very important, so make sure you completely understand this section before continuing with the next tutorial.

To restore your practice file system before leaving this session, type the commands shown in **boldface** in the following screen. Finally, you should verify everything with **ls**.

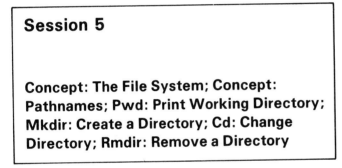

```
$ mv letter4 temp
$ rm letter?
$ ls
letter          message temp
$ □
```

Time to log off until the next session.

Session 5

Concept: The File System; Concept: Pathnames; Pwd: Print Working Directory; Mkdir: Create a Directory; Cd: Change Directory; Rmdir: Remove a Directory

---

Concept: The File System

The file system is arranged as a hierarchy of directories, in the form of an upside-down tree. The source of the tree is the *root,* or the root directory, denoted by "/". Each directory can contain any number of directories, developing a branching structure.

Figure 3-3 illustrates a typical file system.

Concept: Pathnames

A *pathname* specifies the complete name of a directory or file by starting at the root and tracing the hierarchy of the file. For instance, in our sample file system in Figure 3-3, the file in parentheses has the full

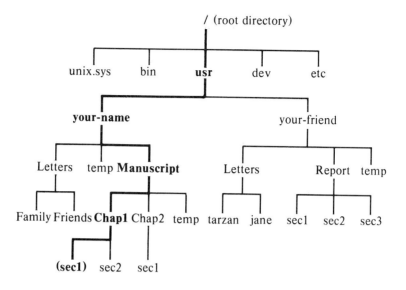

FIGURE 3-3: A typical file system

pathname of **/usr/your-name/Manuscript/Chap1/sec1**. Start at the root (/), trace the **boldface** lines down through the directories **usr, your-name, Manuscript, Chap1**, finally reaching the file **sec1**.

Each file and directory has a unique pathname which identifies that file. Pathnames can be used wherever file or directory names are used. Partial pathnames are constructed by starting at a lower level than the root in the directory hierarchy. For instance, from your login directory called **your-name**, the pathname to the same file in our example would be **Manuscript/Chap1/sec1**.

Pwd: Print Working Directory

Your current directory is the directory in which you are working. The **pwd** displays the complete pathname, starting at the root and proceeding through any intermediate directories until it reaches your current directory. Type "pwd<CR>" to display a complete pathname.

```
$ pwd
/usr/your-name
$ □
```

The exact response to this command varies from system to system, but the forms are similar to our example. On our system the pathname to our login directory is **/cb/rathomas**.

You will find **pwd** to be a valuable utility when you are moving around in the directory hierarchy. It is easy to get "lost" in this complex two-dimensional maze. Use the **pwd** command to learn where you are, at any time, from any directory.

Mkdir: Create a Directory

You may wish to organize several files in a single directory. To create the new directory, use the following command form:

$ **mkdir** *dirname* ...

You created one or more directories named *dirname* in your current directory. We will now create one directory named **Sample** for some sample files. Simply type "mkdir Sample<CR>", then list your current directory to verify.

```
$ mkdir Sample
$ ls
Sample    letter      message temp
$ □
```

Note: We prefer to capitalize the name of a directory to distinguish it from a filename. You do not have to capitalize a directory name when you use **mkdir**.

Cd: Change to a Directory

To change to a subdirectory of your current directory, use the following command form:

$ **cd** *subdirname*

Subdirname is a subdirectory name. Change to the **Sample** directory you created in the last section by typing the command "cd Sample<CR>", then verify your location with **pwd**.

```
$ cd Sample
$ pwd
$ /usr/your-name/Sample
$ □
```

You can always return to your login directory from any other directory by simply typing the **cd** command without an argument. Type "cd<CR>", then verify that you are back in your home directory.

```
$ cd
$ pwd
$ /usr/your-name
$ □
```

Now change to the directory **Sample** as before by typing "cd Sample<CR>". As long as you are in **Sample**, any filename you specify (unless you use a pathname) will be taken to mean a file in that directory. Now type "cat temp<CR>".

```
$ cd Sample
$ cat temp
cat: can't open temp
$ □
```

This error message indicates that the **cat** command cannot find the file **temp** in the current directory, which is **Sample**. Recall that **temp** was created within your login directory. **Sample** is a subdirectory of your *login* directory, so your *login* directory is the *parent* of the **Sample** directory. Since a parent directory is denoted by two periods (..), you can display **temp** by employing a partial pathname to **temp** from **Sample**. The partial pathname is **../temp**, so you should type "cat ../temp<CR>".

```
$ cat ../temp
Now is the time
for all good citozens
to come to the aid
of their country.
$ □
```

Note: "cat ../temp" is interpreted as "print (cat) the file obtained by moving to the parent directory (..) and selecting the file **temp** (/temp)."

We will now show you how to move around in your subdirectories. You must first create another subdirectory. Type the commands shown in **boldface** below, and you should see the following responses shown in regular type.

```
$ cd
$ pwd
/usr/your-name
$ mkdir Manuscript
$ ls
Manuscript Sample       letter      message      temp
$ cd Sample
$ pwd
/usr/your-name/Sample
$ □
```

Visualize the parent directory as a "bridge" to another directory at the same level of the directory hierarchy. Consider the partial diagram in Figure 3-4 of your practice file system.

To get to the **Manuscript** directory from the **Sample** directory, type "cd ../Manuscript <CR>". You move "up" one level to your parent directory (..), which is **your-name** in this case, then "down" one level to the subdirectory **Manuscript**. Verify the move with **pwd**.

```
$ cd ../Manuscript
$ pwd
/usr/your-name/Manuscript
$ □
```

Now move back "up" to your home directory again by typing either the command "cd<CR>", which always returns you to your login directory, or "cd ..<CR>", which returns you to your login directory in

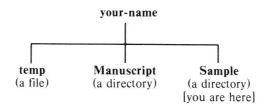

FIGURE 3-4: A practice file system

this instance, because your login directory is the parent directory of **Manuscript**. Verify again with **pwd**.

While remaining in your login directory, move a copy of the file **temp** to the subdirectory **Sample**, then verify its location.

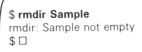

```
$ cp temp Sample/temp
$ cat Sample/temp
Now is the time
for all good citozens
to come to the aid
of their country.
$ □
```

Note: If the filename is not changed, it need not be respecified in the **cp** command; the command could be shortened to "cp temp Sample<CR>".

Rmdir: Remove a Directory

If you decide you no longer need the directory **Sample** which you created in the last section, you can use a special form of the **rm** command, **rmdir**, to remove directories. To remove one or more subdirectories named *subdirname,* use the following command form:

$ **rmdir** *subdirname...*

From your login directory, type "rmdir Sample<CR>".

```
$ rmdir Sample
rmdir: Sample not empty
$ □
```

You received an error message. **Rmdir** cannot remove the directory until it is empty. This convention prevents you from accidentally removing text you want to keep. Remove **temp** with the command "rm temp<CR>" and try again.

```
$ rm temp
$ rmdir Sample
rmdir: Sample not empty
$ □
```

The directory is still not empty, even though you just removed **temp**. That is because you removed it from the wrong directory. Remember that you are in your login directory and wish to remove **temp** in the **Sample** directory. You can correct this mistake in one step. Move **temp**, which is in directory **Sample**, back to your login directory by typing "mv Sample/temp temp<CR>". Verify that **temp** is no longer in **Sample** with the command "ls Sample<CR>".

```
$ mv Sample/temp temp
$ ls Sample
$ □
```

No response means that **Sample** is empty. Now that directory **Sample** is empty, you can remove it. Type "rmdir Sample<CR>" and verify with "ls<CR>".

```
$ rmdir Sample
$ ls
Manuscript letter      message      temp
$ □
```

To restore your practice file system, remove **Manuscript** by typing "rmdir Manuscript <CR>".

Session 6

Concept: User Process Control;
&: Run a Process in the Background;
Ps: User Process Status;
Kill: Abort the Background Process;
At: Execute a Process at a Specific Time

Concept: User Process Control

The UNIX system is a *multi-tasking* operating system. This means that several processes can be scheduled to run simultaneously. For example, the computer can execute your commands while it executes commands for everyone else logged in, seemingly simultaneously. In reality, the computer only executes one process at any one time. However, it is able to switch between different processes very rapidly. The computer divides its attention among all the execution processes requested by multiple users. This operation is called *time-sharing*.

&: Run a Process in the Background

The UNIX system not only allows different users to execute commands simultaneously, but also allows a single user to perform more than one task at once. You might prefer to run a long task in the "background." This is easy to do in the UNIX system. Simply type the ampersand character (&) at the end of the command line you wish to execute in the background. The system will then print a number on your terminal and immediately prompt ($) for the next command. This *process number* identifies the background process. You can inquire about the status of that process or perhaps terminate it before it finishes. The "&" directs the shell not to wait for the command to finish before prompting for another command.

For example, let's select a task which requires more than a minute to complete, say sorting the 24,000-word on-line spelling dictionary in reverse. We will direct the result of the sort to a file so your terminal display is not interrupted by the sort output. The **sort** program utility is discussed further in Chapter 4. For this example, type the command line "sort -r /usr/dict/words -o word.sort &<CR>" and make a written note of the process number which appears.

```
$ sort -r /usr/dict/words -o word.sort &
800
$ □
```

Your process number will probably not be 800. In the examples which follow, use the process number your system indicates.

Ps: User Process Status

You can monitor a background process with the **ps** (process status) command. Type the process status command in the following form:

$ **ps** *process number*

Process number is the value you noted for the sorting process you are running in the background. In a few seconds you should see a display similar to the following screen.

```
$ sort -r /usr/dict/words -o word.sort &
800
$ ps 800
800 tty5          0:04 sort -r /usr/dict/words -o word.sort
$ □
```

Note: Your display for **ps** may be different. This command is implementation-dependent.

Here the **ps** command displays the process number (800), the terminal designation (tty5), the elapsed CPU time so far in minutes and seconds (0:04), and the name of the process (sort -r /usr/dict/words -o word.sort).

Now enter **ps** several times, and watch the accumulated execution time in the third column increase as the sorting process continues running sporadically in the background.

```
$ ps 1022
800 tty5          0:19 sort -r /usr/dict/words -o word.sort
$ ps 800
800 tty5          0:36 sort -r /usr/dict/words -o word.sort
$ ps 800
800 tty5          0:52 sort -r /usr/dict/words -o word.sort
$ ps 800
800: No such process
$ □
```

Eventually, the process numbered 800 will no longer exist and the **ps** program will convey that message. Now consider the file **word.sort**, where the output from the sorting process was stored.

```
$ cat word.sort
zucchini
zounds
zoom
zoology
zoo
zone
zombie
zodiacal
[ Interrupt ]
$ □
```

We aborted the long printout of this file with the interrupt (DEL) key, indicated as [Interrupt]. (You won't see anything displayed when you press the interrupt key.) The on-line dictionary has been sorted in reverse order.

Kill: Abort the Background Process

You will occasionally need to halt the execution of the background process. The interrupt (DEL) key only works for the "foreground" process. To abort the background process use the following command form:

$ **kill** *process number*

Process number refers to the background process. If you forget the background process number, you can find it out by typing "ps<CR>"; all currently active processes associated with your terminal (tty5 in these examples) will be listed.

Next, type in the same **sort** command used in the previous section. Then type the command "ps<CR>", without a process number, to display all processes.

```
$ sort -r /usr/dict/words -o word.sort &
803
$ ps
PID   TTY          TIME CMD
803   tty5         0:08 sort -r /usr/dict/words -o word.sort
145   tty5         0:04 -sh
$ □
```

Note: Your screen may also display the process (denoted by "-ps" in the right-hand column) which is executing the **ps** command itself.

Two active processes can be seen: the shell (labeled "-sh" in the right-hand column) runs in the foreground, and the sorting process runs in the background. There is no way to distinguish foreground from background by this **ps** display.

Now press the interrupt key (DEL) a few times. The interrupt character doesn't appear on the screen. To see if the background sorting process was affected, type "ps<CR>" again.

```
$ [ Interrupt ]
$ [ Interrupt ]
$ ps
PID   TTY      TIME CMD
803   tty5     0:18 sort -r /usr/dict/words -o word.sort
145   tty5     0:06 -sh
$ □
```

As you can see, the background process (803) was not interrupted when you pressed the interrupt key.

To demonstrate that the **kill** command does indeed abort the background process, type in quick succession the commands shown in **boldface**. Substitute your process number for the "814" shown in the example below.

```
$ rm word.sort
$ sort -r /usr/dict/words -o word.sort &
814
$ ps
PID   TTY      TIME CMD
814   tty5     0:10 sort -r /usr/dict/words -o word.sort
145   tty5     0:06 -sh
$ kill 814
$ ps
PID   TTY      TIME CMD
145   tty5     0:05 -sh
$ □
```

After entering the **kill** command, the background process disappears from the screen. To further verify that the sorting process was killed, try to print out the contents of **word.sort** with **cat**. You should either get the error message "cat: can't open word.sort" (file not created yet) or see nothing (file created but not written yet). The background process was aborted before **sort** could complete its task and store the result in the file.

At: Execute a Process at a Specific Time

Use the **at** command to run a command file at a specified time and date. Consider the following command form:

at *time* [*day*] [*file*]

Time consists of one to four digits. An optional A, P, N, or M represents AM, PM, noon, or midnight. One- and two-digit numbers represent hours; three- and four-digit number represent hours and minutes. If no letters follow the digits, a 24-hour clock time is assumed. The *day* can be either a month name followed by a day number, or a day of the week. If you specify **week** then the process will be executed a week later. Names of months and days may be abbreviated. Consider the following examples of valid specifications of the date and time:

at 8am	Today, at 8 o'clock in the morning
at 2130	Today, at 9:30 PM
at 12N fri week	Noon, a week from next Friday
at 2PM apr 3	Next April 3rd at 2 PM

The command to be executed at the specified time must be placed in the file before entering the **at** command. In our example we will use the command "date >> timefile". You will learn in the shell tutorial session that " >> timefile" will cause the output of the **date** command to be *appended to* (stored at the end of) the file named **timefile**.

You need to invoke your editor to create a file named **storetime**, containing "date >> timefile". We use the **ed** editor in our example.

```
$ ed storetime
? storetime
a
date  > >timefile
.
w
16
q
$ □
```

You are now ready to use the **at** command. Choose a time at least one hour from now to start your delayed execution series. Start with an even hour. In our example we chose 2 PM. Type the commands shown in the screen, substituting the time you choose for 1400 if you don't use 2 PM as a starting point.

```
$ at 1400 storetime
$ at 1410 storetime
$ at 1420 storetime
$ at 1430 storetime
$ at 1440 storetime
$ at 1450 storetime
$ at 1500 storetime
$ □
```

Now wait until the hour has elapsed (until after 3 PM in our example) then display the contents of the file **timefile**. Consider our results.

```
$ cat timefile
Sat   Oct   3 14:00:04 PDT 1981
Sat   Oct   3 14:20:08 PDT 1981
Sat   Oct   3 14:40:04 PDT 1981
Sat   Oct   3 15:00:08 PDT 1981
$ □
```

The accuracy of **at**-files is installation-independent. On our system, **at**-files are checked only on the hour, 20 minutes after the hour, or 20 minutes before the hour. On this system, if you requested the command to run at ten minutes after the hour, the system would wait until 20 minutes past the same hour before running the **at**-file.

Session 7

Shell Tutorial; Multiple Commands on a Command Line; Redirecting Output to a File; Reading Input from a File; Pipelines: Connecting Command Processes; Wild Cards and Other Special Characters; Echo: Expand Command-Line Arguments

---

Shell Tutorial

You learned earlier that the shell is the program through which you communicate with the UNIX system. The shell is a command interpreter; it translates your command into a sequence of actions and directs the UNIX system to fulfill your request. The Bourne Shell is the command interpreter supplied with UNIX Edition 7 from Western Electric Company. There are other command interpreters from the UNIX operating system, most notably the "C" Shell written by William Joy at the University of California at Berkeley. Our discussion will be restricted to the simpler and more commonly used Bourne Shell.

This tutorial session introduces some of the shell's features. We demonstrate entering multiple commands on a single line, redirecting output to a file, reading input from a file, and connecting commands in a "pipeline." We also discuss the shell's special interpretation characters.

Multiple Commands on a Command Line_____

Two or more commands can be typed on a single command line if they are separated by semicolons (;). The semicolon tells the shell to execute the first command, wait for its completion, then execute the next command.

As an example, type "date;who<CR>" and observe the following display.

```
$ date; who
Wed Sep   2 15:40:30 PDT 1981
veronica        bx066      Aug 27 13:28
rathomas        dz24       Aug 28 07:42
jlyates         tty5       Aug 28 07:39
$ □
```

The commands **date** and **who** were executed in sequence. After the current date and time of day, a list of all the users currently logged into your system was displayed.

You can separate the commands from the semicolon with blanks or tabs if you wish to improve readability. The shell will ignore these "white space" characters.

Redirecting Output to a File_____

The output of the programs discussed earlier has appeared on the terminal. The UNIX system sends the output of commands to a file called the *standard output file*. Normally, the standard output file is assigned to your terminal. The shell has the ability to "redirect" standard output to another file which you specify in the command line.

command >file

This command form indicates *file* as the standard output for the *command*. The information will not be displayed on your terminal, but will be stored in *file*. If *file* does not already exist it will be created by the shell. If *file* does exist, the shell destroys its contents in preparation for storing the output of *command*.

For example, type "who >who.now<CR>". Another shell prompt immediately appears with no display from the **who** command.

```
$ who >who.now
$ □
```

Print the contents of **who.now** with **cat** to verify that the ouput of **who** was indeed stored in that file.

```
$ who >who.now
$ cat who.now
veronica      bx066      Aug 27 13:28
rathomas      dz24       Aug 28 07:42
jlyates       tty5       Aug 28 07:39
$ □
```

When you need to redirect the output of two or more commands to a file, enclose the commands in parentheses. For example, type "(date; who) >who.now<CR>." Now display the contents of the **who.now**.

```
$ (date;who) >who.now
$ cat who.now
Wed Sep          2 15:40:30  PDT 1981
veronica      bx066      Aug 27 13:28
rathomas      dz24       Aug 28 07:42
jlyates       tty5       Aug 28 07:39
$ □
```

Note: If you do not enclose both **date** and **who** in parentheses the shell will execute **date**, displaying the result on the terminal, then execute **who**, saving the result in the file **who.now**.

To add the output of a process to a file without deleting what is already there type the alternate command form.

command >> file

In this case, the shell redirects the standard output to the end of *file,* so the output of *command* will be appended to the file. If *file* does not already exist, the shell creates it.

For example, type "date >>who.now<CR>" then print the contents of **who.now**.

```
$ date  > >who.now
$ cat who.now
veronica        bx066      Aug 27 13:28
rathomas        dz24       Aug 28 07:42
jlyates         tty5       Aug 28 07:39
Wed Sep         2 15:40:30 PDT 1981
$ □
```

Reading Input from a File

The shell can also reassign the "standard input" to a command. A command normally obtains the standard input from your terminal keyboard. You can store data or text in a file with an editor, and then direct the shell to use this file as the standard input for your command. Consider the following command format:

command < file

Type the command "cat <temp<CR>" to display the file **temp**.

```
$ cat <temp
Now is the time
for all good citozens
to come to the aid
of their country.
$ □
```

Use **ed** to create a reminder message for yourself. Store the message in a file named **reminder**. Direct the **mail** program to read the contents of **reminder** as its standard input and to send it to you. To accomplish this, type the commands shown in **boldface** on the screen (replace **your-name** with your own login name).

```
$ ed reminder
? reminder
a
This is a reminder.
.
w
20
q
$ mail your-name <reminder
$ □
```

Invoke **mail** and read the message you just sent yourself.

You can place the <, > and >> directives almost anywhere and the shell will correctly interpret your request. Remember to keep the filename *file* in close association with the appropriate directive. You can also use "white space" characters to separate the command names and filenames.

You can practice redirecting output using our directives. Try these practice examples.

```
$ man sh  >sh.doc
$ cat sh.doc
SH(1) UNIX Programmer's Manual ... [ Interrupt ]
$ □
```

The output of the **man sh** command was stored in the file **sh.doc**, as you can see by displaying the latter with **cat**. Note: [Interrupt] stands for the interrupt signal generated by pressing the DEL key, and is not seen on the screen. You can edit the contents of **sh.doc** at your leisure, since it is now in a file in your directory.

Try the following example.

```
$ crypt secret  <reminder  >classified
$ □
```

Recall that you created the file **reminder** with **ed**. The shell inputs the contents of **reminder** (<reminder) to the **crypt** program, which encrypts the text using key "secret." The shell directs the encrypted letter to the disk file named **classified**. If you tried to use **cat** to display **classified**, gibberish would appear on your terminal.

You can rearrange the command line for the example shown above and get the same result. Type the following command.

```
$ crypt secret >classified2 <reminder
$ □
```

To verify that **classified** and **classified2** are identical, use the **cmp** command. If the two files specified on the **cmp** command line are identical, no output appears.

```
$ cmp classified classified2
$ □
```

Pipelines: Connecting Command Processes

The shell allows you to extend the idea of redirection. In particular, the standard output of one command can serve as the standard input of a second. Consider the following command form:

command 1 | command 2

The output from *command 1* does not appear on the terminal, nor is it stored in some intermediate file. Rather, the UNIX system "buffers" the output of the first process for input to the second command.

This connection between commands is called a *pipeline*. The term "pipe" is often used loosely as a verb: "the output of the **who** command is 'piped' into the **sort** utility.'' The pipeline concept is one of the novel and powerful features of the UNIX system.

As an example, let's connect the output of the **who** command to be sorted by login name (the first field) and then displayed on your terminal.

```
$ who | sort

jlyates      tty5      Aug 28 07:39
rathomas     dz24      Aug 28 07:42
veronica     bx066     Aug 27 13:28
$ □
```

You can perform extensive manipulations in a single command line using the pipeline facility. Our example may at first appear rather complex, but it is composed of a number of simple single-task command steps.

```
$ cat temp
Now is the time
for all good citozens
to come to the aid
of their country.
$ cat temp | tr -cs A-Za-z '\012' | sort -d | uniq -c
   1 Now
   1 aid
   1 all
   1 citozens
   1 come
   1 country
   1 for
   1 good
   1 is
   1 of
   2 the
   1 their
   1 time
   2 to
$ □
```

In this example, four commands work together in a pipeline. The **cat** command reads the file **temp** and sends the output to the **tr** command. This form of the **tr** command will cause each word in the file to be placed on a line by itself. This list of words is sent to **sort**, which orders them in increasing ASCII sequence (upper-case letters come before lower-case, "a" comes before "b", etc.). The output of **sort** is sent directly to **uniq**, which removes all duplicate words and indicates how many times each word occurred. The end result is an ordered list of the words from the file **temp**. A number telling how many times each word occurred in **temp** precedes the word.

Notice that you did not see any results from the intermediate steps of the pipeline; only the final result (output) was displayed. In fact, the intermediate results were not stored anywhere in the system, but were passed directly from one command to the next. Try substituting a different text file for **temp** in the pipeline and see what happens.

Wild Cards and Other Special Characters

There are a number of characters which have special meanings to the shell. They are

* ? [ ] < > ; | ' " &

Because of their special command interpretation you should not use these characters in filenames. Also avoid using ^, /, and - when naming files.

In the majority of the examples in these tutorials we have specified files by filenames. You may also use "wild cards" to name a file or a group of files in an abbreviated fashion. Consider the following wild-card characters:

* ? [ ]

When the shell encounters these characters in a command word, it replaces the word with a sorted list of matching filenames. The filenames come from your current directory or an indicated directory. Consider the following *pattern matching* (also called *expansion*):

- Most characters match themselves
- The ? matches any single character

•The * matches any string of characters (except '/')

•The set of characters in [. . .] will match any one character in that set. A pair of characters separated by a dash (-) includes all the characters in the alphabetic or numeric range of the pair.

The following examples show wild-card characters used in commands:

$ ls *	List all files in the current directory.
$ rm *.doc	Remove all files ending in ".doc".
$ pr sec?	Print all files whose name begins with "sec" followed by any single character.
$ ls Chap[1-3]	List the directories Chap1, Chap2, and Chap3.

Caution: The wild-card characters should be used carefully. For instance, **cat *** will display the files in your current directory, but **rm *** will erase them all.

Whenever single quotes ('), and in most cases double quotes ("), enclose a special character, that character loses its special significance to the shell. Also, the shell treats a special character preceded with the backslash (\) as an ordinary character.

For instance, compare the results of typing "cat *<CR>" and "cat '*'<CR>". In the first case, the shell expands the abbreviation by finding a match with every file in your current directory; the contents of all files will be displayed consecutively. In the second case, the shell treats '*' as a single unique filename which doesn't exist in your directory. **Cat** will display "cat: can't open *" and nothing will be displayed.

Echo: Expand Command-Line Arguments

The **echo** command is useful for learning about "wild cards" and other special characters. It performs no action except to write its arguments to the standard output. In this way you can preview exactly how the shell will interpret a wild card or other special character.

The use of **echo** is best illustrated by example. Assume your current directory contains the following files:

chap1 chap2 chap3 ed.doc man.doc

Type the following commands shown in **boldface**.

```
$ echo *
ed.doc chap1 chap2 chap3 man.doc
$ echo *.doc
ed.doc man.doc
$ echo chap?
chap1 chap2 chap3
$ echo chap[2-3]
chap2 chap3
$ echo ??.doc
ed.doc
$ echo ?????
chap1 chap2 chap3
$ □
```

Session 8

**Ed Text Editor; Position in Buffer;
Append Text; Locating Text;
Substitute Function; Undo;
Write to a Different File**

Ed Text Editor_____

We will continue our study of **ed** in this tutorial. After logging in, call up the **ed** program. Specify the file which you created and saved on disk in Session 3 with the command "ed temp<CR>". First **ed** reads the file **temp** into its edit buffer, then it displays the number of characters in this file.

```
$ ed temp
75
□
```

If "?temp" appears, instead of a numerical quantity, then the file **temp** does not exist in your directory. Perhaps you erased it by mistake. If so, follow the instructions in Session 3 to enter text and save it on disk (as **temp**). Without leaving **ed,** continue with this tutorial. The desired copy of **temp** will be in the edit buffer.

Position in the Buffer

You will not usually know where the current line is located in the text buffer without displaying a line of text. To determine your position in the edit buffer, construct the command to display the current line. Remember that all **ed** commands use this form:

address range command-letter [parameter]

Recall that the period addresses the current line. The edit buffer contents are displayed with the **print** command which includes the "p" *command-letter.* No parameters are needed for the "p" function, so the most verbose form of the command becomes ".p<CR>". Type this command directly after invoking **ed** to edit **temp**:

.p
of their country.
□

The current line is the last line in the buffer. This is always the case after reading a file into the edit buffer.

Since the default address for the "p" command is the current line, a shorthand command for displaying the current line is simply "p".

```
p
of their country.
□
```

To move to the beginning of the file, change the current line to line address 1. You can enter the desired line number without a command-letter: "1<CR>". Since "p" is a default case, line 1 will also be displayed:

```
1
Now is the time
□
```

This illustrates a general case. When you specify a line address in an **ed** command line, the current line number reflects that specified position in the edit buffer. The operation indicated by the command-letter is carried out. In the last example, the print operation was performed even though you did not type "1p<CR>", because the "p" command-letter is implied by default.

Practice positioning the current line to line addresses 2, 3, and $ (remember that the $ addresses the last line of the edit buffer).

Return to the first line of the buffer and type successive carriage returns. You will observe the successive display of each line until the end of the buffer. This illustrates a convenient way to move through the text a line at a time.

```
Now is the time

for all good citozens

to come to the aid

of their country.

?
□
```

When you reach the last line and type another <CR>, **ed** will display a ?. You are requesting a line address past the end of the buffer, which is a command error.

To successively display previous lines, type successive -'s. After you reach the first line in the buffer and attempt to continue backward with another -, **ed** will display a ?, again indicating a command error.

```
–
to come to the aid
–
for all good citozens
–
Now is the time
–
?
□
```

You can also move forward by typing successive +'s:

```
+
for all good citozens
+
to come to the aid
+
of their country.
?
□
```

To skip forward or backward by more than a single line, type a decimal number after the + or -. This example leads us to a general conclusion: if an address begins with a + or -, the addition or subtraction is made *relative to* the current line. To illustrate the previous statement, position yourself on the first line of the buffer, then type "+2".

```
1
Now is the time
+2
to come to the aid
□
```

To display the line number of your current line without changing position in the buffer, use the command ".=<CR>".

```
.=
3
□
```

To determine the total line count, enter the command to display the line number for the last line of the edit buffer.

```
$=
4
□
```

In summary, you can reposition the current line to an absolute buffer address by typing the decimal number corresponding to that address, followed by a <CR>. You can also position the current line to an address relative to the current line by typing a + or - sign before the desired decimal number displacement (a "1" displacement is understood if no number is specified).

Append Text

Now position yourself at the end of the buffer using one of the methods we have described. To enter text entry mode, type the **append** command, "a<CR>", then enter the sample text. Exit the append or text entry mode by typing ". <CR>" on a line by itself.

```
$p
of their country.
a
This is the time
to get on the UNIX bandwagon.
.
□
```

Now you are back in command mode. Display the entire contents of the edit buffer to verify that the append was carried out correctly. Remember, to construct the command use the address range from 1 to $ with the "p" command-letter as "1,$ p<CR>".

```
1,$ p
Now is the time
for all good citozens
to come to the aid
of their country.
This is the time
to get on the UNIX bandwagon.
□
```

The following screen summarizes all the steps we have performed for appending the specified text to the end of the edit buffer.

```
$p
of their country.
a
This is the time
to get on the UNIX bandwagon.

.
1,$ p
Now is the time
for all good citozens
to come to the aid
of their country.
This is the time
to get on the UNIX bandwagon.
□
```

$p	Move to last line and display
of their country.	Display of current line
a	Enter append mode
This is the time	Enter a line
to get on the UNIX bandwagon.	Enter another line
.	Leave append mode
1,$ p	Display entire edit buffer
Now is the time	Line 1 of buffer
for all good citozens	Line 2 of buffer
to come to the aid	Line 3 of buffer
of their country.	Line 4 of buffer
This is the time	Line 5 of buffer
to get on the UNIX bandwagon.	Line 6 (last line)
□	Cursor waiting for next command

Locating Text

You can also locate a particular line in the edit buffer without moving from line to line. You can search for a particular pattern of text using the following command form:

"/pattern /<CR>"

The editor searches for the pattern in the file, stops at the first occurrence and displays the line where the match occurred. This line becomes the current line.

For example, position yourself at line 3 of the edit buffer by typing "3<CR>", and then enter the command "/the time/<CR>".

```
3
to come to the aid
/the time/
This is the time
□
```

The match occurred in "This is the time", the first line after line 3 which contained the characters "the time". **Ed** remembers the pattern "the time" until you enter a different search pattern. To find the next occurrence of "the time" in the buffer, simply enter the command "//<CR>".

```
//
Now is the time
□
```

This is the next line in which the pattern occurs. Notice that **ed**, after reaching the end of the buffer (line 6), "wrapped around" to the beginning (line 1) in order to find the line.

You can cause **ed** to search backward through the buffer by bracketing the search pattern with ? characters. Position yourself at the end of the edit buffer by typing "$<CR>", and enter the command "?the time?<CR>".

```
$
to get on the UNIX bandwagon.
?the time?
This is the time
□
```

Next, enter the command "??<CR>".

```
??
Now is the time
□
```

Ed found the line shown in our screen after searching backward through the buffer to line 1.

To print all lines containing the search pattern in the edit buffer, precede the /*pattern* / with the letter "g" (for *global search*) and add the suffix "p" (for *print*). All lines in the buffer which contain the pattern will be displayed. For instance, type "g/the time/p<CR>" and observe the following display.

```
g/the time/p
Now is the time
This is the time
□
```

The following screen summarizes this section on locating text.

```
3
to come to the aid
/the time/
This is the time
//
Now is the time
?the time?
This is the time
??
Now is the time
g/the time/p
Now is the time
This is the time
□
```

Substitute Function

Recall that earlier you were asked to mistype "citizen" in the second line, entering it as "citozen". We will now correct this misspelling to illustrate the **substitute** command. This command looks similar to the pattern search function. The general format of the **substitute** command is as follows: s/*old pattern* /*new pattern* /**p** <CR>

The "p" (for print) suffix displays the result of the **substitute** function.

Before using the **substitute** command, position yourself at the line where the error is located. Locate and display the line with the **search** command "/citozens/p<CR>" and then use the **substitute** command.

```
/citozens/p
for all good citozens
s/citozens/citizens/p
for all good citizens
□
```

Alternatively, consider how the following two commands can be combined on the same line.

```
/citozens/s/citozens/citizens/p
for all good citizens
□
```

Note: The "p" command-letter at the end of the command line is optional, and causes **ed** to display the corrected result.

The last **search**-and-**substitute** command is further abbreviated because **ed** will remember "citozens" as the last pattern.

```
/citozens/s//citizens/p
for all good citizens
□
```

A line generally includes only one command. However, most commands allow you to append the "p" command-letter to display the current line, and reflect the command's action. Thus **ed** responds to our sample commands by displaying "for all good citizens", indicating a successful correction.

You may include special characters in the **substitute** command to denote the beginning (^) or end ($) of a line. **Ed** knows from the context that $ doesn't mean the end of the buffer. Some examples will help illustrate.

Type the command "1s/^/Right /p<CR>". **Ed** moves to line 1 of the edit buffer, substitutes "Right" for "^" (which indicates the beginning of the line) and then prints the result.

```
ls/^/Right /p
Right Now is the time
□
```

Move to line 5 and append the phrase "before it is too late" to the end of the line by typing the command "5s/$/ before it is too late/ p<CR>".

```
5s/$/ before it is too late/p
This is the time before it is too late
□
```

Don't forget to enter a space character after "Right" and before "before", to create a space between "Right Now. . ." and ". . .time before. . .".

At this point, display the entire buffer.

```
1,$ p
Right Now is the time
for all good citizens
to come to the aid
of their country.
This is the time before it is too late
to get on the UNIX bandwagon.
□
```

The **substitute** command changes only the first occurrence of a pattern on a given line. To illustrate, type "5s/is/IS/p<CR>", and you will see the following display:

```
5s/is/IS/p
ThIS is the time before it is too late
□
```

Use the "g" (global) suffix to change all occurrences of a pattern.

```
5s/is/IS/gp
ThIS IS the time before it IS too late
□
```

To substitute multiple-line occurrences, precede the **substitute** command with an address range. For example, if you wish to replace "the" with "THE" on all lines, type the command "1,$ s/the/THE/g<CR>" and verify correct execution by displaying the entire edit buffer.

```
1,$ s/the/THE/g
1,$ p
Right Now is THE time
for all good citizens
to come to THE aid
of THEir country.
ThIS IS THE time before it IS too late
to get on THE UNIX bandwagon.
□
```

As an exercise, imagine dividing the edit buffer in half. Use the **substitute** command twice to convert all occurrences of "THE" back to "the". Let's convert the first four lines with "1,4 s/THE/the/g<CR>" and display the buffer.

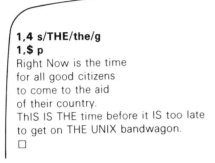

```
1,4 s/THE/the/g
1,$ p
Right Now is the time
for all good citizens
to come to the aid
of their country.
ThIS IS THE time before it IS too late
to get on THE UNIX bandwagon.
□
```

Then restore the last two lines with "5,$ s/THE/the/g<CR>".

```
5,$ s/THE/the/g
1,$ p
Right Now is the time
for all good citizens
to come to the aid
of their country.
ThIS IS the time before it IS too late
to get on the UNIX bandwagon.
□
```

Undo

To return the edit buffer to the state it was in prior to the last **substitute** command, type the **undo** command "u<CR>". The **undo** command can only reverse the effect of the most recent substitution, and works only if **ed** is currently positioned on the affected line. Type the **undo** command "u<CR>" and display the entire buffer.

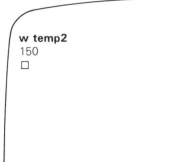

```
u
1,$ p
Right Now is the time
for all good citizens
to come to the aid
of their country.
ThIS IS the time before it IS too late
to get on THE UNIX bandwagon.
□
```

Notice that only line 6 (or $) , which was the last line affected by the **substitute** command, was undone. The one intervening print command had no effect on **undo** because **print** does not change the buffer and does not reposition the current line.

Write to a Different File

This is a good time to use the **write** command and save the modified text. If you specify a different filename than the one you used to read in the file **temp**, you can have a copy of both the original and the modified text. With the **write** command-letter "w", type a space followed by the parameter "temp2", which is the desired filename for saving the modified text. Typing "w temp2 <CR>" requests a display of the number of characters written to the disk.

```
w temp2
150
□
```

Now exit the editor with the "q" command and request a listing of your directory.

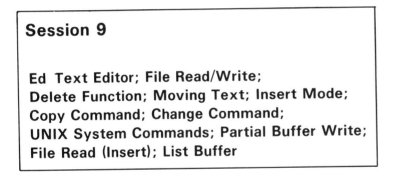

```
q
$ ls
letter          message temp          temp2
$ □
```

Next, use the **cat** command to verify the contents of the files **temp** and **temp2**.

This is the end of Session 8. Unless you wish to continue with the next session, log off your UNIX system with the ^D logout code.

Session 9

Ed Text Editor; File Read/Write;
Delete Function; Moving Text; Insert Mode;
Copy Command; Change Command;
UNIX System Commands; Partial Buffer Write;
File Read (Insert); List Buffer

Ed Text Editor

Log into the UNIX system and invoke **ed** without a filename. To verify you are in **ed**, press a ".." and **ed** will respond with "?". Tell **ed** to edit the file **temp2** by typing "e temp2<CR>".

```
$ ed
.
?
e temp2
150
□
```

This erases all text from the edit buffer, and reads the file **temp2** into the buffer. The current line, ".", is set to the last line of the buffer. The filename **temp2** will now be "remembered" by **ed** as a default filename for any subsequent file commands.

File Read/Write

Use a combination of the "e" and "w" commands to read and write files without leaving **ed**. This is useful if you wish to edit several files in one editing session. You can also use the "e" command to create a new file.

Caution : Remember to write the contents of the edit buffer to disk before using the "e" command, since the buffer will be overwritten when another file is read in. Used alone (without specifying a file name) the "e" command will not erase the buffer.

Delete Function

The **delete** command, command-letter "d", removes one or more addressed lines from the buffer. **Ed** automatically renumbers all the lines left in the buffer.

In our first example we will delete one of the two lines added in the last session. We can delete one line at a time by prefacing the "d" command-letter with the line number. Type "5d<CR>" and display the entire buffer.

```
5d
1,$ p
Right Now is the time
for all good citizens
to come to the aid
of their country.
to get on THE UNIX bandwagon.
□
```

Now delete the last line and display the buffer.

```
$d
1,$ p
Right Now is the time
for all good citizens
to come to the aid
of their country.
□
```

To restore the edit buffer to its previous condition, read in **temp2** again. Verify by displaying the entire buffer.

```
e temp2
150
1,$ p
Right Now is the time
for all good citizens
to come to the aid
of their country.
THIS IS the time before it IS too late
to get on THE UNIX bandwagon.
□
```

To delete the last two lines in one step, use an address range with the **delete** command. Type the command "5,6d<CR>" and display the buffer to verify.

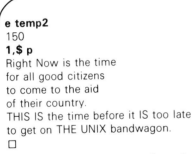

```
5,6d
1,$ p
Right Now is the time
for all good citizens
to come to the aid
of their country.
□
```

Moving Text

There is a command to move one or more lines around in the buffer. The line address specification is more complex than those you've used before, but it is straightforward. Use the following command format:

move from line, to line inclusive **m** *to after line*

To move the last two lines of the buffer to the beginning of the buffer, use the command "$-1,$ m0 <CR>". **Ed** allows the destination address to be 0 since the line after 0 is address 1, which is a valid address in the buffer. Note that we have used spaces in the command for greater clarity. Now list the buffer contents and look at your screen.

```
$-1,$ m 0
1,$ p
to come to the aid
of their country.
Right Now is the time
for all good citizens
□
```

To move the lines back, type "1,2 m $<CR>" and verify.

```
1,2 m $
1,$ p
Right Now is the time
for all good citizens
to come to the aid
of their country.
□
```

Try moving other lines yourself and verify the moves by printing the entire buffer before and after each operation. Restore the buffer to its original sequence before proceeding to the next section.

Insert Mode

A command related to **append** is used to insert text in the edit buffer. The **append** and **insert** commands differ in the placement of the new text. The **insert** command adds text *before* the addressed line; the **append** command adds text *after* the addressed line. For both commands, terminate text entry by typing a period as the first character of the line, then pressing <CR>.

To see the difference between these two commands, consider this simple example. To **append** the text "who are patriotic" after the second line of the buffer and to verify the execution, type the following commands.

```
2a
who are patriotic
.
1,$ p
Right Now is the time
for all good citizens
who are patriotic
to come to the aid
of their country.
□
```

Delete the line you just added by typing "3d<CR>". To **insert** the same text before the same line and verify execution, type the following commands.

```
3i
who are patriotic
.
1,$ p
Right Now is the time
for all good citizens
who are patriotic
to come to the aid
of their country.
□
```

Note: You can insert as much text as your wish. The buffer automatically moves previous text to accommodate the insert.

Transfer Command

To duplicate one or more lines in the buffer without moving the original lines use the **transfer** command, with the command-letter "t". For instance, to make a copy of the last two lines, use the command "$-1,$ t 0<CR>" at the beginning of the file, and verify execution by displaying the buffer.

```
$-1,$ t 0
1,$ p
to come to the aid
of their country.
Right Now is the time
for all good citizens
who are patriotic
to come to the aid
of their country.
□
```

To move text to the beginning of the buffer, use address 0 for the destination.

Before proceeding with the session, delete the two extra top lines with the **delete** command "1,2 d<CR>".

Change Command

If you wish to replace lines of text successively, enter either the **delete** and **insert** commands, or the **delete** and **append** commands. You may also use the single **change** line command. The editor deletes the indicated lines and then enters text entry mode, and you add the new text. You do not have to add the same number of lines that you deleted. You add text until you terminate the text entry mode by typing ".<CR>" as the first entry on a line.

For practice, remove the line "who are patriotic" and insert the two lines "whose skills are needed" and "in the peace effort". Use the **print** function to verify execution.

```
3 c
whose skills are needed
in the peace effort
.
1,$ p
Right Now is the time
for all good citizens
whose skills are needed
in the peace effort
to come to the aid
of their country.
□
```

UNIX System Commands

To enter shell commands without leaving the editor, precede the shell command with an exclamation mark (!). For instance, to display your current directory, type "! ls<CR>". After the shell executes the **ls** command, **ed** will type a second "!" and you will again be in ed command mode.

```
! ls
letter      message temp      temp2
!
□
```

Try other shell commands to see how this feature works.

Partial File Write

Use the **write** command to save the two lines you previously inserted in the file named **temp3**. Type "3,4 w temp3<CR>" and verify that the edit buffer is unchanged by the disk write operation.

```
3,4 w temp3
44
1,$ p
Right Now is the time
for all good citizens
whose skills are needed
in the peace effort
to come to the aid
of their country.
□
```

Now delete these same lines with the command "3,4 d<CR>" and display the buffer.

```
3,4 d
1,$ p
Right Now is the time
for all good citizens
to come to the aid
of their country.
□
```

File Read (Insert)

The **read** command enables you to read text into the buffer without first erasing the buffer, as the "e" **read** command requires. The file contents will be placed after the indicated line address. You do not have to specify a filename if the "remembered filename" is appropriate. In this example, you do have to specify a filename, because when we started this **ed** session we specified **temp2** as the filename.

Since we saved the same two lines on disk which were deleted in the last example, we can use the "r" command to read the contents of the file **temp3**. The text will appear after the current second line, restoring the original state of the edit buffer. Type "2 r temp3<CR>" and the number of characters will be displayed if the read operation is successful. Display the buffer for verification.

```
2 r temp3
44
1,$ p
Right Now is the time
for all good citizens
whose skills are needed
in the peace effort
to come to the aid
of their country.
□
```

List Buffer

The **list** command displays not only *ASCII* text characters, but also non-printing characters, such as *control characters*. The non-printing characters will be represented by either their two-digit *octal* equivalent or by a special symbol. This command will list long text lines which exceed 72 characters by folding the lines into two or more lines. Like the "p" command, the "l" command can appear as a suffix for many other commands. Table 3-1 lists some of the "invisible" characters which the **list** command displays.

As an example, delete the contents of the edit buffer with the "1,$ d" command and append the following text:

```
            tab:^ I<CR>
           bell:^ G <CR>
      form feed:^ L <CR>
     backspace:^ H<CR>
```

Note: You may not be able to enter a backspace on your system.

TABLE 3-1: Invisible characters displayed by **list**

Character	Representation
Tab	>
Backspace	<
Bell	\ 07
Form feed	\ 14

```
1,$ d
a
tab:
bell:
form feed:
backspace
.
□
```

Notice that none of the non-printing characters is visible, and also that the backspace character may have erased the colon you typed. (This depends on your terminal.)

Display the edit buffer with the "p" command.

```
1,$ p
tab:
bell:
formfeed:
backspace:
□
```

Finally, display the contents of the buffer with the **list** command "1,$ l".

```
1,$ l
tab:>
bell:\07
form feed:\14
backspace:<
□
```

You have completed your introduction to **ed** with this tutorial. You can now create and change text files, and you have a solid foundation for further instruction from your UNIX system documentation.

COMMONLY USED
UNIX SYSTEM COMMANDS

Chapter 4

COMMONLY USED
UNIX SYSTEM COMMANDS

IN THIS CHAPTER WE PRESENT 40 UNIX system commands. The screen displays reflect System III, and may be slightly different from other system implementations. However, the content or operation of each command will be essentially the same.

The command descriptions assume an understanding of the material presented in Chapter 3. We continue to use the conventions introduced in Chapter 3 as well. Each command section begins with brief descriptions and screen displays of the command operation, the command line options, and command-specific error messages. The Notes sections offer more detailed explanations of the options, and the Tutorials present several examples you can enter on your computer.

The interrelated nature of the UNIX system becomes apparent in this chapter. Many of our examples use several commands to perform a realistic task. We suggest you focus on the command being addressed, and keep in mind that additional information on related commands will be addressed in subsequent sections.

In order to provide a consistent naming convention for the examples in this chapter, assume you are using the *file system* illustrated in Figure 4-1.

To construct the *your-name* section of this particular file system from your login (personal) directory, enter the commands shown in **boldface** in the following screen:

```
$ mkdir Letters Manuscript
$ ed temp
?temp
a
Now is the time
for all good citizens
to come to the aid
of their country.
.
w
75
q
$ cd Letters
$ mkdir Family Friends
$ cd ../Manuscript
$ mkdir Chap1 Chap2
$ cd Chap1
$ ed sec1
?sec1
a
These lines are in file sec1 of Chap1 subdirectory
of the Manuscript directory.
.
w
80
e sec2
?sec2
a
These lines are in file sec2 of Chap1 subdirectory
of the Manuscript directory.
.
w
80
q
$ cd ../Chap2
$ ed sec1
?sec1
a
These lines are in file sec1 of Chap2 subdirectory
of the Manuscript directory.
.
w
80
q
$ cd
$ □
```

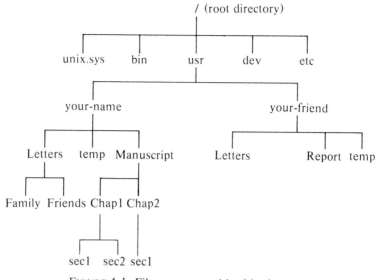

FIGURE 4-1: File system used in this chapter

Access Control

Passwd — Change Login Password

This command changes your password for logging into the UNIX system.

$ passwd

Changes your password.

```
$ passwd
Old password:
New password:
Retype new password:
$ □
```

$	Shell prompt
Old password:	System query for current password
	You type your current password (no echo)
New password:	System query for desired password
	You type new password (no echo)
Retype . . .	System query to verify new password
	You retype new password (no echo)
$ □	Next prompt and cursor

Notes on passwd

This command changes or installs the password associated with your account. In a small local system, your account may be created without any password at all. On a larger system, where your account is established on paper and you must specify a password in writing, be sure to use this utility command to change the password in your first session and prevent unauthorized use of your account.

New passwords must be at least four characters long if a rich alphabet of upper- and lower-case characters and numerals is used, and at least six characters long if exclusively lower-case or exclusively upper-case characters are used. Control characters and punctuation can be used; however, do not include ^H, @, #, ^M, and ^D in your new password.

Only the owner of the password or the *superuser* may change a password, and the owner must prove that he or she knows the old password.

Remember your password. You cannot log into the system without it. If you do forget it, you will have to ask the person in charge of system accounts to delete your account password so that you may log in.

Tutorial

If you wish to change your password from an old password to a new password, type the command and answer the system's prompt for the old password.

```
$ passwd
Old password: □
```

You will not be able to see the password you typed since the system will not echo your response for security reasons. If all went well and you typed in your current password correctly, the system will then prompt you to type the new password, followed by a carriage return.

```
$ passwd
Old password:
New password: □
```

Finally, since you cannot see what you typed, the system will verify that your entry is the password you wanted by prompting you to type it again.

```
$ passwd
Old password:
New password:
Retype new password: □
```

If both responses are the same, your login password file will be changed to reflect your new password.

Communication

Mail — Send or Receive Electronic Mail Among Users

Use this command to communicate with other users in your system. Note: The exact form of the output indicated below may differ from your UNIX system implementation. The content, however, will be the same.

Receiving Mail: $ mail [-r] [-q] [-p] [-f *file*]

Reads each message in your mailbox in last-in, first-out order. After each message is displayed, **mail** reads the instructions you type and directs disposition of the message.

Options:

-r   Reverses order in which **mail** displays messages to first-in, first-out.

-q   Causes **mail** to exit after you type an interrupt character without changing the mailbox.

-p   Displays entire contents of mailbox without queries.

-f *file*   Displays the named *file* as if it were the mail file.

The examples that follow assume these three messages are in your mailbox:

From rathomas Mon Sep 7 09:00:34 1981
Labor Day party at the hot tubs.

From jlyates Fri Sep 4 09:56:30 1981
Don't forget the Labor Day party at Heavenly hot tubs.

From d:consult Mon Aug 10 10:34:45 1981
Dear Dr. Thomas:
. . .

$ mail

Examines contents of mailbox and displays the most recent message first.

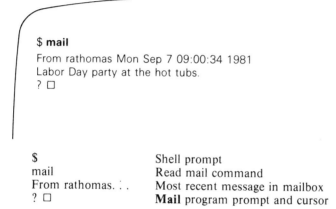

```
$ mail
From rathomas Mon Sep 7 09:00:34 1981
Labor Day party at the hot tubs.
? □
```

$	Shell prompt
mail	Read mail command
From rathomas. . .	Most recent message in mailbox
? □	**Mail** program prompt and cursor

$ mail -r

Reads contents of mailbox and displays oldest message first.

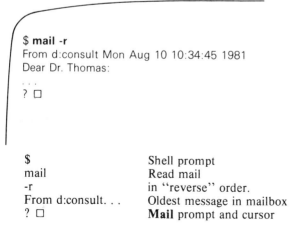

```
$ mail -r
From d:consult Mon Aug 10 10:34:45 1981
Dear Dr. Thomas:
. . .
? □
```

$	Shell prompt
mail	Read mail
-r	in "reverse" order.
From d:consult. . .	Oldest message in mailbox
? □	**Mail** prompt and cursor

$ mail -p

Displays all messages in your mailbox, without distribution queries, then exits from mail.

```
$ mail -p
From rathomas Mon Sep 7 09:00:34 1981
Labor Day party at the hot tubs.

From jlyates Fri Sep 4 09:56:30 1981
Don't forget the Labor Day party at Heavenly hot tubs.

From d:consult Mon Aug 10 10:34:45 1981
Dear Dr. Thomas:
. . .
$ □
```

$	Shell prompt
mail	Read contents of mailbox,
-p	displaying all messages without inquiries.
From rathomas . . .	Most recent message in mailbox
Remember . . .	
From jlyates . . .	Next most recent message
Don't forget . . .	
From d:consult . . .	Oldest message in mailbox
Dear Dr. Thomas:	
. . .	
$ □	Next prompt and cursor

Unless the **mail** program was invoked with the **-p** option on the command line, the program will wait for you to direct disposition of the message after it displays the first message. Use one of the following commands after the **mail** program prompt (?) appears to direct message disposition:

<CR>	Continues to next message or exits from the **mail** program after the last message.
d	Deletes the last message displayed and goes on to the next.
p	Display the message again.
-	Displays the previous message again.
s [file]. . .	Saves the messages in your current directory under the name specified (file **mbox** by default if no filename specified), then exits to the shell. The shell prompt ($) appears.

w [file]. . .　　Saves the messages, without a header (sender's login name and postmark), in the named file in your current directory. If no filename is given, the message(s) are saved under the name **mbox**. Then exits to the shell.

m [person(s)]. . .　　Mails the message to the named **person(s)**. You are the default person.

EOT (^D)　　Leaves unexamined mail in mailbox and exits from **mail**.

q　　Same as **EOT**.

x　　Exits without changing the mailbox file.

!command　　Escapes temporarily to the shell to execute a *command*.

?　　Prints this command summary for message disposition on your terminal.

Sending Mail: $ mail *loginname. . .*

Sends a message to one or more users on your UNIX system.

```
$ mail jlyates
Thank you for the reminder.
I had completely forgotten.
.
$ □
```

$	Shell prompt
mail	Invoke **mail** program to send a message
jlyates	to user with login name of **jlyates**.
Thank you. . .	Message to be sent
.	End-of-message code: a single "." on a line by itself, or ^D
$ □	Next prompt and cursor

$ mail *your-name*

Sends a reminder message to your mailbox to be read the next time you log in. *Your-name* is your account login name.

```
$ mail rathomas
Remember the Labor Day party at the hot tubs.
.
$ ▯
```

$	Shell prompt
mail	Invoke **mail** program to send a message
rathomas	to yourself (login name of **rathomas**).
Remember the. . .	Message to be sent
.	End-of-message code: a single "." on a line by itself, or ^D
$ ▯	Next prompt and cursor

Error Messages

The error messages displayed on your system may not appear exactly like those shown here, but the meaning of the messages should be similar.

```
$ mail gened
Hi gene! Done with the commands yet?

mail: can't send to gened
Mail saved in dead.letter
```

There is no login name "gened."

```
$ mail
From rathomas Sat Sep 26 10:08:44 1981
This is a reminder message to myself.
? a
usage:
q           quit
x           exit without changing mail
p           print
s [file]    save (default mbox)
w [file]    save without header
-           print previous
d           delete
+           next (no delete)
m user      mail to user
! cmd       execute cmd
? □
```

"a" was not a valid **mail** command. **Mail** listed
the valid mail commands and returned the **mail**
prompt for valid input.

Notes on mail

After you log into the UNIX system, you will be informed if you have
mail:

You have mail

Use the **mail** command to both read and write messages. When users
log into the system they are advised if they have mail. The messages are
actually stored in the **/usr/spool/mail** directory in a file with the same
name as the recipient's login name. In the following discussions, we will
call this system directory the UNIX system mailbox or simply
"mailbox."

There are two basic formats for invoking the **mail** command. One
sends a message or messages, and the other reads the message(s) in
your mailbox. To send a message to another user (or even to yourself
for a reminder) use the following form:

$ mail person. . .

Mail will receive your typed text until it reads an end-of-file character, a
^D, or, on some systems, a line containing only a period. It places the

message in the proper mailbox. A header listing the sender's login name and a postmark precedes each message. A *person* is a user's login name. To read the contents of your mailbox, use the following command form:

$ mail [-r] [-q] [-p] [-f *file*]

If no options are specified, the last messages received are the first messages displayed. This can be reversed with the **-r** option when invoking **mail**. You can read all your messages at once and then exit to the shell ($ prompt) with the **-p** option. With another option, **-q**, you can exit from **mail** without changing the mailbox contents, after typing an interrupt character (DEL or RUBOUT).

Tutorial

The **mail** function is convenient for leaving yourself a reminder to read when you next log in. Simply type "mail", a space, then your login name, and press <CR>. Now type a message. When you are finished, press ^D to exit from **mail**.

```
$ mail your-name
( Your message )
[^D]
$ □
```

Note: The ^D enclosed in brackets indicates that the system does not display this entry.

To conveniently write longer messages you may use an editor, save the message on disk, and then instruct **mail** to send the disk file containing the message. Use an editor to write a short message and save the text as the file **reminder**. To send the message to yourself use the **mail** command form with redirected input:

$ **mail** *your-name* < *filename*

Replace *your-name* with your login name and *filename* with **reminder**.

```
$ ed reminder
? reminder
a
( Your message )
.
w
( Number of characters saved )
q
$ mail your-name <reminder
$ □
```

You can communicate with any user on your system by using the **mail** command. The commands cited above are used with references to *your-name* replaced by the login name of the recipient.

Now log off the system and log in again. You should see a message from the system informing you that "You have mail". To read your mail simply type "mail<CR>", and the most recent message will be displayed. When the display has finished type "?<CR>" and read the command summary **mail**.

Type "-<CR>" to reread the previous message. If you have more than one message, press the <CR> to read the next. Save the message which you have just read by typing "s<CR>" and when you exit **mail** the same message will be in a file named **mbox** in your login directory. When you have returned to the shell ($ prompt), type "cat mbox <CR>" to read the message you saved from **mail**.

When invoking the mail command to read your messages there are a number of options you can specify. If you want to read all the messages in your mailbox one after the other without your intervention and then leave **mail**, use the **-p** (print) option.

```
$ mail -p
( Newest message )
. . .
( Oldest message )
$ □
```

To "reverse" the order of the messages so that you read the first message (oldest chronologically) in your mailbox, type "mail -r <CR>". You could concatenate this option with the "print" option to read all your messages oldest first.

```
$ mail -pr
( Oldest message )
. . .
( Newest message )
$ □
```

Mesg — Permit or Deny Messages

This command permits or denies access to your terminal for the **write** communication utility.

$ mesg [n] [y]

Revokes or reinstates "write" permission to other system users on your terminal. Reports the current permission if no option argument is given.

Options:

n   Revoke non-user write permission.

y   Reinstate non-user write permission.

```
$ mesg
is y
$ □
```

$	Shell prompt
mesg	Report the current status for your terminal's write permission
is y	Write permission is enabled
$ □	Next prompt and cursor

```
$ mesg n
$ mesg
is n
$ □
```

$	Shell prompt
mesg	Alter non-user write permission
n	to deny access to your terminal.
mesg	Verify by requesting non-user status
is n	Now there is no write permission
$ □	Next prompt and cursor

```
$ mesg y
$ □
```

$	Shell prompt
mesg	Alter non-user write permission
y	to enable access to your terminal.
$ □	Next prompt and cursor

Error Messages

```
$ mesg x
mesg: usage: mesg [y] [n]
```

Invalid option.

Notes on mesg

This utility provides a convenient way to prevent other users from writing on your terminal with the **write** command. You may wish to "write protect" your terminal when you are editing a document to prevent others from interfering with your screen display.

If you invoke **mesg** without an argument it displays the status of your terminal's write permission. The response "is y" means your terminal is write enabled, and "is n" means your terminal is write protected. Other system users cannot communicate with you by using the **write** command when your terminal is write protected.

Invoke **mesg** with the argument **n** to forbid message reception, and with the argument **y** to reenable message reception. To verify that the write permission was correctly set or reset after changing the permission, invoke **mesg** without an argument and check the terminal status.

Tutorial

First, type "mesg<CR>" to see your current terminal write permission status.

```
$ mesg
is y
$ □
```

Note: You should enable your terminal's write permission before proceeding with this tutorial. Type "mesg y<CR>" and check the status again.

Next, you need to determine your current terminal number. Give the **tty** command by typing "tty<CR>", and the response will be the number of the terminal file for your present session. To verify the number, type "who<CR>" and you should see your owner (login) name and the same terminal number. For example, if your terminal designation is "tty5" then you would observe the following responses.

```
$ tty
tty5
$ who
. . .
your-name    tty5 . . .
. . .
$ □
```

The UNIX system treats your terminal as a file. The terminal is a special type of file called a *character device file.* To observe the permission modes for this file you simply list the terminal permissions by invoking the **ls** (list) command with the **-l** option. Type "ls -l /dev/*ttyname*<CR>", where *ttyname* is your current terminal number. Continuing with our example, you will observe something similar to the following display.

```
$ /ls -l /dev/tty5
crw--w--w-    1 your-name 23, 98 Oct 14 11:11 /dev/tty5
$ □
```

The "c" to the left of the permission modes indicates that the file **/dev/tty5** is a character file. The presence of a "w" character indicates that write permission is enabled for either you (the login owner), other users in your group, or all other users. In the screen above, write permission is enabled for all three classes of users. More information on file permissions is available in the **ls** command summary in this chapter.

Next, write protect your terminal by typing "mesg n<CR>". Invoke **mesg** without an argument to verify the change.

```
$ mesg n
$ mesg
is n
$ □
```

Examine the permission modes by typing "ls -l /dev/*ttyname*<CR>". The "w" characters have been replaced by dashes, indicating that there is no write permission for other system users.

```
$ ls -l /dev/tty5
crw------- 1 your-name 23, 98 Oct 14 11:11 /dev/tty5
$ □
```

To see how your system enforces the terminal write protection feature, type "write *your-name*<CR>" and another "<CR>" if needed. An error message will appear on the screen.

```
$ write your-name
Permission denied.
$ □
```

Finally, before leaving this tutorial, reenable your terminal's write permission by typing "mesg y<CR>".

Write — Write to Another User

This command permits direct on-line communication with other users currently logged into your UNIX system.

$ **write** *user* [*ttyname*]

Initiates message transmission to *user* on *ttyname*.

Terminal Display of rathomas:	**Terminal Display of jlyates:**

```
$ write jlyates

Message from jlyates tty6 . . .
Hello!
Thanks for the present -o-


Glad you liked it! -o-
I've got to go now. -oo-

[^D]


EOF
```

```
Message from rathomas tty4
$ write rathomas

Hello!

Thanks for the present. -o-
Glad you liked it. -o-


I've got to go now. -oo-

EOF
[^D]
```

$ **write jlyates**	User **rathomas** initiates write
Message from rathomas tty4 . . .	System announces **rathomas** is writing
$ **write rathomas**	User **jlyates** establishes return communication link
Message from jlyates tty6 . . .	System announces **jlyates** is writing
Hello!	First line sent by **rathomas**
Hello!	First line appears on recipient's terminal
Thanks for the present. -o-	Second line sent by **rathomas** ("-o-" indicates message is over)
Thanks for the present. -o-	Second line appears on recipient's terminal
Glad you liked it. -o-	User **jlyates** sends a reply
Glad you liked it! -o-	Reply received by **rathomas**

I've got to go **now. -oo-**	User **rathomas** sends last line (''-oo-'' means ''over and out'')
I've got to go now. -oo-	Recipient receives last line
^**D**	User **rathomas** exits **write** by pressing ^**D** (doesn't appear on screen)
EOF	User **jlyates** receives ''EOF'' (end-of-file) from system
^**D**	User **jlyates** exits with ^**D**
EOF	User **rathomas** receives ''EOF''

Error Messages

```
$ write gened
gened not logged in.
```

Attempt to write to a user who is not on-line.

```
$ write -x rathomas
/dev/rathomas: No such tty
```

There are no options for **write**, so in this case ''-x'' was
thought to be a user and ''rathomas'' a terminal.

```
$ write rathomas
Permission denied
```

Other user is write-protected with **mesg**

Notes on write

This utility permits direct communication between on-line users. First, use the **who** command to see if the desired recipient is currently on-line. Since a user can be logged into more than one terminal at a time, you may need to specify the recipient's terminal name.

To initiate transmission use the following command form:

write *user* [*ttyname*]

Here *user* is the recipient's login name and *ttyname* should be supplied if *user* is logged in on more than one terminal.

The recipient will receive a message on his/her screen indicating your attempt to communicate:

Message from yourname yourttyname. . .

Inter-terminal messages cannot be received if the recipient is using a program such as **nroff** or **pr**. These programs temporarily disallow such messages in order to prevent outside influence over the terminal output. Also, the recipient can deny non-user write permission on his/her terminal by using the **mesg** program.

If the recipient wishes to return your communication, he/she needs to invoke **write** specifying your login name and terminal:

write *yourname* [*yourttyname*]

Messages are sent a line at a time when the carriage return is pressed. The Bell Laboratories documentation recommends using the following protocol to prevent messages from crossing and producing confusing displays:

• When you first write to another user, wait for that user to respond before you start to send your message.

• Each party should end *each* message with a distinctive signal such as "-o-" for "over."

• Each party should use "-oo-" for "over and out" when he or she wishes to terminate the conversation.

To execute a shell *command* without leaving the **write** program, type the following as the first expression on a line:

!*command*

To exit the **write** program and return to the shell ($ prompt) press a

^D. The **write** program will transmit the message "EOF" to the recipient's terminal, telling the recipient that you have exited **write**.

Tutorial

As a first example, try writing to yourself. This will help you become familiar with the protocol. To initiate transmission type "write *yourname*<CR>". Substitute your login name for *yourname*. Then type the messages shown in **boldface** in the following screen.

```
$ write yourname
Message from yourname tty5. . .
This is a test of write.-o-
This is a test of write.-o-
I'm writing to myself.-o-
I'm writing to myself.-o-
```

After invoking the **write** program to write to yourself (designated by yourname) you received a message "Message from yourname tty5. . ." telling you that yourname was initiating transmission from terminal tty5. On the next line you typed yourself the message "This is a test of write.-o-". After pressing <CR> you saw that the message was received. This was repeated again on the next two lines. Note that the "-o-" is a voluntary protocol, *not* a signal recognized by **write**.

Execute the shell command to list your directory while still in the **write** program by typing "!ls<CR>".

```
!ls
Letters    Manuscript temp
!
```

After the shell command was complete an exclamation mark "!" appeared on your terminal. Although there is no prompt, you are still in the **write** program. Send yourself a sign-off message and then leave **write** by pressing a control-D.

Now it's time to end transmission.-oo-
Now it's time to end transmission.-oo-
EOF
$ □

Note: ^D does not appear, but **write** displays "EOF" before you return to the shell.

When you have mastered the protocol, send a message to a friend on-line. Use the **who** command to see if you know anyone currently logged in. Use the **ps** command with the **a** (for all) option to learn what process a user is executing. You might choose to write to someone who is using the shell (indicated by -sh) rather than an editor to prevent confusing that person's display.

Documentation

Man — Display On-Line UNIX Programmer's Manual

This command displays sections of the on-line *UNIX Programmer's Manual,* for study of command descriptions. The exact behavior of the **man** program will depend on your UNIX implementation.

$ **man** *title*

Displays occurrences of *title.*

```
$ man date <CR>
DATE(1) . . .
. . .
[ Press any key to continue ]
$ □
```

$	Shell prompt
man	Display *UNIX Programmer's Manual* for
date	the **date** command.
DATE(1) . . .	Display of the on-line version of this command.
[Press . . .]	Pause so you can catch up reading
	(Implementation-dependent)
$ □	Next prompt and cursor

$ man *title* > *filename*

Saves the manual section *title* on disk as *filename*.

```
$ man date >date.doc
$ □
```

$	Shell prompt
man	Display *UNIX Programmer's Manual* for
date	the **date** command,
>	redirecting the output to
date.doc	the disk file named **date.doc**.
$ □	Next prompt and cursor

$ **man** *-options section title . . .*

Locates and displays the pages of the *UNIX Programmer's Manual* named *title* in the specified *section.*

Options:

-t Phototypesets the section using **TROFF**.

-n Prints the section on the standard output using **NROFF**.

-e If concatenated with **-t** or **-n** causes the manual section to be preprocessed by **neqn** or **eqn**; **-e** alone means **-te**.

-w Displays the pathnames of the manual sections, but does not display the manuals themselves.

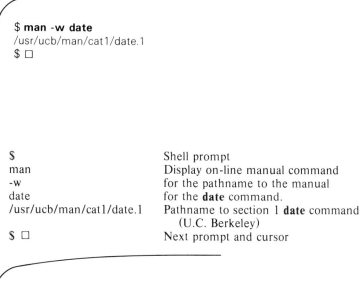

```
$ man -w date
/usr/ucb/man/cat1/date.1
$ □
```

$	Shell prompt
man	Display on-line manual command
-w	for the pathname to the manual
date	for the **date** command.
/usr/ucb/man/cat1/date.1	Pathname to section 1 **date** command (U.C. Berkeley)
$ □	Next prompt and cursor

```
$ cat  /usr/ucb/man/cat1/date.1

DATE(1)        UNIX Programmer's Manual    DATE(1)

NAME
[ Interrupt ]
$ □
```

$	Shell prompt
cat	Display command
/usr/ucb/man/cat1/date.1	Pathname to the desired manual
DATE(1) . . .	Display of manual . . .
[Interrupt]	Interrupt character typed
$ □	Next prompt and cursor

Error Messages

```
$ man 6 date
No entry found for date
```

There is no section 6 entry for date.

```
$ man -x date
man: unknown option 'x'
```

There is no -x option.

Notes on man

This command and its options appear to be implementation-dependent.
Some systems do not display certain sections of the *UNIX Programmer's
Manual* because these sections are not operational in that system implementation, or they operate in a substantially different way. Check your
particular UNIX system installation for pertinent details.

The *title* is entered in lower case. The *section* number does not need a letter suffix. If no *section* is specified, the whole manual is searched for *title* and some or all occurrences of it are displayed on your terminal (implementation-dependent).

If no options are specified, previously formatted manual sections will be displayed. If no terminal is available, the **-n** option is assumed, and the manual sections are printed rather than displayed. A filter program may be required to adapt the output to a particular terminal's characteristics.

Tutorial

To display the on-line description of a UNIX system command, use the following command form:

$ **man** *command*

The command description from section 1 of the *UNIX Programmer's Manual* appears. If you wish to keep a copy of the manual section on your disk for subsequent editing, use the following form:

$ **man** *command* > *command*.doc

Start by displaying the on-line description for **man**; type either "man man<CR>" or "man > man.doc" followed by "cat man.doc".

```
$ man man
MAN(1)        UNIX Programmer's Manual            MAN(1)
[ Interrupt ]
$ □
```

In this example we began listing the on-line *UNIX Programmer's Manual* entry for the command **man**. By default the first section is listed. [Interrupt] shows that we pressed the interrupt character to abort the display. The interrupt character did not appear on the terminal.

To display entries for sections other than the default (1) you must explicitly specify the section. Type "man 7 man<CR>":

```
$ man 7 man
MAN(7)              UNIX Programmer's Manual           MAN(7)

NAME
    man - macros to typeset manual

SYNOPSIS
    nroff -man file . . .
    troff -man file . . .

DESCRIPTION
    . . .[ Interrupt ]
$ □
```

Type "man 7 ascii<CR>" and a chart of the set of ASCII characters and their octal equivalents will be displayed. Another informative manual section is a description of the file system hierarchy, obtained by typing "man 7 hier<CR>".

You may find the on-line manuals difficult to understand when you first read them. The descriptions in these manuals tend to be terse and filled with technical jargon. Study the on-line manuals for the commands covered in this book to learn how to interpret the on-line descriptions of the other commands.

Manual sections are searched in a particular order to locate commonly used information quickly. Section numbers, in the order searched, and their meanings are listed below:

1	General commands
3	Standard subroutine library
3s	Standard I/O subroutine library
3m	Mathematical subroutine library
2	UNIX system calls
3f	f77 subroutine libraries
1g	Graphics-related commands
3x	Various specialized subroutine libraries
3f4p	f4p introduction and subroutine libraries

Im	System maintenance commands
1c	Communication-related commands
5	Include files and formats
6	Games
7	Special files
4	Device driver descriptions
8	UNIX system procedures

Note: Your implementation may organize or select section headings in a different manner than those shown above.

File Management

Cat — Concatenate and Print

Cat, short for concatenate, successively displays the contents of one or more files. The resulting output is directed to your terminal or a file, or piped to another command.

$ **cat** *filename*

Displays the contents of the file *filename* on your terminal (standard output).

```
$ cat temp
Now is the time
for all good citizens
to come to the aid
of their country.
$ □
```

$	Shell prompt
cat	Display the contents
temp	of the file **temp**.
Now is. . .	File contents (text) being displayed
$ □	Next prompt and cursor

$ cat *file1 file2. . .*

Reads *file1, file2,* and any other files you specify, in sequence and displays them successively on your terminal.

```
$ cat sec1 sec2
This is section 1 of chapter 1.
This is section 2 of chapter 1.
$ □
```

$	Shell prompt
cat sec1 sec2	Concatenates the display of **sec1** and **sec2**
This is section 1 . . .	Display of **sec1** followed immediately by
This is section 2 . . .	the display of **sec2**.
$ □	Next prompt and cursor

$ cat *file1 file2* >*file3*

Concatenates the contents of *file1* and *file2* and places the result in disk file named *file3*.

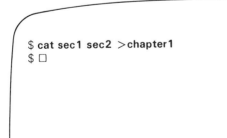

```
$ cat sec1 sec2 >chapter1
$ □
```

$	Shell prompt
cat sec1 sec2	Prints files **sec1** and **sec2** in succession to standard output
>	Redirects standard output
chapter1	to the file **chapter1**.
$ ☐	Next prompt and cursor

$ **cat** >*filename*

This form of the **cat** command will accept subsequent lines directly from the keyboard and write them onto the file named *filename*. Terminate **cat** by pressing ^D. You can use character erase (#) and line kill (@) to make corrections while entering lines.

```
$ cat>testfile
This is text stored in testfile.
[^D]
$ ☐
```

$	Shell prompt
cat >testfile	Copy standard input (keyboard) to **testfile**
This is. . .	One line as entered from keyboard
[^D]	Control-D (not echoed back)
$ ☐	Next prompt and cursor

Error Messages

```
$ cat temp2
cat: can't open temp2
```

The file **temp2** does not exist, or exists but is unreadable.

```
$ cat temp temp2
cat: can't open temp2
Now is the time
for all good citizens
to come to the aid
of their country.
```

File **temp2** does not exist, but **temp** does and is displayed.

```
$ cat -x temp
cat: can't open -x
Now is the time
for all good citizens
to come to the aid
of their country.
```

Cat interprets ''-x'' to be a file.

```
$ cat <temp 2
temp2: cannot open
```

The shell cannot open **temp2** to redirect it for input to **cat**.

Notes on cat

A file you wish to concatenate should contain only printable characters. If you request files containing non-printable characters (such as control characters), garbage will appear on the screen. You may successfully use **cat** to list files which contain ASCII text. You may use a text editor or word processing program to display or print a file, but if you just want to take a quick look at your program or data, the **cat** program is a timesaver.

You may use **cat** to combine two or more files into another single file by redirecting the command output. Files are copied in the same sequence you specified on the command line.

If you wish to title or paginate a listing, employ the related **pr** command.

Tutorial

Type the command "cat temp<CR>" to display the contents of **temp**.

```
$ cat temp
Now is the time
for all good citizens
to come to the
aid of their country.
$ □
```

Since **temp** is an ASCII text file you are able to read its contents. If **temp** were an object program or a directory, only cryptic characters would be displayed on the screen. Finally, if **temp** were empty, nothing would be displayed.

You may wish to display just a few lines of a file to determine its contents. In that case, press the interrupt character (usually labeled RUBOUT or DEL) to abort further output. Type "cat /usr/dict/words<CR>" to display the on-line dictionary. Use the DEL key to abort the display. A shell prompt ($) will then appear.

In our tutorial file system **Letters** is a directory. If you typed "cat Letters<CR>" the system would display garbage characters intermixed with filenames, proving that you cannot effectively display the contents of a directory with **cat**. Use the **ls** command to list the contents of a directory file.

If no filename is specified, or if the argument "-" is entered, then **cat** reads from the standard input keyboard. To illustrate, type "cat<CR>". The information you type will be displayed on the standard output (terminal). Now try typing a few lines. You will see the line as you type it (an echo of your input). After typing each <CR> you will see the line duplicated on your terminal. This redirection capability of the **cat** command offers a rapid method of entering data into a file without using an editor. To exit the **cat** program, type ^D.

To illustrate redirecting the output of **cat** to a file, type "cat >testfile<CR>", then type the line "This is one way to enter text into a file<CR>", and finally press ^D to return to the shell.

You have just entered another text file, **testfile**, into your login directory. Type "ls<CR>" and observe the display.

```
$ ls
letters    Manuscript    temp    testfile
$ □
```

Concatenate the display of the contents of the files **temp** and **testfile** by typing "cat temp testfile<CR>".

```
$ cat temp testfile
Now is the time
for all good citizens
to come to the
aid of their country.
This is one way to enter text into a file
$ □
```

The **cat** program will read and display the file **temp**, then immediately read and display the file **testfile**.

To concatenate the files **temp** and **testfile** and write them to a third file named **togetherfile,** type "cat temp testfile >togetherfile<CR>".

```
$ cat temp testfile >togetherfile
$ □
```

To verify the results, use **cat** to display the contents of **togetherfile.** Type "cat togetherfile<CR>" and you will observe the original contents of **temp** and **testfile** displayed in immediate succession.

Bugs

Note that when you use ">" to redirect the output to a file, as in the following command line, the shell will erase the contents of the file named *file1* just before the command is executed.

cat *file1 file2. . . >file1*

Generally speaking, you never use the same filename as input and output in the same command.

Cd — Change Working Directory

Use this command to change the current working directory.

$ **cd**

Returns you to your login directory from any other directory.

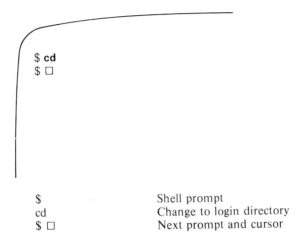

$	Shell prompt
cd	Change to login directory
$ ☐	Next prompt and cursor

$ **cd** *fullpathname*

Moves you to the last directory in the complete *fullpathname.*

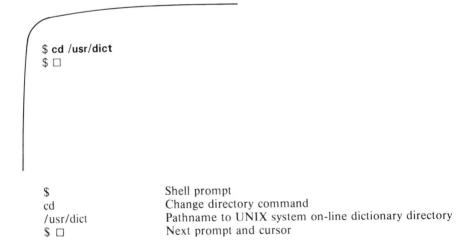

$	Shell prompt
cd	Change directory command
/usr/dict	Pathname to UNIX system on-line dictionary directory
$ ☐	Next prompt and cursor

$ **cd** *subdir*

Moves from the current directory down to the subdirectory named *subdir.* Here, *subdir* must exist in your current "working" directory.

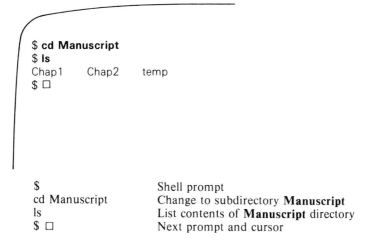

```
$ cd Manuscript
$ ls
Chap1      Chap2      temp
$ □
```

$	Shell prompt
cd Manuscript	Change to subdirectory **Manuscript**
ls	List contents of **Manuscript** directory
$ □	Next prompt and cursor

$ cd . .

Changes to the "parent" directory. You move upward one level in the directory hierarchy.

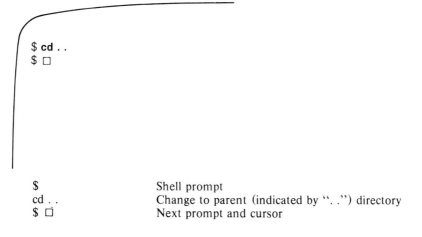

```
$ cd . .
$ □
```

$	Shell prompt
cd . .	Change to parent (indicated by ". .") directory
$ □	Next prompt and cursor

Error Messages

```
$ cd temp
temp: bad directory
```

There is no directory named **temp**.

```
$ cd -x Manuscript
-x: bad directory
```

There are no options to the **cd** command;
cd tried to interpret "-x" as a directory.

Notes on cd

When you log into the UNIX system, your working directory will be your personal (or login) directory. You can keep all files in your login directory or you may choose to separate files into subdirectories, according to particular projects. For instance, in our practice file system, all files related to the manuscript are kept in the **Manuscript** directory while all correspondence files are in the **Letters** directory.

You can access files in another directory without specifying a file pathname each time. Typing pathnames rather than moving to a different directory creates more opportunities to make typographical errors. Just move from your current directory to the directory that contains the desired files. You must have execute (search) permission to move to the desired directory (see the **ls** command for a discussion of file system permission).

Tutorial

Suppose you wish to edit several of the files contained in the practice subdirectory **Manuscript**. Move to the **Manuscript** directory for these operations to avoid specifying long pathnames for every file. From the practice login directory move to the **Manuscript** subdirectory by typing "cd Manuscript<CR>". To verify that you are in the **Manuscript** directory, use the **pwd** and **ls** commands. Type "pwd; ls<CR>".

```
$ cd Manuscript
$ pwd; ls
/usr/your-name/Manuscript
Chap1     Chap2
$ □
```

You may occasionally need to move from one subdirectory to another. You can change from the **Manuscript** to the **Letters** directory by jumping "up" to their common parent directory (. .) and then jumping "down" into the **Letters** directory. To do this, type the command "cd ../Letters<CR>". Verify the change with the **pwd** command.

```
$ cd . ./Letters
$ pwd
/usr/your-name/Letters
$ □
```

It is easy for a novice to get "lost" in the complex hierarchical file system. If that happens, you can easily return home to your login directory at any time from any directory by typing "cd<CR>". Try this and then give the command "pwd<CR>".

```
$ cd
$ pwd
/usr/your-name
$ □
```

Chmod — Change Mode

The change mode command is used to alter the permission modes of one or more files or directories. The permissions include read, write, and execute. The permissions for **user** (login owner), a **group** of users, and all **others** can be changed independently.

$ **chmod** [*Who*] *Op-code Permission. . . file. . .*

Changes the permission modes for *file*.

Who:

u	Login owner (user)
g	Group
o	All others
a	All (default): user, group, and all others

Op-codes:

+	Add permission of files mode
-	Remove permission of files mode
=	Assign absolute permission for file

Permissions:

r   Read
w   Write
x   Execute

Note: Each set of [*Who*] *Op-code Permission* must be entered without intervening spaces.

```
$ ls -l temp
-rwxrwxrwx   1 rathomas        75 Oct 1 20:18 temp
$ chmod go-w temp
$ ls -l temp
-rwxr-xr-x   1 rathomas        75 Oct 1 20:18 temp
$ □
```

$	Shell prompt
ls -l	List file in long format and observe
-rwxrwxrwx	all permissions enabled.
chmod	Change mode for
go	owner's group and all others,
-w	restricting write permission
temp	for the file **temp**.
ls -l	List file in long format and observe
-rwxr-xr-x	the file is "write protected."
$ □	Next prompt and cursor

```
$ ls -l command.script
-rw------   1 rathomas        36 Oct   4 10:51 command.script
$ chmod +x command.script
$ ls -l command.script
-rwx------   1 rathomas        36 Oct   4 10:51 command.script
$ □
```

$	Shell prompt
ls -l	List in long format and observe
-rw-------	no execute permission.
chmod	Change the mode

+x	to make executable the
command.script	file named **command.script**.
ls -l	List in long format and observe
-rwx------	file can now be executed.
$ □	Next prompt and cursor

```
$ ls -l command.script
-rwx------   1 rathomas              36 Oct 4 10:51 command.script
$ chmod a=rwx command.script
$ ls -l command.script
-rwxrwxrwx   1 rathomas              36 Oct 4 10:51 command.script
$ □
```

$	Shell prompt
ls -l	List in long format and observe
-rwx-----	permissions on for owner only.
chmod	Change mode for
a	all users,
=	assigning permission for
rwx	read, write and execute
command.script	for the file **command.script**.
ls -l	List in long format and observe
-rwxrwxrwx	permissions on for everyone.
$ □	Next prompt and cursor

$ chmod [*who*] *Op-code Permission. . . directory. . .*

Changes the permission mode for the specified directory or directories.

```
$ ls -l
drwx------   2 rathomas        48 Oct   1 20:30 Test
$ chmod -x Test

drw------   2 rathomas        48 Oct   1 20:30 Test
$ □
```

$	Shell prompt
ls -l	List directory in long format.
drwx------	Permissions set by **umask**
chmod	Change mode for all (default),
-x	restricting search permission
Test	in newly created directory **Test**.
ls -l	List directory and observe
drw------	no search permission for owner.
$ □	Next prompt and cursor

```
$ ls -l
total  3
drwx------   4 rathomas        80 Sep 24 19:49 Letters
drwx------   4 rathomas       112 Sep 26 12:40 Manuscript
-rw-------   1 rathomas        75 Oct  3 13:16 temp
$ chmod a=rwx *
$ ls -l
total  3
drwxrwxrwx   4 rathomas        80 Sep 24 19:49 Letters
drwxrwxrwx   4 rathomas       112 Sep 26 12:40 Manuscript
-rwxrwxrwx   1 rathomas        75 Oct  3 13:16 temp
$ □
```

$	Shell prompt
ls -l	List login directory in long format
drwx------	Default modes for **Letters**,
drwx------	**Manuscript**,
-rw-------	and **temp**.
chmod	Change mode for
a=rwx	all users, enabling all permissions
*	for all visible files in current directory.
$ ls -l	List in long format
drwxrwxrwx	All permissions on for **Letters**,
drwxrwxrwx	**Manuscript**,
-rwxrwxrwx	and **temp**.
$ □	Next prompt and cursor

Error Messages

```
$ chmod u + x temp
chmod: can't access +
chmod: can't access x
```

Can't separate *Who* from *Permission.*
Can't separate *Op-code* from *Permission.*

```
$ chmod x+x temp
chmod: invalid mode
```

Not a valid *Who.*

```
$ chmod u.x temp
chmod: invalid mode
```

Not a valid *Op-code.*

```
$ chmod -y temp
chmod: invalid mode
```

Not a valid *Permission.*

```
$ chmod u+ x temps
chmod: can't access temps
```

The file **temps** doesn't exist.

```
$ chmod a=rw a-x temp
chmod: can't access a-x
```

One set of concatenated *Who Op-code Permission*
allowed per **chmod** command.

Notes on chmod

There are three major categories of access privileges: read, write, and
execute. The **chmod** command allows you to change these permissions

for a file or directory. Read permission grants access to print a file's contents or list a directory. Write permission enables you to add characters to a file, or add entries to a directory by creating or moving files and directories. Execute permission has a different meaning for files and directories. If a file has execute permission, you can invoke it like a command. If a directory has execute permission, you can access its filenames or search through it.

The access privileges are independent of one another; the presence or absence of any access mode does not affect any other mode. One or more of these access permissions may be assigned to the owner (specified by **u**), his/her user group (**g**), and all others (**o**). Only the file owner or the *superuser* may change the permission modes of a file. In theory the access modes can be assigned in any combination, but in practice certain combinations are more useful than others. For instance, if you were granted write permission for a file or directory you would usually have read permission as well.

When you create a file or directory, your system assigns a certain pattern of permission modes as a default situation. This is referred to as a *umask* or user mask. The umask can be reset to any combination of permissions. Ask your system administrator to reset it for you. On our system the default umask displays the **-rw------** pattern for the permission modes when we create a file. Now whenever we specify a **chmod** command which uses the default case for *Who* we start with the **-rw------** pattern and add or subtract the desired permissions. If we request a change mode of -w+x (short for u-w+x) then the resulting pattern would be **-r- x------**.

After scanning the permissions for your files and directories you may decide to change the mode(s) from the default case (set by your umask) to a different combination. For instance, it is advisable to write protect your files and directories from destruction by other system users. To restrict access by other users, remove the "execute" permission on directories you do not want searched.

Chmod can designate a program file as "executable." Executable files can contain compiled programs ready for loading into the computer memory, or they can be text files of instructions for programming the shell.

The change operations can be conveniently specified with the symbolic format depicted in this command summary. There is also an equivalent *octal* representation for the same options which will not be discussed in this introductory text.

Tutorial

For the examples which follow it is helpful to examine permissions for the files and directories using the **ls** command with the "long" format option before and after each **chmod** command. The permissions are listed in the first field printed.

In the first set of examples we change the permissions modes for a file and observe the effect. Since umasks may differ, set your **temp** file to enable read and write, but deny everyone execute permission. Type "chmod a=rw-x temp" and list in long format to verify.

```
$ chmod a=rw -x temp
$ ls -l temp
-rw-rw-rw-      1 rathomas           75 Oct 1   20:18 temp
$ □
```

You can allow others to read your files, but to prevent accidental removal or alteration you should write protect the files which you share with other system users. For example, let's allow everyone to read but not to write by invoking the command "chmod a-w temp<CR>" and verifying the change with "ls -l temp<CR>"·

```
$ chmod a-w temp
$ ls -l temp
-r--r--r--      1 rathomas           75 Oct   1 20:18 temp
$ □
```

Enter the commands in the following display to see how the absence of write permission for a file is enforced by the system.

```
$ ls -l temp
-r--r--r-- temp
$ mv temp temp2
$ ls
Letters        Manuscript temp2
$ mv temp2 temp
$ cp temp temp2
$ ls -l temp*
-r--r--r--   temp
-r--------   temp2
$ mv temp temp2
$ ls -l temp*
-r--r--r--   temp2
$ mv temp2 temp
$ cat >temp
temp: cannot create
$ cat >>temp
temp: cannot create
$ cat test
This is a test file.
$ mv test temp
mv: temp: 444 mode n
$ cp test temp
cp: cannot create temp
$ rm temp
rm: temp 444 mode n
$ □
```

$ ls -l temp	List **temp** in long format
-r--r--r-- temp	Verify that write is disabled
$ mv temp temp2	Rename **temp** to **temp2**
$ ls	Verify
Letters Manuscript temp2	Ability to rename not affected
$ mv temp2 temp	Change name back now
$ cp temp temp2	Make a copy named **temp2**
$ ls -l temp*	Verify
-r--r--r-- temp	Source file
-r-------- temp2	Destination file permissions influenced by owner's "umask"
$ mv temp temp2	Rename to **temp2**
$ ls -l temp*	Verify that permissions
-r--r--r-- temp2	are the same if renamed.

$ **mv temp2 temp**	Change name back
$ **cat >temp**	Attempt to write to **temp**
temp: cannot create	Shell can't open for writing,
$ **cat >>temp**	nor for
temp: cannot create	appending.
$ **cat test**	Another file named **test**
This is a test file.	contains this text.
$ **mv test temp**	Attempt to rename **test** to **temp**
mv: temp: 444 mode **n**	is queried. Answer **n** (for no).
$ **cp test temp**	Attempt to copy **test** onto **temp**
cp: cannot create temp	unsuccessful.
$ **rm temp**	Remove **temp** file
rm: temp 444 mode **n**	Not permitted without query
$ □	Next prompt and cursor

Note: the octal mode value shown above may be different for your system, depending on the umask setting.

To see how the system enforces the absence of read permission for a file, observe the following screen.

```
$ chmod a+w-r temp
$ ls -l temp
--w--w--w-   temp
$ cat temp
cat: can't open temp
$ pr temp
$
$ ed temp
?temp
q
$ □
```

$ **chmod a +w-r temp**	Change mode to disable reading
$ **ls -l temp**	and verify.
--w--w--w- temp	
$ **cat temp**	
cat: can't open temp	**cat** can't open **temp** to print,
$ **pr temp**	
$	nor can **pr**.
$ **ed temp**	Attempt to read file with **ed**
? temp	is also unsuccessful.
q	
$ □	Next prompt and cursor

To designate the shell *command files* as executable, use the **chmod** command. Unless a file is flagged as executable, the shell will not "see" your directory files. For example, use an editor (such as **ed**) to create the file **test.script** containing the command "echo This is a test.". Then use the **chmod** command "chmod +x test.script<CR>". Now "run" or execute the file by simply typing its name.

```
$ ed test.script
?test.script
a
echo This is a test.
.
w
21
q
$ test.script
test.script: cannot execute
$ chmod +x test.script
$ test.script
This is a test.
$ □
```

$ **ed test.script**	Invoke **ed** to edit
?test.script	**test.script** (not yet created).
a	Enter append mode
echo This is a test.	Add this one-line command
.	Back to **command mode**
w	Write buffer to disk
21	21 characters written
q	Exit **ed**
$ **test.script**	Try to execute **test.script**
test.script: cannot execute	Error message
$ **chmod +x test.script**	Need to mark it "executable"
$ **test.script**	Try to execute again
This is a test.	This time it works
$ □	Next prompt and cursor

The following examples examine the effects of **chmod** on your directories. First create a new directory named **Test** in your login directory and enable all modes with "chmod a=rwx Test<CR>". Now list your login directory in long format to verify the permission status.

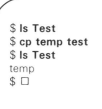

```
$ mkdir Test
$ chmod a=rwx Test
$ ls -l
drwxrwxrwx   2 rathomas      48   Oct 1 20:30 Test
$ □
```

Note: As before, we only show the one line from the **ls** command that pertains to the directory **Test**.

All permissions are enabled. Move a copy of the text file **temp** in **Test** and verify.

```
$ ls Test
$ cp temp test
$ ls Test
temp
$ □
```

Note: The first command in the preceding screen gave no output because there were no files in **Test**.

To restrict your (owner) execute (search) permission for **Test,** type "chmod -x Test<CR>" and verify.

```
$ chmod -x Test
$ ls -l
drw-rwxrwx   2 rathomas
$ □
```

Consider how the system enforces the absence of execute permission for a directory. Observe the effects of the commands given from your login directory shown in **boldface** on the following screen.

```
$ ls Test
temp
$ ls -l Test
Test/temp not found
total 0
$ rm Test/temp
rm: Test/temp nonexistent
$ cd Test
Test: bad directory
$ mv Test/temp x
mv: cannot access Test/temp
$ □
```

$ ls Test	List directory contents
temp	for the name is possible
$ ls -l Test	Long directory listing
Test/temp not found	not permitted.
total 0	
$ rm Test/temp	
rm: Test/temp nonexistent	Can't access **temp** in **Test**
$ cd Test	
Test: bad directory	Can't change to **Test** directory
$ mv Test/temp x	
mv: cannot access Test/temp	Can't rename file **temp** in **Test**
$ □	Next prompt and cursor

Now give the command to enable your search permission, but turn off your write permission and see how the system enforced this restriction on a directory file.

```
$ chmod +x-w Test
$ ls -l
dr-xrwxrwx Test
$ ls -l Test
total 2
-rw------ temp
$ rm Test/temp
rm: Test/temp not removed
$ mv temp Test
cp: cannot create Test/temp
$ □
```

```
$ chmod +x-w Test
$ ls -l
'dr-xrwxrwx Test                    Verify no write permission for Test
$ ls -l Test
total 2
-rw------ temp                      Can read temp for long listing
$ rm Test/temp
rm: Test/temp not removed           Can't rename temp in Test
$ mv temp Test
cp: cannot create Test/temp         Can't rename file into Test
$ □                                 Next prompt and cursor
```

Note: You entered all the commands in the preceding screen while still in your login directory.

Restricting the read permission to one of your directories produces a different set of responses. To enable **write** and restrict **read**, type the command "chmod +w-r Test<CR>". Now observe what the commands invoked from your login directory produce in the following screen.

```
$ chmod +w-r Test
$ ls -l
d-wxrwxrwx Test
$ cat Test
cat: can't open Test
$ cat Test/temp
Now is the time
for all good citizens
to come to the aid
of their country.
$ ls Test
Test unreadable
$ ls -l Test
Test unreadable
total 2
$ rm -r Test
rm: Test: cannot read
$ cd Test
$ mkdir Test2
mkdir: cannot access
$ cd
$ □
```

```
$ chmod +w-r Test
$ ls -l
```

```
d-wxrwxrwx Test          Verify no read permission for Test
$ cat Test
cat: can't open Test     Can't print Test with cat
$ cat Test/temp
Now is the time          You can access a file within Test
for all good citizens       and print it with cat.
to come to the aid
of their country.
$ ls Test
Test unreadable          Can't list Test either
$ ls -l Test
Test unreadable
total 2
$ rm -r Test
rm: Test: cannot read    Can't recursively remove Test
$ cd Test                Change to Test directory
$ mkdir Test2            Attempt to create directory in Test
mkdir: cannot access     Mkdir cannot access the current directory,
                            which is Test, to create a directory.
$ cd                     Change back to login directory
$ □                      Next prompt and cursor
```

Restore your practice file system to its original state before leaving this tutorial session by executing the following commands.

```
$ chmod +r Test
$ rm -r Test
$ ls
Letters  Manuscript  temp
$ □
```

The examples in this tutorial demonstrate the effects of changing the permission modes for yourself (**user** category). However, the results apply analogously for **group** and **others**. You may verify your system's enforcement of the permissions modes for the **group** and **others** permissions, too. After changing the mode(s), ask other system users to verify that the permissions have been successfully altered. Also ask them to attempt the access-related commands demonstrated in this tutorial.

Caution: If you do something foolish like "chmod -x .<CR>", you can no longer log into the system or access your login directory. You will need to ask the system administrator to enable the execute permission in your login directory.

Comm — Common Lines in Two Files

The **comm** command is used to display the lines which are identical in two sorted files. Lines which are unique to either file can also be displayed.

$ **comm** *file1 file2*

Displays in three columns all lines which are unique to *file1*, lines unique to *file2*, and lines contained in both files.

For the following example assume that we have two customer mailing lists, customer.A and customer.B. Each list was created by a sales representative in the same territory. The sales manager wishes to review the lists and then remove names which are duplicated on the two lists.

Customer.A	Customer.B
Anderson	Barnes
Flemming	Haws
Haws	Hunt
Ingold	Smith
Jones	Thomas
Smith	Wainwrite
White	White
Wright	Williams

Note: The lists do not need to have the same number of entries.

```
$ comm customer.A customer.B
Anderson
        Barnes
Flemming
                Haws
        Hunt
Ingold
Jones
                Smith
        Thomas
        Wainwrite
                White
        Williams
Wright
$ □
```

$	Shell prompt
comm	Select lines common to the files
customer.A	**customer.A**
customer.B	and **customer.B**.
Anderson	Entries in mailing list A
Flemming	but not in B are listed in the
Ingold	left-hand column.
Jones	
Wright	
Barnes	Entries in mailing list B
Hunt	but not in A are listed in the
Thomas	middle column.
Wainwrite	
Williams	
Haws	Entries common to both lists
Smith	are in the right-hand column.
White	
$ □	Next prompt and cursor

$ comm [**-123**] *file1 file2*

Displays unique and common lines in sorted files *file1* and *file2*. Use the flags **1**, **2**, or **3** to suppress the display of the corresponding column. Note: **comm -123** will display nothing.

```
$ comm -12 customer.?
Haws
Smith
White
$ □
```

$	Shell prompt
comm	Display line entries common
-12	to both files
customer.?	given by shell expansion of **customer.?**, which is **customer.A** and **customer.B.**
Haws	Entries common to both files
Smith	
White	
$ □	Next prompt and cursor

Error Messages

```
$ comm -x rec del
comm: illegal flag
```

Not a valid option.

```
$ comm temp temp2
comm: cannot open temp2
```

File **temp2** doesn't exist or can't
be opened for reading by **comm**.

Notes on comm

This command is useful for selecting information obtained by comparing two files. All lines of the two files must be previously sorted in *ASCII collating sequence,* possibly by using the **sort** utility. This program can display three columns of information: entries unique to each file and entries common to both files. Three "flag" options allow you to restrain the display of any one of these columns of information.

Tutorial

Employ this utility to rapidly select data from two ordered files.

Three columns of output are generated: lines unique to file A, lines unique to file B, and lines common to both A and B.

Comm is useful for manipulating words, prefixes, roots, and suffixes. For example, create two files, one containing words with the prefix "em" and the other containing words ending in "tion." Use the on-line dictionary and the **grep** pattern-matching program.

```
$ grep '^em' /usr/dict/words >em.words
$ grep 'tion$' /usr/dict/words >tion.words
$ □
```

To list the words common to both categories use the **comm** utility.

```
$ comm -12 em.words tion.words
emotion
$ □
```

Only the word "emotion" is displayed. The on-line spelling dictionary does not have entries for emaciation, emanation, emancipation, emendation, emigration, or emulation.

Practice using the **comm** program on these and other word lists. Create two more short files named **receivables** and **delinquent**. Add several names to the **receivables** file and use **sort** to order them. Make a copy of **receivables,** call it **delinquent,** and delete several of the entries from **delinquent. Delinquent** is a subset of **receivables.** Now execute **comm** on the two files. In one case collect entries who have paid their bills (receivables) and in the other entries who will receive dunning letters (delinquent).

Use these lists to run the example:

Receivables	Delinquent
Anderson	Flemming
Barnes	Hunt
Flemming	Smith
Haws	Williams
Hunt	
Ingold	
Jones	
Smith	
Thomas	
Wainwrite	
White	
Williams	

To print a list of all the people who have paid their bills, type the line shown in boldface in the following screen.

```
$ comm -23 receivables delinquent | pr -h "Payment Acknowledge"
Oct 4 15:57 1981  Payment Acknowledge Page 1

Anderson
Barnes
Haws
Ingold
Jones
Thomas
Wainwrite
White
. . .
$ □
```

Print a list of all those who haven't paid their bills.

```
$ comm -12 receivables delinquent | pr -h "Dunning Letters"
Oct  4 15:58 1981  Dunning Letters Page 1

Flemming
Hunt
Smith
Williams
. . .
$ □
```

Cp — File Copy

This command copies one file to another file or copies several files to a
directory.

$ **cp** *file1 file2*

Make a copy of *file1* and name it *file2*.

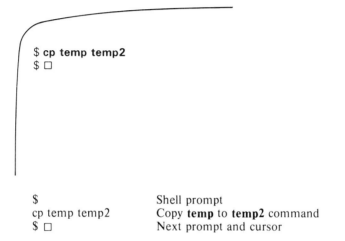

$	Shell prompt
cp temp temp2	Copy **temp** to **temp2** command
$ □	Next prompt and cursor

$ **cp** *file1 file2. . . dirname*

Copy one or more files into the specified directory.

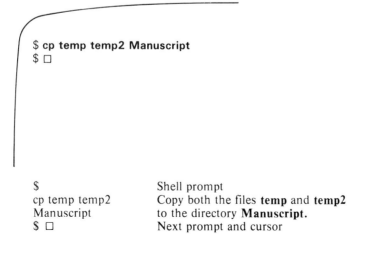

$	Shell prompt
cp temp temp2	Copy both the files **temp** and **temp2**
Manuscript	to the directory **Manuscript.**
$ □	Next prompt and cursor

Error Messages

```
$ cp temp2 Letters
cp: can't open temp2
```

File **temp2** can't be read.

```
$ cp temp temp
cp: cannot copy file to itself
```

Cp doesn't allow writing when destination
file is the same as the source file.

```
$ cp -s temp temp2
Usage: cp: f1 f2; or cp f1 ... fn d2
```

There are no options for this command.

Note: **cp** should, but does not, give an error message if you direct it to
copy a directory.

Notes on cp

This command creates "backup" copies of files. With backups you can manipulate the original file without worrying that "all will be lost" if you irreparably damage it. For example, to backup **temp** you can type "cp temp oldtemp<CR>". If you damage **temp,** simply copy the backup file with "cp oldtemp temp<CR>" and try again.

The following command form is used to copy *file1* onto *file2:*

cp *file1 file2*

If the destination file already exists, its contents are erased before the contents of the *file1* are copied. Otherwise a new file is created with the new name. Had *file2* already existed, the owner and permission modes of *file2* would be preserved. Otherwise the permission modes of the source file are used.

To copy one or more files into the specified directory with their original filenames, use the following command form:

cp *file1 file2. . . dirname*

This is useful for moving an entire group of files with a single command. (See also the **mv** command.)

Tutorial

Make a copy of **temp** and name it **temp2.** Enter "cp temp temp2<CR>", then list the directory with "ls<CR>".

```
$ cp temp temp2
$ ls
Letters   Manuscript   temp   temp2
$ □
```

The directory now contains **temp2** as well as **Letters, Manuscript,** and **temp.**

Now copy both temporary files into the **Manuscript** directory by typing "cp temp temp2 Manuscript<CR>". To verify that the copies are in the **Manuscript** directory, type "ls Manuscript<CR>". To verify that the original copies are still in your login directory type "ls<CR>".

```
$ cp temp temp2 Manuscript
$ ls Manuscript
Chap1     Chap2         temp      temp2
$ ls
Letters   Manuscript    temp      temp2
```

Before leaving this tutorial session, restore your practice file system to its original state. Erase the files you created for this session with the command "rm temp2 Manuscript/temp*<CR>".

Diff — Differential File Comparator

This command compares two files and searches for differences on a line-by-line basis.

$ **diff** [**-efbh**] *file1 file2*

Find the differences between *file1* and *file2*.

Options:

-e   Obtains a script of append, change, and delete **ed** commands which will recreate **file2** from **file1**.

-b   Causes trailing blanks (spaces and tabs) to be ignored; also, other strings of blanks will compare as equal.

-f   Produces a script of differences in the opposite order (not useful with **ed**).

-h   Use for files of "unlimited" length. Does a fast job, but only works when the changed stretches are short and well separated.

Note: Some of these options may be concatenated, e.g., **-eb.**

For the examples which follow, create the file **temp2** from **temp** by deleting the fourth line in **temp.** See the Tutorial section for a detailed explanation.

```
$ diff temp temp2
4d3
< of their country.
$ □
```

$	Shell prompt
diff	Difference command
temp temp2	to change **temp** to **temp2.**
4	4 refers to line 4 of file **temp**
d	for delete of that line (4).
3	3 refers to line 3 of file **temp2**
<	Refers to the line affected in **temp**
of their country.	Line in **temp** affected
$ □	Next prompt and cursor

```
$ diff temp2 temp
3a4
> of their country.
$ □
```

$	Shell prompt
diff	Difference command
temp temp2	to change **temp2** to **temp.**
3	3 refers to line 3 of file **temp2**
a	for append to that line (3)
4	refers to the line 4 in **temp** after append.
>	Refers to the line affected in **temp**
of their country.	Line in **temp** affected
$ □	Next prompt and cursor

```
$ diff -e temp temp2
4d
$ □
```

$	Shell prompt
diff	Difference command
-e	using **-e** (for **ed**) option
temp temp2	to change **temp** into **temp2**.
4d	Delete line 4 in **temp** (an **ed** command)
$ □	Next prompt and cursor

```
$ diff -e temp2 temp
3a
of their country.
.
$ □
```

$	Shell prompt
diff	Difference command
-e	using **-e** (for **ed**) option
temp2 temp	to change **temp2** into **temp.**
3a	Append after line 3:
of their country.	"of their country."
.	Terminate append mode
$ □	Next prompt and cursor

Error Messages

```
$ diff temp temp3
diff: cannot open temp3
```

File **temp3** can't be read.

Note: The **diff** command does not give an error message if you give it an incorrect option.

Notes on diff

Use the **diff** utility to economically store several versions of a file. Each time you produce a new version, run **diff** between the original and new version to collect the "difference" file. The smaller difference file can be used at any time to recreate the latest version of the file from the original. In this way you need only keep several small "diff" files (along with your original) instead of the same number of the larger complete versions of the original file. Consider the following command form:

diff *file1 file2*

When *file1* and *file2* are not identical, the **diff** command produces output similar to the **ed** editor commands which convert *file1* into *file2*. If they are identical, no output is produced.

Specify the **-e** option (mnemonic for **ed**) to obtain an exact "script" of the commands **a** (append), **c** (change), and **d** (delete) which **ed** uses to create *file2* from *file1*.

Tutorial

Use an editor (such as **ed**) to delete the last line, "of their country.", from the file **temp** to create the new file **temp2.**

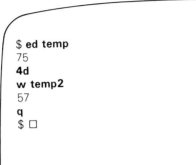

```
$ ed temp
75
4d
w temp2
57
q
$ □
```

Employ the **-e** option to produce a "script" of **ed** commands to create **temp2** from **temp.** Type "diff -e temp temp2<CR>".

```
$ diff -e temp temp2
4d
$ □
```

Recall that you used this **ed** command to produce **temp2** from **temp.**

To find the **ed** commands used to recreate **temp** from **temp2,** type the converse, "diff -e temp2 temp<CR>".

```
$ diff -e temp2 temp
3a
of their country.
.
$ □
```

You must append (**a**) the line "of their country." after line 3 of the first file (**temp2**) to recreate the second file (**temp**).

Unless you use the -**b** option, unequal numbers of blanks will also be flagged. -**b** equally compares trailing blanks (both space and tab characters) and other strings of blanks. Use the **diff** command, without the -**b** option, on two files which only differ by the number of blank characters.

On a very large file you may wish to employ the -**h** option. This works best when the changed stretches are short and well separated. A drawback is that the -**e** and -**f** options are not available when you use -**h.**

For more practice interpreting the results of **diff,** try the command on two files which differ by one or more characters, words, or lines.

Find — Find Files

Use this command to locate files which meet certain specifications including filename, number of links, login owner, group name, block size, time of last access or modification, and so forth.

$ **find** *pathname-list. . . conditions*

Starting with the directories listed in *pathname-list,* search these and their subdirectories to find all files which meet the specified *conditions*.

Pathname-list

Lists one or more directory pathnames separated by "white space" characters (blanks and tabs).

Conditions:

-**name** *filename*   Specify the name(s) of the file(s) to be *filename.*

-**type** *x*   Specify file type to be **d** for directory and **f** for a plain file.

-**links** *n*   Locate file(s) with *n* links to it/them.

-**user** *uname*   Find file(s) with the owner name *uname.*

-group *gname*	Find file(s) with the group name *gname*.
-size *n*	Find file(s) of size *n* blocks.
-atime *n*	Find file(s) accessed *n* days ago.
-mtime *n*	Find file(s) modified *n* days ago.
-exec *command* {}	Execute the UNIX system *command* for the file(s) meeting the conditions. The "{}" which appear in the command line represent a command argument. The files which are found to meet the specified conditions become arguments on which the *command* will operate.
-ok *command*	Execute the UNIX system *command* when you type **y** in response to the query for each file meeting the other conditions.
-print	Display the pathname for the file(s) which meet all the criteria.
-newer *file*	Find the file(s) starting with *pathname* which have been modified more recently than the argument *file*.

Arguments and Conventions of the Conditions:

n	Decimal integer meaning "exactly *n*."
-n	*Less than n.*
+n	More than *n*.
-	All conditions start with "-".
.	"Find" starts at your login directory.
-a	If more than one condition is specified, files will be selected which fulfill all of the criteria simultaneously (logical AND condition).
( )	Parentheses are used to group the conditions to be simultaneously met by files found.
-o	Precedes a set of conditions for finding files. If either condition is met by a file, the file is found. -o denotes the OR operator.

```
$ find . -name 'sec?' -print
./Manuscript/Chap1/sec1
./Manuscript/Chap1/sec2
./Manuscript/Chap2/sec1
$ □
```

$	Shell prompt
find	Locate in
.	your login directory
-name 'sec?'	all files named sec? (? = any character)
. . ./sec1	Three files were found in second-level
. . ./sec2	subdirectories.
. . ./sec1	
$ □	Next prompt and cursor

```
$ find . -mtime +14 -print
./Letters
.Manuscipt
./Manuscript/Chap1/sec2
./Manuscript/Chap2
./Manuscript/Chap2/sec1
$ □
```

$	Shell prompt
find	Locate all files starting with
.	your login directory
-mtime	which have not been modified
+14	for 14 days and
-print	display the result.
./Letters	Display of files meeting these criteria
./. . .	
. . .	
$ □	Next prompt and cursor

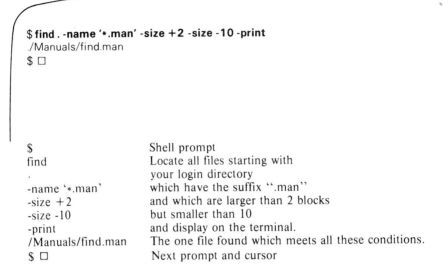

```
$ find . -name '*.man' -size +2 -size -10 -print
./Manuals/find.man
$ □
```

$	Shell prompt
find	Locate all files starting with
.	your login directory
-name '*.man'	which have the suffix ".man"
-size +2	and which are larger than 2 blocks
-size -10	but smaller than 10
-print	and display on the terminal.
/Manuals/find.man	The one file found which meets all these conditions.
$ □	Next prompt and cursor

Error Messages

```
$ find -name 'sec?' -print
Usage: find path-list predicate-list
```

No pathlist specified.

```
$ find . -size +2 -10 -print
find: bad option -10
```

Must use -size -10.

```
$ find . 'sec?' -print
find: bad status -- sec?
```

Forgot -name before 'sec?'.

```
$ find . -name 'sec?' -ok rm { };
find: incomplete statement
```

Must escape ; with \.

Notes on find

This command searches every subdirectory of the directories named in *pathname-list* for files which satisfy the specified conditions. The syntax for the options is awkward but consistent.

Conditions for **find** can be combined logically in the operations listed below. The operations are listed in order of decreasing precedence (or consequence):

• Group the conditions together with parentheses. Parentheses are given special interpretation by the shell and thus must be "protected" or escaped as follows: \ (and \ ).

• Negate or reverse the logical meaning of condition or a parenthetical grouping of conditions with the *unary* NOT operator. An exclamation mark "!" means find all files that do not meet the specified conditions.

• Linking together conditions in a logical AND operation which is denoted by their juxtaposition.

• Alternate conditions can be specified by a logical OR operator, the **-o** option.

Tutorial

We have chosen examples to demonstrate the principles of using the complex syntax for the **find** command. You can become more conversant with this command by trying all the options which make this a powerful and versatile utility.

You can find every directory and file in your personal file system with the command "find . -name '*' -print<CR>".

```
$ find . -name '*' -print
./Letters
./Letters/Family
./Letters/Family/parents1
./Letters/Friends
./Letters/Friends/john1
./Letters/Friends/jane1
./Letters/Friends/jane2
./temp
./Manuscript
./Manuscript/Chap1
./Manuscript/Chap1/sec1
./Manuscript/Chap1/sec2
./Manuscript/Chap2
./Manuscript/Chap2/sec1
$ □
```

In the previous command line we requested **find** to locate all files beginning with your login directory (*pathname-list* = .). The shell interprets the wild card '*' to mean all possible filenames. You must explicitly ask that the result be displayed on your terminal by entering the condition, "-print". Note: When you wish to find all files you may omit the option "-name '*'", since the default case specifies all files. Type "find . -print<CR>" to obtain the same display of all files.

To manipulate files using wild cards, make a certain part of the filename constant. One common technique is to use an optional alphabetical extension after a punctuation character such as a period ".". For example, you might use ed.man to reference the on-line **ed** manual. We use a numeral suffix with a name to indicate a certain ordering, such as Chap1 for the first of several chapters. In your practice file system the Manuscript chapter sections are indicated by **sec1, sec2,** etc. You can find all occurrences of "sec" filenames by typing "find . -name 'sec?' -print<CR>".

```
$ find . -name 'sec?' -print
./Manuscript/Chap1/sec1
./Manuscript/Chap1/sec2
./Manuscript/Chap2/sec1
$ □
```

In the preceding example, **find** interprets the wild card filename 'sec?' to mean all occurrences of 'sec' and displays the specific names **sec1** and **sec2.**

You can concatenate more conditions together in a logical AND sense by adding them to the command line. This enables you to narrow your search for specific types of files with the given name. Before beginning the next example, list all your level 1 subdirectories with the command "ls -l */*", as illustrated at the top of the following page. (Your current directory is considered level 0. Level 1 is a subdirectory of your current directory.)

We will now search for the files in your practice file system which have not been modified within the last two weeks. Use the command "find . -mtime +14 -print<CR>".

```
$ find . -mtime +14 -print
./Letters
./Manuscript
./Manuscript/Chap1/sec2
./Manuscript/Chap2
./Manuscript/Chap2/sec1
$ □
```

```
$ ls -l */*
Letters/Family:
total 1
-rwx------   1rathomas        92     Sep 13 10:54 parents1
Letters/Friends:
total 3
-rwx------   1 rathomas       88     Sep 13 10:56 jane1
-rwx------   1 rathomas       97     Sep 13 10:57 jane2
-rwx------   1 rathomas       88     Sep 13 10:55 john1
Manuscript/Chap1:
total 2
-rw------    1 rathomas      269     Sep 14 17:59 sec1
-rw------    1 rathomas      215     Jul  4 20:14 sec2
Manuscript/Chap2:
total 1
-rwx------   1 rathomas      239     Jul  4 20:17 sec1
$ □
```

Reading the command from left to right, it is interpreted to mean "find, starting with your login directory (.), all files whose modification time (-mtime) is greater than (+) fourteen days (14), and display them (-print)."

To verify that the files listed have not been modified in the last 14 days, check the right-hand columns in the previous screen which list the time of last modification. For this example, the current date is Sept 14.

To follow the next example we will create a new directory, **Manuals,** to store a few large files from the on-line *UNIX Programmer's Manual.* Name the files **ed.man,** for **ed** manual, **find.man,** for **find** manual, and **cat.man,** for **cat** manual. Type the commands exactly as shown in the following screen.

```
$ mkdir Manuals
$ man ed  >Manuals/ed.man
$ man cat >Manuals/cat.man
$ man find  >Manuals/find.man
$ ls -s Manuals
total 52   2 cat.man   42 ed.man   8 find.man
$ □
```

The last command, "ls -s Manuals", verifies that the files exist and displays their sizes in 512-character blocks. To continue with this example, display all files in your file system which are currently larger than two blocks by typing "find . -size +2 -print <CR>".

```
$ find . -size + 2 -print
./Manuals/ed.man
./Manuals/find.man
$ □
```

Now type "find . -size +10 -print" to locate all files which are larger than 10 blocks.

```
$ find . -size +10 -print
./Manuals/ed.man
$ □
```

To demonstrate the concatenation of two options in a logical AND sense, type "find . -size +2 -size -10 -print". **Find** displays all files in your file system which are larger than two blocks (-size +2) AND smaller than 10 (-size -10).

```
$ find . -size +2 -size -10 -print
./Manuals/find.man
$ □
```

Another useful feature of this command permits you to execute shell commands on the "found" files. To illustrate the syntax, type "find . -name '*.man' -ok rm { } \; <CR>". This command finds all files with the extension ".man" and queries for your "-ok" to execute the command "rm { }", which means **rm** (remove) file found satisfying the conditions. (The **rm** command is discussed in another section.)

```
$ find . -name '*.man' -ok rm { } \;
< rm . . . .Manuals/ed.man >? y
< rm . . . .Manuals/cat.man >? n
< rm . . . .Manuals/find.man >? n
$ □
```

Since we answered "y" (yes) to the first query and "n" (no) to the last two questions, only the removal of the file **ed.man** was carried out. To demonstrate, type: "ls -s Manuals<CR>".

```
$ ls -s Manuals
total 10      2 cat.man      8 find.man
$ □
```

As our last example we will demonstrate the syntax for using parentheses and the logical OR operator. To prepare for this example, give the command "find . -name 'sec?' -mtime -7 -print<CR>" to display all the files with the prefix "sec" followed by one additional character (represented by "?") which have been modified (-mtime) within the last seven days (-7).

```
$ find . -name 'sec?' -mtime -7 -print
./sec1
./Manuscript/Chap1/sec1
$ □
```

Then display all the files with the suffix ".man" which have also been modified within the last seven days by typing "find . -name '*.man' -mtime -7 -print<CR>".

```
$ find . name '*.man' -mtime -7 -print
./Manuals/cat.man
./Manuals/find.man
$ □
```

We combine the above two searches in a logical OR sense by using parentheses to group the filename specifications. Type the command "find . \(-name 'sec?' -o -name '*.man' \) -mtime -7 -print<CR>".

```
$ find . \( -name 'sec?' -o -name '*.man' \) -mtime -7 -print
./sec1
./Manuals/cat.man
./Manuals/find.man
./Manuscript/Chap1/sec1
$ □
```

This is interpreted, reading from left to right, as "find in your login directory (.) files which have the name 'sec?' (-name 'sec?') OR (-o) the name '*.man' (-name '*.man') which have been modified within the last seven days (-mtime -7) and display them (-print)." Note: The parentheses group the name specifications together in their logical OR combination. What happens if you omit the parentheses? Try it and see. Also, the parentheses must be "escaped" by the backslash "\" or quoted (like '*.man') in order to be correctly interpreted by the shell.

Finally, to restore your login directory to its original state erase all files in **Manuals** as well as the directory itself with the command 'rm -r Manuals<CR>'' and verify with "ls<CR>", to list all files in your directory.

Ln — Make Link

Use the **link** command to add synonyms for a file or directory, without changing the original file.

$ **ln** *name1* [*name2*]

Establish a link to a file *name1*, and call the link *name2*.

```
$ ln temp  temp2
$ □
```

$	Shell prompt
ln	Establish a link to
temp	file named **temp** and
temp2	name the link **temp2.**
$ □	Next prompt and cursor

```
$ ls
Letters    Manuscript temp
$ ln  Manuscript/Chap1/sec1
$ ls
Letters        Manuscript sec1      temp
$ □
```

$	Shell prompt
ls	List directory before making link,
Letters Manuscript	observing two directories and a file.
temp	
ln	Establish a link to the file
Manuscript/Chap1/sec1	which will be named **sec1**.
ls	Verify with a directory listing
Letters Manuscript sec1 temp	that the link is named **sec1**.
$ □	Next prompt and cursor

Error Messages

```
$ ln temp
ln: File exists
```

Attempt to establish another link with the same name.

```
$ ln -x temp
ln: -x does not exist
```

There are no options for this command.

```
$ ln tempfile temp2
ln: tempfile does not exist
```

Tempfile not in current directory.

```
$ ln Manuscript Manuscript2
ln: Manuscript is a directory
```

Can't link to a directory file.

```
$ cp temp /tmp
$ ln /tmp/temp tmp.temp
ln: Cross-device link
```

Can't link between file systems.

Notes on ln

Each file in the UNIX file system has a unique identification number, the i-number. For our purposes, the i-number refers to the physical file on the disk or tape. Each entry in a directory associates an i-number with a filename. This connection is called a *link*. Nothing prevents two or more directory entries from having the same i-number, creating multiple links. Hence several files can be associated with the same physical file.

The **ln** utility program can establish additional links to a file. You cannot establish a link to a directory file, nor can you link across file systems on different devices. Use the following format for the **ln** command:

$ **ln** *name1* [*name2*]

Here *name1* is the filename for the file to which you wish to establish an additional link. If you specify *name2* then this new link will be called *name2*. If you do not indicate a *name2* then *name1* must be in the form of a file pathname so that the last component (the filename itself) will become the name of the new link. If *name1* is not specified as a pathname, you will get an error message since you would be attempting to give both links the same name, which is prohibited.

The **rm** command "removes" files by breaking the link between the filename and the i-number. When the number of links to any physical file becomes zero, the UNIX system reallocates the physical space so it can be used for another file.

Tutorial

You can display the i-number for a file by using the **-i** option when you invoke the **ls** utility. Type "ls -il<CR>" and observe a directory listing similar to this one:

```
$ ls -il
total 3
  413 drwx------   4 rathomas        80      Sep 24 19:49 Letters
 7975 drwx------   4 rathomas       112      Sep 26 12:40 Manuscript
 5738 rw  ------   1 rathomas        75      Oct  4 11:04 temp
```

Note: The actual i-numbers given in the first column will almost certainly be different for your files.

Establish another link, called **temp2,** to the file **temp** by typing "ln temp temp2<CR>". Then list the directory again.

```
$ ln temp temp2
$ ls -il
total 4
  413 drwx------   4 rathomas        80      Sep 24 19:49 Letters
 7957 drwx------   4 rathomas       112      Sep 26 12:40 Manuscript
 5738 -rw  ------   2 rathomas        75      Oct  4 11:04 temp
 5738 -rw  ------   2 rathomas        75      Oct  4 11:04 temp2
$ □
```

The **temp2** link appears to have all the same characteristics as the original link to 5738 named **temp.** Note also that the number of links to **temp** increased from one in the first screen to two in the second screen.

If you change the contents of **temp2** with an editor, then you will change the contents of **temp,** since the names are really aliases for the same physical file. To demonstrate, invoke **ed** to edit **temp2,** delete the last line, save the edit buffer, exit, then print **temp2** by typing the commands exactly as shown in boldface.

```
$ ed temp2
75
$d
w
57
q
$ cat temp2
Now is the time
for all good citizens
to come to the aid
$ □
```

To verify that **temp** was also changed, use **cat** again.

```
$ cat temp
Now is the time
for all good citizens
to come to the aid
$ □
```

Now use the **rm** command and erase **temp.** Then list the file in "long" format. Although one of the links was broken, the physical file is still accessible because one link remains.

```
$ rm temp
$ ls -il
total 6
 413 dwx ------ 4 rathomas      80     Sep 24 19:49 Letters
7975 drwx------ 4 rathomas     112     Sep 26 12:40 Manuscript
5738 -rw ------ 1 rathomas      75     Oct  4 11:04 temp2
$ □
```

Consider how this linking process differs from the **cp** command. Make a copy of **temp2,** call it **temp,** and list the files again.

```
$ cp temp2 temp
$ ls -il
  total 4
    413 drwx------   4 rathomas        80     Sep 24 19:49 Letters
   7975 drwx------   4 rathomas       112     Sep 26 12:40 Manuscript
  10956 -rw  ------   1 rathomas        75     Oct  6 16:55 temp
   5738 -rw  ------   1 rathomas        75     Oct  4 11:04 temp2
$ □
```

Temp and **temp2** are two physically distinct files. The date of last access reflects that **temp** was created by reading and then writing a copy of **temp2**. If **temp** was established as another link to **temp2**, the contents of **temp2** would not have been accessed and they would both share the same time for the last modification. (See the second screen in this tutorial.)

To restore your practice file system, use an editor and append "of their country." to the file **temp.** After returning to the shell, remove **temp2** by typing "rm temp2<CR>".

Alternate file links provide a convenient means of manipulating files. Let's say you have a group of files representing a manuscript such as an early version of this book. The files can have descriptive names such as **intro, basic.concepts, tutorials,** etc. Let's establish a set of links with names useful for sorted wild card manipulation such as **ch0, ch1, ch2,** as shown here:

```
$ ln intro ch0
$ ln unixinfo ch1
$ ln basic.concepts ch2
$ ln tutorials ch3
$ ln command.sum ch4
$ ln word.process ch5
$ ln resources ch6
$ ln appendix ch7
$ □
```

When you are ready to proof the entire Manuscript, send all the files to the line printer with the following command.

```
$ pr ch? | lpr
$ □
```

The shell interprets the wild card abbreviation **ch?** to include **ch0, ch1,. . ., ch7. Pr** paginates the contents. **Lpr** sends (l) the files to the line printer queue.

Using **ln** we can create a link to a file which is "buried" in a directory hierarchy for handy reference. For instance, from your login directory you can establish a link to **/usr/your-name/Manuscript/ Chap1/sec1** by typing the command "ln /usr/your-name/Manuscript/ Chap1/sec1<CR>". Then list the directory.

```
$ ln /usr/your-name/Manuscript/Chap1/sec1
$ ls
Letters      Manuscript    sec1     temp
$ □
```

Note: The link in your login directory is named **sec1** because that was the last component of the pathname by which you specified the file.

Finally, to restore your practice file system to its original condition, type "rm sec1<CR>".

Lpr — Line Printer Spooler

This command sends a file to the line printer queue to be printed in "background."

$ lpr *-options file. . .*

Options:

-r   Remove the file(s) after they have been *queued.*

-c   Make another copy of the file for the printer queue. (Usual default option.)

-m   Report by **mail** when the printing is complete.

-n   Do not report by **mail.** (Usual default options).

$ lpr *filename*

Print the file *filename.*

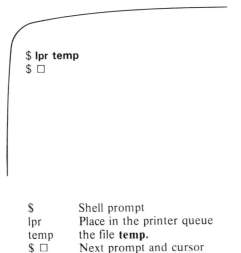

```
$ lpr temp
$ □
```

$	Shell prompt
lpr	Place in the printer queue
temp	the file **temp.**
$ □	Next prompt and cursor

$ lpr -r *filename*

Remove the file *filename* from your directory after it has been placed in the printer queue.

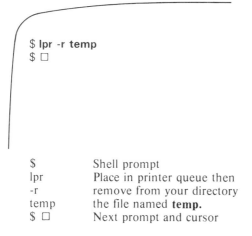

```
$ lpr -r temp
$ □
```

$	Shell prompt
lpr	Place in printer queue then
-r	remove from your directory
temp	the file named **temp.**
$ □	Next prompt and cursor

$ lpr -c *filename*

Make a copy of the file *filename* just for the printer queue and leave the original intact and available for change. This is a default option on many systems.

```
$ lpr -c temp
$ □
```

$	Shell prompt
lpr	Place in printer queue
-c	a copy of the file
temp	named **temp.**
$ □	Next prompt and cursor

$ lpr -m *filename*

Print the file *filename* and request **mail** to inform you when the task is complete.

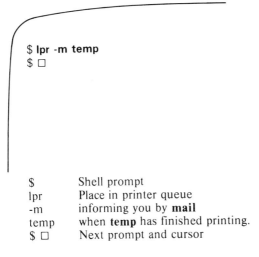

$	Shell prompt
lpr	Place in printer queue
-m	informing you by **mail**
temp	when **temp** has finished printing.
$ □	Next prompt and cursor

$ **lpr** *file1 file2. . .*

Place the files *file1, file2,* and more if specified, in the line printer queue.

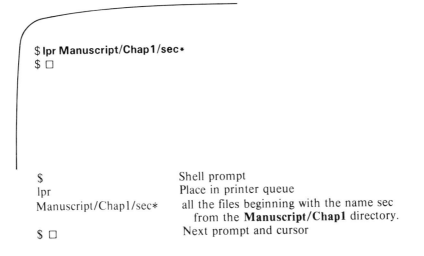

$	Shell prompt
lpr	Place in printer queue
Manuscript/Chap1/sec*	all the files beginning with the name sec from the **Manuscript/Chap1** directory.
$ □	Next prompt and cursor

Notes on lpr

The operation of this command is implementation-dependent. Check your system documentation.

This command places the specified files in line for printing on a line printer.

You will frequently use the **lpr** command at the tail end of a pipeline. You will probably want to format the file with **pr** before sending it to the printer. The **pr** command and its formatting options are discussed in another section. In this example the **-h** option specifies a custom header is to be printed. (The vertical bar " | " means "to pipe" the header to the printer queue.) To identify the printer output you might use the following command:

$ **pr** -h "Your custom title" | **lpr**

Tutorial

First read your system documentation concerning use of the **lpr** command and its options, since this command tends to be more implementation-dependent than most.

To illustrate why some sort of header is helpful in identifying what you print, first type "lpr temp<CR>". Then compare this with the result you obtain with the command "pr -h temp | lpr<CR>".

If the **-m** option is available on your system, type "lpr -m temp <CR>". The next time you log in, **mail** will inform you that the printing task is complete and, in large installations, where to pick up the output.

If the **-r** option is available on your system, type "lpr -r temp<CR>", then after the file is printed, examine your directory with **ls** to see if **temp** was removed.

If you have a number of files to print, it is convenient to name them so you can use "wild cards" such as "lpr sec*<CR>" to print all files in your current directory whose names begin with "sec".

Ls — List Contents of Directory

This command lists the contents of a directory. It displays the names of all files and directories in a specified directory, providing information on read/write permissions, date of last change, etc.

$ **ls** [-**ltasdru**] *filename...*

Options:

   -**l**   List in long format.

   -**t**   List in order of last modification (most recent first).

   -**a**   List all entries, including "." entries.

   -**s**   Report the size in blocks (512 characters = one block).

   -**d**   Report directory status information.

   -**r**   List in reverse order.

   -**u**   List in order of last access (most recent first).

Note: Options may be concatenated, e.g., -**ltasdru.** Also, the form of the output for this command may be implementation-dependent.

$ **ls**

Lists the filename of the current directory alphabetically.

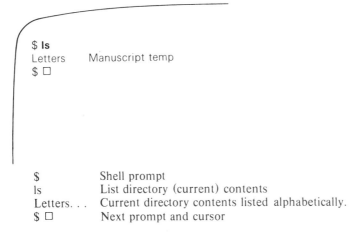

```
$ ls
Letters       Manuscript temp
$ □
```

$	Shell prompt
ls	List directory (current) contents
Letters...	Current directory contents listed alphabetically.
$ □	Next prompt and cursor

$ **ls -l**

Lists the filenames of the current directory in "long" format.

```
$ ls-l
total 3
drwx ------ 4 your-name        64      Jul 4 20:02 Letters
drwx ------ 4 your-name        96      Aug 9 13:06 Manuscript
-rw  ------ 1 your-name       134      Jul 4 20:05 temp
$ □
```

$	Shell prompt
ls	List directory in
-l	"long" format.
total 3	Total number of 512-byte blocks
drwx--------	Permission mode for first entry (**Letters**)
4	Number of links to **Letters**
your-name	Owner of **Letters**
64	Number of characters (or bytes) in **Letters**
Jul 4	Date of last modification
20:02	Time (24-hour system) of last modification
Letters	Name of file
. . .	Analogous information for other files
$ □	Next prompt and cursor

$ ls -t

Lists filenames in order of last modification date/time (most recent first).

```
$ ls -t
Manuscript temp     Letters
$ □
```

$	Shell prompt
ls	List contents of current directory
-t	by time last modified (latest first).
Manuscript . . .	Current directory contents listed, most recently changed first.
$ □	Next prompt and cursor

$ ls -a

Lists all entries, including "invisible" files (preceded by ".").

```
$ ls -a <CR>
.   ..  .profile  Letters  Manuscript temp
$ □
```

$	Shell prompt
ls	List for the current directory
-a	all files.
.	Denotes current directory
..	Denotes parent directory
.profile	Login file
Letters . . .	Continue listing alphabetically
$ □	Next prompt and cursor

$ ls -s

Lists files, and gives their sizes in 512-character blocks.

```
$ ls -s
total 3  1 Letters  1 Manuscript  1 temp
$ [ ]
```

$	Shell prompt
total 3	Total of three blocks (1536 characters or bytes)
1 Letter	One block for **Letters,**
1 Manuscript	**Manuscript,** and
1 temp	**temp.**
$ □	Next prompt and cursor

$ ls -r

Reverses order of sort for directory listing. If used alone it causes reverse alphabetic listing. The -r option is frequently concatenated with other options to reverse the sort order.

```
$ ls -r
temp      Manuscript Letters
$ □
```

$	Shell prompt
ls	List current directory alphabetically
-r	in reverse order.
temp . . .	Listed in reverse order
$ □	Next prompt and cursor

$ ls -u

Lists files, beginning with the most recently accessed for reading or writing.

```
$ ls -u
temp   Letters   Manuscript
$ □
```

$	Shell prompt
ls	List current directory contents
-u	in order last accessed (most recent first).
temp . . .	Most recent. . .
$ □	Next prompt and cursor

Error Messages

The **ls** command does not usually give any error messages, even for incorrect options, etc.

Notes on ls

When no filenames are given, the current directory is listed. When several filename arguments are given, the arguments are first sorted appropriately. File arguments are listed before directories and their contents. For each directory argument, **ls** lists the contents of the directory. For each file argument, **ls** repeats its filename and any other information requested. The output is sorted alphabetically by default.

Permission Modes

The permission mode printed with the **-l** option contains ten characters to be interpreted as follows. If the first character is

d	The entry is a directory;
b	The entry is a block-type special file;
c	The entry is a character-type special file;
-	The entry is a plain file.

The next nine characters are interpreted as three sets of three characters each. The first set of three refers to owner permissions, the next set indicates permissions to other users in the same group as the owner, and the last to all other users. Within each set the three characters indicate permission respectively to read, modify, or execute the file as a program. For a directory, "execute" permission means permission is given to search the directory for a specified filename. The permissions letters are indicated as follows:

r	The file is readable;
w	The file is modifiable (writable);
x	The file is executable;
-	The indicated permission is not granted.

Tutorial

Type only "ls<CR>" after the shell prompt ($) for an alphabetical listing of the current directory's contents.

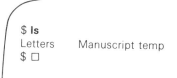

```
$ ls
Letters     Manuscript temp
$ □
```

Note: Your **ls** command display format may differ from those depicted in this command summary. For instance, all the directory entries may be listed in one vertical column.

Any or all of these names in the directory could refer to a file or to another directory. A file entry can be distinguished from a directory entry by the use of an appropriate **ls** option. The "long" option (**-l**) is one of the most commonly used **ls** options. For this option **ls** will provide the total number of 512-character blocks, the permission mode for each file or directory, the number of links, owner (login name), size in bytes (or characters), and the date and time of last modification for each file. Consider the following example. When in your personal directory, type "ls -l <CR>".

```
$ ls -l
total 3
drwx------  4 your-name       64   Jul 4 20:02 Letters
drwx------  4 your-name       96   Aug 9 13:06 Manuscript
-rw-------  1 your-name      134   Jul 4 20:05 temp
```

Total 6 refers to the total occupied disk space. The date and time refer to the last change made to the file. The numbers 64, 96, and 134 are the number of characters (or bytes) in the file. The owner of the file is designated as your-name. The number preceding the owner is the number of links to the file. The **drwx------** etc. is the permission mode, in which the "d" at the left indicates that **Letters** and **Manuscript** is a directory, and the "-" means that **temp** is an ordinary file. The pattern of permissions says that all directory entries are read, write, and execute enabled for the owner and the file **temp** is read and write enabled for the owner only.

You will find that after a directory or file is created, it will have a certain pattern of permission modes which reflects the "umask" set by the system administrator. You can then use the **chmod** command to extend or restrict the permissions as desired. (The **chmod** command is discussed in another section.)

You can request directory information about a particular file, directory, or group of files or directories by specifying names on the command line. This is especially powerful when a "*" wild card is used to list a group of filenames. For instance, let's say that you would like a listing of all the chapters in the **Manuscript** directory. To simplify matters, move to that directory, using the command "cd Manuscript<CR>". Type "ls Chap*" and observe the display.

```
$ cd Manuscript
$ ls Chap*
Chap1:
sec1 sec2
Chap2:
sec1
$ □
```

Recall that we labeled our chapter heading subdirectories as Chap1, Chap2, etc. The "*" wild card abbreviates any and all names for chapters in the **Manuscript** directory. The shell expands the abbreviation **Chap*** into **Chap1** and **Chap2**, so that command actually becomes "ls Chap1 Chap2". To verify this, type the equivalent longer command "ls Chap1 Chap2<CR>" to display the same results without using the "*" wild card. Now return to your original working directory by typing "cd<CR>".

You can also display directory information about a file or directory which is not in the current directory by entering the pathname to that file or directory. Continuing with the example used above, type from your login directory "ls Manuscript/Chap*<CR>". The same information appears in a slightly different display without changing your working directory.

```
$ ls Manuscript/Chap*
Manuscript/Chap1:
sec1 sec2

Manuscript/Chap2:
sec1
$ □
```

To list the files in the order in which they were changed, most recent first instead of alphabetically, type "ls -t<CR>".

```
$ ls -t
Manuscript temp      Letters
$ □
```

To list all files including the "invisible" files (files whose name begins with a period, such as **.profile** or **.login**) use the **-a** option.

```
$ ls -a
.   ..   .profile  Letters  Manuscript  temp
```

The **ls** option **-s** gives the size in 512-character blocks for each entry. Type "ls -s<CR>".

```
$ ls -s
total  3  1 Letters  1 Manuscript 1 temp
```

In this case, the system displays the file size in blocks and indicates that each of the three entries occupies one block. Any number of characters from 1 to 512 inclusive will occupy *one* block on the disk.

Use the **-r** option to reverse the order for the sort used by **ls.** Used alone, **-r** simply lists the file contents in reverse alphabetical order.

```
$ ls -r
temp        Manuscript Letters
$ □
```

The **-r** option is usually concatenated with other options to reverse the order of the sort for other qualities. For instance, type "ls -rt<CR>" to reverse the temporal order and list the oldest first.

```
$ ls -rt
Letters   temp   Manuscript
$ □
```

The files are still listed in the order in which they were last modified (specified by the **-t** option) but the oldest is listed first (due to the **-r** option).

Mkdir — Make a Directory

This command makes one or more specified directories.

$ **mkdir** *dirname. . .*

Creates one or more directories in your current directory.

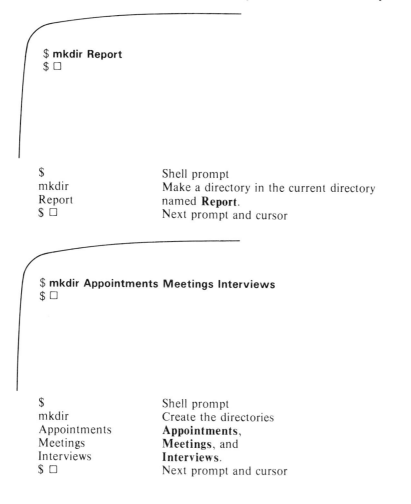

```
$ mkdir Report
$ □
```

$	Shell prompt
mkdir	Make a directory in the current directory
Report	named **Report**.
$ □	Next prompt and cursor

```
$ mkdir Appointments Meetings Interviews
$ □
```

$	Shell prompt
mkdir	Create the directories
Appointments	**Appointments**,
Meetings	**Meetings**, and
Interviews	**Interviews**.
$ □	Next prompt and cursor

Error Messages

```
$ mkdir -x Sample
$ ls
-x      Manuscript   Sample   temp    temp2
```

If you try to specify an option the command
will take it to be a directory name.

Notes on mkdir

Mkdir creates the directories you specify on the command line. This
command requires permission to write in the current directory to create
the new subdirectories. The pattern of the permission modes for the
directories will depend on your particular system. List the newly created
directory in long format using the command **ls -l**. You may need to
extend or restrict the access permission of your new directories with the
chmod command. (**Chmod** is discussed in another section.) The newly
created directories are ''empty'' except for two ''invisible'' files (''.''
and ''. .'') used exclusively by the system.

Tutorial

To create a new empty subdirectory named **Report** in the current directory, type ''mkdir Report<CR>'' and then enter the command ''cd
Report<CR>'' to move to this new directory. Finally, type ''ls<CR>''
and you will see no output but instead obtain another shell prompt.

```
$ mkdir Report
$ cd Report
$ ls
$ □
```

There were no files listed by the **ls** command because there are no "visible" files in the newly created directory **Report**. However, an **ls** option permits you to list all the files. Type "ls -a<CR>" where the **-a** option means "all."

```
$ ls -a
.    ..
$ □
```

The "current" and "parent" directories are revealed as entries.

You can create more than one directory at a time with the **mkdir** command. Type "mkdir Appointments Meetings Interviews<CR>", then list the current directory with "ls<CR>".

```
$ mkdir  Appointments  Meetings  Interviews
$ ls
Appointments  Interviews  Meetings
$ □
```

Mv — Move or Rename Files and Directories

This command renames files or directories. It moves a group of files into another directory.

$ mv *file1 file2*

Changes the name of *file1* to *file2*.

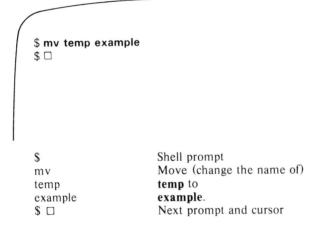

```
$ mv temp example
$ □
```

$	Shell prompt
mv	Move (change the name of)
temp	**temp** to
example	**example**.
$ □	Next prompt and cursor

$ mv *file. . . dirname*

Moves one or more files to the directory *dirname*.

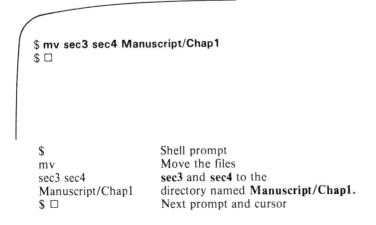

```
$ mv sec3 sec4 Manuscript/Chap1
$ □
```

$	Shell prompt
mv	Move the files
sec3 sec4	**sec3** and **sec4** to the
Manuscript/Chap1	directory named **Manuscript/Chap1.**
$ □	Next prompt and cursor

$ mv *dirname newdirname*

Renames your subdirectory *dirname* to *newdirname*.

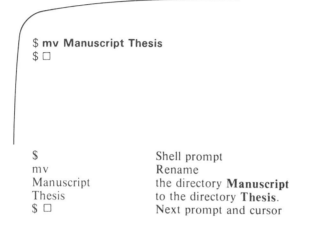

```
$ mv Manuscript Thesis
$ □
```

$	Shell prompt
mv	Rename
Manuscript	the directory **Manuscript**
Thesis	to the directory **Thesis**.
$ □	Next prompt and cursor

Error Messages

```
$ mv temp temp
mv: temp and temp are identical
```

The destination can't be the same as the source file.

```
$ mv -x temp temp2
mv: cannot access -x
```

There are no options for **mv**.

```
$ mv temp2 temp4
mv: cannot access temp2
```

File **temp2** doesn't exist.

Notes on mv

In the UNIX system file system, filenames are not inalterably associated with a file, but rather directories provide the "link" between the filename and file. Therefore, when **mv** "moves" a file it really changes names in directories rather than reading and writing the contents of the file. However, if the destination lies on a different physical file system, **mv** must copy the file between the file systems. Consider the following command:

$ **mv** *file1 file2*

File2 (if it already exists) is deleted and the name of *file1* is changed to *file2*. If *file2* has a mode which forbids writing, **mv** prints the mode (which serves as a warning message) and reads the standard input (terminal keyboard) to obtain your response. If you answer with a "y", the move takes place; if not, **mv** exits.

To "move" one or more files into the specified directory with their original filenames, use the following command form:

$ **mv** *file. . . dirname*

The **mv** command is a useful utility for moving a number of *files* to another directory.

Tutorial

From your login directory type "mv temp example<CR>". The directory will now contain the file **example**, which may be seen by typing the command "ls<CR>".

```
$ mv temp example
$ ls
example      Letters      Manuscript
$ □
```

To move the **temp** file to your friend's directory (/friend-pathname), type "mv temp /friend-pathname<CR>".

```
$ mv temp /friend-pathname
mv: cannot access temp
$ □
```

What happened? This example illustrates an important difference between **cp** and **mv**. Note that **mv** removed **temp** by renaming it **example**. If we had employed the related **cp** command the **temp** file would have remained listed in your directory. The **mv** command removes your link to **temp** so you can no longer reference the file named **temp**.

In summary, **mv** "moves" a file by establishing a link between the physical file reference and the specified name. It creates the new filename in the appropriate directory, and then removes the link between the same file reference and the old filename in the original directory. The **cp** command, on the other hand, actually copies the file, leaving the link in the source directory intact.

Now let's try moving more than one file into another directory with the **mv** command. First create the files **sec3** and **sec4** with an editor. Follow the steps in the next screen.

```
$ ed sec3
? sec3
a
This is Section 3.
.
w
19
e sec4
? sec4
a
This is Section 4.
.
w
19
q
$ □
```

Now type the **mv** command shown in the next screen, then use the **ls** command to verify that the move has occurred.

```
$ mv sec3 sec4 Manuscript/Chap1
$ ls Manuscript/Chap1
sec1 sec2 sec3 sec4
$ □
```

If, for example, your manuscript is a thesis and you wish to call the directory **Thesis**, type "mv Manuscript Thesis<CR>". To verify that **Manuscript** is gone and that **Thesis** contains all the files that **Manuscript** had before the move, type "ls Thesis<CR>".

```
$ mv Manuscript Thesis
$ ls
example     Letters     Thesis
$ ls Thesis
Chap1     Chap2
$ □
```

As a final example, consider what would happen if you attempted to move **example** to itself. Type "mv example example<CR>" and you will get an error message.

```
$ mv example example
mv: example and example are identical
$ □
```

To restore your tutorial practice file system to its original state, perform the operations shown in boldface in the following screen.

```
$ mv example temp
$ mv Thesis Manuscript
$ ls
Letters      Manuscript      temp
$ □
```

Pr — Print File with Pagination

This command executes formatted printing of one or more files.

$ **pr** *file*

Produces a printer-ready listing of *file* with the date and time, the filename, and page headings.

```
$ pr temp

Jul 4 10:56 1981 temp Page 1

Now is the time
for all good citizens
to come to the aid
of their country.
. . .
$ □
```

$	Shell prompt
pr	Print the file
temp	named **temp** on terminal,
	skip two lines then supply a line with
Jul 4	the date the file was last modified,
10:56	time of modification,
1981	and year (part of date) and repeat
temp	the filename and
Page 1	supply the page number.
	Skip two more lines then
Now ...	display the file contents.
. . .	Default of 66 lines in the page
	Trailer of five blank lines at end
$ □	Next prompt and cursor

$ **pr** *-options file. . .*

Print the *file*s, altering the display as shown in the following options.

Options:

-n   Produces *n*-column output.

+n   Prints the file at page *n* into the file.

-h   The next argument or string of characters following this option will become your own customized page header and will be accessed by the **pr** command, e.g., -h "title line".

-wn   Sets the width of the page to be *n* characters instead of the default 72 characters.

-l*n*   Changes the length of the printed page to be *n* lines instead of the default of 66 lines. The number 66 is standard, rising out of six lines per inch on a standard 11-inch long page.

-t   Skips the printing of the five-line header or the five-line trailer normally supplied for each page.

-s*c*   Separates your column output by a single character *c* instead of the usual amount of white space. Without the c, the tab character will separate the columns.

-m   Prints all the files, or one or more files that you specify on the command line, simultaneously and in one column.

Error Messages

The **pr** command does not give error messages for files not found, incorrect options, and so forth.

Notes on pr

This command produces well formatted output for listing one or more specified files. The output is automatically separated into pages with a header which includes the date and time the file was last modified, the name of the file or a different user-specified header, and a page number. If no filename was specified, then the standard input or keyboard input is printed. This command has a number of options which change the appearance of the output listing.

Inter-terminal messages (messages between two users invoked by using the **write** command) are suppressed during the output of the **pr** command. This ensures that the formatted listing is not disturbed.

Tutorial

Type "pr temp<CR>" and you will see something similar to the following display.

```
$ pr temp

Aug 26 08:05 1981 temp Page 1

Now is the time
for all good citizens
to come to the aid
of their country.
. . .

$ □
```

You will see a five-line header: two blank lines, a line containing the text for the header, and two more blank lines. Then **pr** displays the contents of the file. After the 66-line page is printed, a five-line trailer consisting of blank lines is appended. If **temp** contained enough text to require a second page, another header similar to the first would be displayed at the beginning of the second page, indicating Page 2. Note: On terminals with high-speed display rates you will need to *pipe* this command to a utility which lets you view one screenful at a time. Check your system documentation for such a utility. (Use *more* with Berkeley Unix system).

There are a number of options which you can use to customize the formatted output. You must specify the options before the filename.

If you don't want **pr** to print the five-line header or the five-line trailer normally supplied for each page, use the **-t** option. The display will be similar to displays produced with the **cat** printing utility, but it will contain the 66 lines of the default page length. Compare the results shown in the following screen.

```
$ cat temp
Now is the time
for all good citizens
to come to the aid
of their country.
$ pr -t temp
Now is the time
for all good citizens
to come to the aid
of their country.
. . .

$ □
```

You can request **pr** to produce multi-column output by specifying a decimal digit after the dash, such as -*n*, where *n* is the number of columns desired. For an example, let's display a long list of single words in five columns. The on-line spelling dictionary **/usr/dict/words** is a convenient single-column word list which contains over 20,000 entries. To illustrate a five-column display type "pr -5 /usr/dict/words<CR>".

```
$ pr -5 /usr/dict/words

Jan 20 02:55 1979 /usr/dict/words Page 1

10th            abject          abstinent       accountant      across
1st             ablate          abstract        accouter        acrylate
2nd             ablaze          abstractor      Accra           acrylic
[ Interrupt ]
$ □
```

The [Interrupt] above indicates that the display was aborted by pressing the DEL key.

The **pr** command will take the words which will fit on one page and display them from top to bottom down each column beginning with the left-hand column and ending with the column on the extreme right. This procedure provides a means to list all the words in succession from left to right across the page. You should also suppress the page header with the **-t** option and then specify a page length of one line to achieve the desired effect.

```
$ pr -t -5 -l1 /usr/dict/words
10th            1st             2nd             3rd             4th
5th             6th             7th             8th             9th
a               A&M             A&P             a's             AAA
AAAS            Aaron           AAU             ABA             Ababa
[ Interrupt ]
$ □
```

Consider this example for changing the page size: You might want to change the length of the printed page to fit 8½ × 14 inch legal paper. Use

the **-l** option again and multiply 14 inches per page by 6 lines per inch to
get 84 lines per page. Type "pr -l84 /usr/dict/words<CR>".

```
$ pr -5 -l84 /usr/dict/words

Jan 20 02:55 1979 /usr/dict/words Page 1

10th         abound        accessory     acronym       adjoint
1st          about         accident      acropolis     adjourn
. . .
aborning     accessible    acrobat       adjective     advisor
abort        accession     acrobatic     adjoin        advisory

Jan 20 02:55 1979 /usr/dict/words Page 2

advocacy     Agee          airtight      algae         Allstate
advocate     agenda        airway        algaecide     allude
. . .
[ Interrupt ]
$ □
```

Use the **-w***n* option to change the width of the page for multi-column
output. The default value is 72 columns for the page width. Specify 80
columns with the command "pr -4 -w80 /usr/dict/words<CR>" to
utilize the entire 80 columns which are available on most terminals.

```
$ pr -4 -w80 /usr/dict/words

Jan 20 02:55 1979 /usr/dict/words Page 1

10th         abject        abstinent     accountant
1st          ablate        abstract      accouter
2nd          ablaze        abstractor    Accra
. . .
$ □
```

The option **+***n* means begin printing on page *n*. If you were printing a
long document and stopped in the middle, you could use this option to
resume printing at the point of interruption, rather than from the beginning. To illustrate, print a few pages of the spelling dictionary and abort
the listing with the interrupt character (DEL or RUBOUT key). Note
the page number you were on when you aborted. Now resume printing

on that page using the $+n$ option:

```
$ pr -5 /usr/dict/words
Jan 20 02:55 1979 /usr/dict/words Page 1

Jan 20 02:55 1979 /usr/dict/words Page 3

alcohol          align          [ Interrupt ]
$ □
```

We aborted the display when the third page was just beginning. To resume printing starting at Page 3 type "pr $+3$ /usr/dict/words<CR>".

```
$ pr -5 +3 /usr/dict/words

Jan 20 02:55 1979 /usr/dict/words Page 3

alcohol        align        alluvium     alumni       americium
alcoholic      alike        ally         alumnus      Ames
alcoholism     alimony      allyl        alundum      amethyst
[ Interrupt ]
$ □
```

To design your own customized page header, use the **-h** option, as shown in the following display.

```
$ pr -5 -h "SPELLING DICTIONARY" /usr/dict/words

Jan 20 02:55 1979 SPELLING DICTIONARY Page 1

10th           abject       abstinent    accountant   across
1st            ablate       abstract     accouter     acrylate
[ Interrupt ]
$ □
```

You will find **pr** useful in a "pipe" before the **lpr** command. The header serves to identify the file to be printed. For instance, type "pr temp | lpr<CR>" to produce a hard copy of **temp** with an identifying header and a trailer. (The vertical bar " | " means "to pipe.")

If you want to separate the columns by a particular character rather than the appropriate amount of white space, use the **-s**c option where c is the separator character. The separator is taken to be a tab if you do not explicitly designate a character after **-s**. If the separator character normally has a special interpretation by the shell, you must enclose it in single quotes. As an example, list the on-line dictionary in five columns separated by a vertical bar. Type "pr -5 -s' | ' /usr/dict/words<CR>". (The vertical bar must be enclosed in quotes, since the shell normally interprets it to mean "to pipe.")

```
$ pr -5 -s'|' /usr/dict/words
Jan 20 02:55 1979 /usr/dict/words Page 1
10th | abject | abstinent | accountant | across
1st | ablate | abstract | accouter | acrylate
2nd | ablaze | abstractor | Accra | acrylic
[ Interrupt ]
$ □
```

Rm — Remove Files or Directories

This command removes one or more files from a directory, and removes an empty directory.

$ **rm** [-**fri**] *file. . .*

Removes one or more files.

Options:

-**f**   Force the removal of files with no write permission.

-**r**   Recursively delete the entire contents of the directory as well as the directory itself.

-**i**   Interactively ask to delete each file.

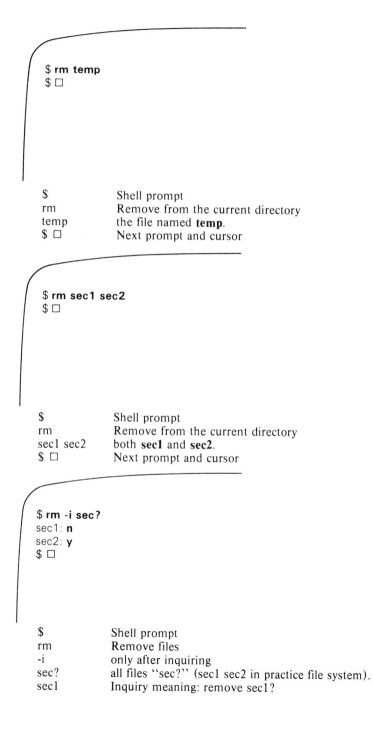

$ **rm temp**
$ □

$	Shell prompt
rm	Remove from the current directory
temp	the file named **temp**.
$ □	Next prompt and cursor

$ **rm sec1 sec2**
$ □

$	Shell prompt
rm	Remove from the current directory
sec1 sec2	both **sec1** and **sec2**.
$ □	Next prompt and cursor

$ **rm -i sec?**
sec1: **n**
sec2: **y**
$ □

$	Shell prompt
rm	Remove files
-i	only after inquiring
sec?	all files "sec?" (sec1 sec2 in practice file system).
sec1	Inquiry meaning: remove sec1?

n	Your response (n for no)
sec2	Inquiry meaning: remove sec2?
y	Your response (y for yes)
$ □	Next prompt and cursor

```
$ rm -ri Family
Family
parents1: y
Family: y
$ [ ]
```

$	Shell prompt
rm	Remove all files
-ri	[and directory (if then empty)] after inquiry
Family	in directory named **Family**.
Family/parents1	Inquiry to remove file **parents1** from **Family**
y	Your response (y for yes)
Family:	Inquiry to remove (now empty) directory **Family**
y	Your response (y for yes)
$ □	Next prompt and cursor

$ **rmdir** *emptydir*

Removes the empty directory *emptydir*. There are no options for this command.

Error Messages

```
$ rm temp2
rm: temp2 nonexistent
```

The file **temp2** doesn't exist in the current directory.

```
$ rm -x temp
rm: unknown option -x
```

The option **-x** doesn't exist.

```
$ rmdir dir
rmdir: dir not empty
```

The directory still has files in it.

Notes on rm(dir)

This command removes the entries for one or more files from a directory. If an entry was the last link to the file, the file is irretrievably lost. Removal of a file requires permission to write in its directory. If you try to remove a file which has no write permission a message will indicate that the file is read-only. If you answer the query to remove the file anyway with a ''y'' as the first letter of the line, the system will delete the file. There is no such query if you invoke the **rm** command with the **-f** (so-called ''force'') option.

Be wary of using the ''*'' wild card. A common mistake is typing ''rm sec *<CR>'' when you meant to type ''rm sec*<CR>''. The former command tells **rm** to remove **sec**. The shell then expands ''*'' to be *all* files, so every file would be removed. *Make sure you don't leave a space here.* Alternatively, you could specify the **-i** option each time you use a

"*" wild card with **rm** in order to catch such a typo before disaster occurs.

Tutorial

Assume that your directory contains the files **Letters**, **Manuscript**, and **temp**. You decide that you don't need **temp** anymore, and delete the file **temp**, leaving only **Letters** and **Manuscript**. But if **temp** has no write permission, the system reponds with a message, "rm temp 400 mode", which means read-only.

```
$ rm temp
rm: temp 400 mode □
```

Note: You may get a different octal mode because your umask is set differently.

If you verify the intended deletion by typing a "y", the file will be removed.

Since **Letters** is actually a directory and not a file, you cannot use the **rm** command alone to remove it. An error message will appear.

```
$ rm Letters
rm: Letters directory
$ □
```

To delete a directory use the closely related command **rmdir**. Here the directory must be empty (as shown by an **ls**); if it is not, an error message will appear.

```
$ rmdir Letters
rmdir: Letters not empty
$ □
```

Alternatively, if you know that **Letters** is not an empty directory you can delete each file from the directory and finally the directory itself by using the **-r** (for recursive) option with the **rm** command: "rm -r Letters<CR>". *Caution:* Make sure you double-check your typing before pressing <CR> when using **rm**, especially with the **-r** option.

The interactive option (**-i**) is another useful option to use with **rm**. This option designates an interactive mode in which **rm** asks you whether to delete each file, and under **-r**, whether to examine each directory. For example, say you have a rather large directory containing several files such as **sec1, sec2, . . . , sec4** and you wish to delete most, but not all of the files. You might invoke **rm** with a wild card for removing all of the **sec** files, but add the **-i** option to query removal of each file. Consider the following example.

```
$ rm -i sec*
sec1: n
sec2: y
sec3: n
sec4: n
$ □
```

Here you deleted **sec2** but left the other **sec** files in the **Manuscript/ Chap1** directory of your sample file system.

Tail — Deliver the Last Part of a File

Use this command to filter all but the last part of a file. This command copies the "tail end" of the file to the *standard output.*

$ tail [±*number* **]** *file*

Copy *file* to the standard output (your terminal) beginning at an offset
+*number* lines from the beginning or -*number* lines from the end of the
file.

```
$ tail /usr/dict/words
zombie
zone
zoo
zoology
zoom
Zoroaster
Zoroastrian
zounds
zucchini
Zurich
$ □
```

$	Shell prompt
tail	Print last part of
/usr/dict/words	the on-line spelling dictionary.
zombie	Last ten lines displayed because no
zone	±*number* was indicated,
zoo	so the default value (**-10**) is used.
. . .	
$ □	Next prompt and cursor

```
$ tail -5 /usr/dict/words
Zoroaster
Zoroastrian
zounds
zucchini
Zurich
$ □
```

$	Shell prompt
tail	Print the last part
-5	starting 5 lines from the end
/usr/dict/words	of the on-line spelling dictionary.
Zoroaster	
. . .	
$□	Next prompt and cursor

$ **tail** [±*number unit*] *file*

Copy *file* to the standard output (terminal) beginning at a distance
+*number* lines, blocks, or characters (determined by the unit letter)
from the beginning or -*number* lines, blocks, or characters from the end
of the file.

Unit:

-**l**   Number is counted in units of lines (default).

-**b**   Number is counted in units of 512-byte blocks.

-**c**   Number is counted in units of characters.

```
$ tail +10c temp
e time
for all good citizens
to come to the aid
of their country.
$ □
```

$	Shell prompt
tail	Print the last part
+10c	starting at the 10th character
	from the beginning
temp	of the file **temp**.
e time	Start display at 10th character
for all . . .	from the beginning of the file
to come . . .	and display the rest on the
of their . . .	terminal.
$ □	Next prompt and cursor

Error Messages

```
$ tail temp1
tail: can't open temp1
```

The file **temp1** doesn't exist or can't be read.

```
$ tail +d temp
usage: tail ±n[lbc] [file]
```

"+d" is not an offset option.

```
$ tail 3 temp
tail: can't open 3
```

Must precede number with + or -.

Notes on tail

This utility enables you to access the end of a file without paging through the entire file from the beginning. You can specify exactly where you wish to begin the display by counting either the number of lines (the default case), blocks, or characters from either the beginning or end of the file.

There are a few applications in which accessing the end of the file is useful. You may wish to place a sentinel (or marker) at the end of a file for some purpose. The **tail** program lets you access that sentinel easily. You may have appended one file to another file and wish to access the end of the appended file first. The **tail** program allows you to check the end of a command pipeline.

Tutorial

Type the command "tail /usr/dict/words<CR>".

```
$ tail /usr/dict/words
zombie
zone
zoo
zoology
zoom
Zoroaster
Zoroastrian
zounds
zucchini
Zurich
$ □
```

Your display may differ depending on the entry included in your on-line dictionary.

The last ten lines were displayed because no offset was indicated. If no ±*number* is named, **tail** assumes the default case, **-10**, and the display begins with the tenth line from the end of the file.

You can specify an offset from the beginning of the file using +*number* or from the end of the file using -*number*. Without the **b** or **c** suffix the offset corresponds to a line count. For example, type "tail + 23997 /usr/dict/words<CR>" and the result will be similar to the following screen.

```
$ tail +23997 /usr/dict/words
Zoroaster
Zoroastrian
zounds
zucchini
Zurich
$ □
```

Here the display began 23,997 lines from the beginning of the file. Compare this with the result obtained by typing the command "tail -5 /usr/dict/words<CR>". The same result appears because the on-line dictionary contains 24,001 entries.

```
$ tail -5 /usr/dict/words
Zoroaster
Zoroastrian
zounds
zucchini
Zurich
$ □
```

If your on-line dictionary contains a different number of entries you will need to readjust the numbers. A simple way to find out the size of your dictionary is to type "wc -l /usr/dict/words<CR>". The display indicates the number of lines (words) in your dictionary.

Lines relative to the end of the file are stored in a buffer which is somewhat limited in length. If you wish to display lines near the beginning of a large file you should specify the starting line relative to the beginning of the file. For example, type "tail +10 /usr/dict/words<CR>" followed by the interrupt signal.

```
$ tail +10 /usr/dict/words
9th
a
A&M
A&P
a's
AAA
AAAS
Aaron
[ Interrupt ]
$ □
```

However, if you give the apparently equivalent command "tail -23992 /usr/dict/words<CR>" you may observe a different display.

```
$ tail -23992 /usr/dict/words
whatever
Whatley
whatnot
whatsoever
wheat
Wheatstone
[ Interrupt ]
$ □
```

In this case, the buffer could only accommodate the last 500+ words, so the display began approximately 500 words from the end of the file.

Consider another example, in which you just used the **spell** program to correct one of your documents. The list of misspelled words for every user is archived in a history file named **/usr/dict/spellhist**. Now use **tail** to access your particular entry. To illustrate, first use your favorite editor and purposely misspell the words "citizen" as "citozen" and "country" as "coumtry" in your **temp** file. Then run the spelling check by typing "spell temp<CR>".

```
$ spell temp
citozens
coumtry
$ □
```

Note: The **spell** program displays the words which it finds in the indicated file that are *not* in the on-line spelling dictionary.

To access the most recent entry in the spelling history file for this
particular case type "tail -3 /usr/dict/spellhist<CR>" and observe the
display.

```
$ tail -3 /usr/dict/spellhist
citozens
coumtry
your-name  tty5 Oct 11 13:45
$ □
```

Note: *your-name* should be your login name. The terminal designation and date will reflect your current login terminal and date.

You can also specify the offset in terms of a character count. Follow
the *number* with the letter **c** (for character) to specify the *number* of
character units. For example, type "tail +20c temp<CR>".

```
$ tail +20c temp
r all good citizens
to come to the aid
of their country.
$ □
```

Here the display begins at the twentieth character from the beginning of the file. As an exercise, try to get this same display by specifying a number of characters from the end of the file. You must count each <CR> as two characters.

You can specify an offset in terms of the number of 512-character units (blocks). For the file **temp**, which is much shorter than one block, if you specified the **b** (for block) suffix with a +*number,* nothing would be displayed. A one-block offset would "reach" past the end of the file. The "block" offset unit is useful for files larger than **temp**. To illustrate, type "tail -1b /usr/dict/words<CR>". A display begins 512 characters from the end of the file.

```
$ tail -1b /usr/dict/words
ngish
youngster
Youngstown
your
yourself
yourselves
youth
[ Interrupt ]
$ □
```

Again your result differs. In any case, to verify that the last block was actually displayed type "tail -1b /usr/dict/words | wc<CR>".

```
$ tail -1b /usr/dict/words | wc
76    76   512
$ □
```

Note: The last column shows that the "tail" file contains 512 characters, which corresponds to one block.

For our final example, we use the **tail** utility to check the end of a command pipeline. Use your favorite editor and append the characters "zz" to the end of the **temp** file. Now print the file to verify the change.

```
$ cat temp
Now is the time
for all good citizens
to come to the aid
of their country.
zz
$ □
```

Now type the command line shown in the following screen. All the words contained in **temp** are displayed one to a line, and are sorted alphabetically with all duplicates removed.

```
$ cat temp | tr -cs A-Za-z '\012' | sort -d | uniq
Now
aid
all
citozens
come
coumtry
for
good
is
of
the
their
time
to
zz
$ □
```

In this case you know that the last line displayed should contain the "word" zz. Another way to verify that the pipeline performed correctly is to employ the **tail** utility at the end to detect the "zz" sentinel.

```
$ cat temp | tr -cs A-Za-z '\012' | sort -d | uniq | tail -1
zz
$ □
```

Tr — Translate Characters

This command substitutes or deletes selected characters while copying text from standard input to standard output.

$ **tr**   *string1 string2*

When copying input to output substitute for any characters in the input which appear in *string1* characters from the corresponding position in *string2*.

```
$ tr abcdefghijklmnopqrstuvwxyz ABCDEFGHIJKLMNOPQRSTUVWXYZ
This line is in all CAPS.
THIS LINE IS IN ALL CAPS.
[^D]
$ □
```

$	Shell prompt
tr	Translate
abc. . .	all lower-case alphabetics to
ABC	upper case.
This line. . .	Keyboard input translated
THIS LINE. . .	as specified.
[^D]	EOT (control-D) terminates command
$ □	Next prompt and cursor

A range of characters from *a* to *b* inclusive in increasing ASCII order can be indicated by the notation *a-b*.

```
$ tr a-z A-Z
This line is in all CAPS.
THIS LINE IS IN ALL CAPS.
[^D]
$ □
```

tr	Translate
a-z	all lower-case letters
A-Z	into upper case.
This line. . .	Keyboard input is
THIS LINE. . .	capitalized in output display.
[^D]	EOT terminates command
$ □	Next prompt and cursor

When *string2* is shorter than *string1*, *string2* is padded to the length of *string1* by duplicating its last character.

```
$ tr 0-9 0-5
0123456789
0123455555
[^D]
$ □
```

$	Shell prompt
tr	Translate
0-9	the entire range of decimal digits
0-5	to a smaller subset.
0123456789	Larger input range mapped to output
0123455555	duplicating last character (5).
[^D]	EOT terminate character
$ □	Next prompt and cursor

$ **tr** [**-cds**] *string1* *string2*

Options:

Three options modify the translation of characters from input to output.

-c This option complements the sense of *string1,* that is, all characters *except* those in *string1* are translated to the corresponding characters in *string2.*

-d This option deletes all the input characters specified in *string1.*

-s This option squeezes all strings of repeated output characters that are in *string2* to single characters.

```
$ tr -c abc ABC
ABCDEFabcdef
CCCCCCabcCCCC
[^D]
$ □
```

$	Shell prompt
tr -c	Translate all characters *except*
abc	"abc"
ABC	to "C" (duplicating its last character).
ABCDEFabcdef	Keyboard input translated
CCCCCCabcCCCC	to give this display. Note: The last "C" comes from the <CR> being translated.
[^D]	EOT terminate code
$ □	Next prompt and cursor

```
$ tr -cs abc ABC
ABCDEFabcdef
CabcC
[^D]
$ □
```

$	Shell prompt
tr -cs	Translate all characters *except*
abc	"abc"
ABC	to "C" (collapsing duplicates to single character).
ABCDEFabcdef	Keyboard input translated
CabcC	to give this display.
[^D]	EOT terminate code
$ □	Next prompt and cursor

```
$ tr -d abc
ABCDEFabcdef
ABCDEFdef
[^D]
$ □
```

$	Shell prompt
tr -d	Translate by deleting
abc	"abc" when copying to output.
ABCDEFabcdef	Keyboard input translated
ABCDEFdef	to this display.
[^D]	EOT terminate code
$ □	Next prompt and cursor

The following example renders a text file into one word per line.

```
$ tr -cs A-Za-z '\012' <temp
Now
is
the
. . .
country
$ □
```

$	Shell prompt
tr -cs	Translate all characters except
A-Za-z	alphabetics
'\012'	to a single "squeezed" newline character
temp	from the file **temp**.

Now	A single list of words is displayed
is	because all spaces between words
the	have been translated to newline
. . .	characters (value: octal 012).
country	
$ ☐	Next prompt and cursor

Error Messages

There are no error messages for incorrectly specified string arguments or options.

Notes on tr

This command copies the standard input (what is typed at the keyboard) to the standard output (what is displayed on the terminal) with substitution, deletion, or compression of selected characters. Thus, you can use this command as a filter program. The **tr** command commonly takes two string arguments, designated *string1* followed optionally by *string2*. The characters specified in *string2* will be substituted for the corresponding characters in *string1* when the input is copied to the output. You can use the shorthand notation, *a-b,* to specify a range of characters from *a* to *b* in increasing ASCII order. Furthermore, you can specify a special character using a backslash followed by one, two, or three octal digits corresponding to its ASCII code. A backslash followed by any other character stands for that character.

Three options modify this command's interpretation. Use the **-c** (complement) option to specify all characters except those in *string1*. Generally the complement of *string1* is a set of characters larger than *string2,* so *string2* will be padded to the length of *string1* by duplicating its last character. The **-s** (squeeze) option "squeezes" all strings of repeated characters in *string2* to single characters. Concatenating these two options (**-cs**) produces a unique and easily interpreted translation when using the complement feature. Use the **-d** option to delete all the characters listed in *string1* when copying input to output. Using *string2* with the **-d** option is meaningless and is ignored by **tr**.

Tutorial

In many of the following examples, after you type the command line the cursor will be poised at the beginning of the next line without a prompt. Type the command line "tr abc ABC<CR>" and note that the cursor appears at the beginning of the next line.

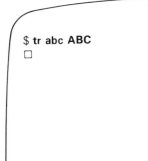

```
$ tr abc ABC
□
```

Now continue typing some text such as "The quick brown . . ." and end the line with a <CR>. The system will then immediately display the translated input.

```
$ tr abc ABC
The quick brown fox jumps over the lazy dog.
The quiCk Brown fox jumps over the lAzy dog.
□
```

Notice that the cursor is waiting at the beginning of the next line. You can either type more lines to continue the translation process or press ^D to exit **tr**.

You specify a range of characters by the notation *a-b*, where *b* is greater than *a* in ASCII value. For example, to convert all lower-case a-z letters to the corresponding upper-case A-Z, type the command "tr a-z A-Z<CR>". Input text, end the line with a <CR>, and exit with ^D.

```
$ tr a-z A-Z
The quick brown fox jumps over the lazy dog.
THE QUICK BROWN FOX JUMPS OVER THE LAZY DOG.
[^D]
$ □
```

The input and/or output for the **tr** command can be a disk file. For instance, the contents of the file **temp** can be translated to upper case and stored in another file **tempUC** by redirecting the standard input and standard output. Type "tr a-z A-Z < temp > tempUC <CR>". Now examine the result with the **cat** program.

```
$ cat tempUC
NOW IS THE TIME
FOR ALL GOOD CITIZENS
TO COME TO THE AID
OF THEIR COUNTRY.
$ □
```

Three options modify the **tr** command. The **-d** option deletes characters indicated in *string1* when copying to the output. For example, you can remove all "-" characters with the command "tr -d '-'<CR>".

```
$ tr -d '-'
It's a bargain — $3.00!
It's a bargain $3.00!
□
```

Note: It is not necessary to specify a *string2* here. If you do, it will be ignored.

What happens if *string1* has more characters than *string2?* The **tr** command will then pad *string2* to the length of *string1* by duplicating the last character in *string2*. An example is shown in the following screen display.

```
$ tr 0-9 0-4
0123456789
0123444444
□
```

Here all numerals are mapped into a smaller subset duplicating the test character (4) in *string2*.

You can use the complement option (**-c**) to specify all characters *except* those in *string1*. That will usually be a set of characters larger than *string2,* so *string2* will be effectively padded by **tr** to the new length of *string1* by duplicating its last character. Since this may produce a confusing display, the **-s** (squeeze) option is usually concatenated with the complement option to produce a unique and meaningful interpretation. The following screen shows an example.

```
$ tr -cs A-Z '\40'
PO BOX 22411 SAN FRANCISCO 94122
PO BOX SAN FRANCISCO
$ □
```

Here all characters which are *not* letters (specified using the range A-Z) are "squeezed" into a space character which is represented as octal 040 using the notation '\040'. The **tr** command requires the backslash character to indicate that the octal value is to follow, and the single quotes are necessary to protect the backslash from incorrect interpretation by the shell.

Bugs

This command will not accept the ASCII NUL character in either *string1* or *string2*. This command always deletes the NUL character from the input.

Running Programs

At — Execute Commands at a Later Time

This command is used for scheduling a file of one or more commands to be run at a specified time and date.

$ **at** *time* [*day*] [*file*]

Executes commands in *file* at *time* on *day*.

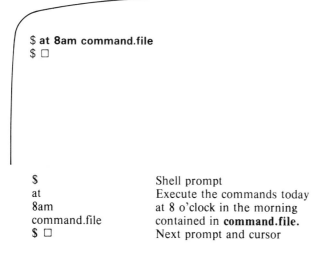

```
$ at 8am command.file
$ □
```

$	Shell prompt
at	Execute the commands today
8am	at 8 o'clock in the morning
command.file	contained in **command.file.**
$ □	Next prompt and cursor

```
$ at 2130 command.file
```

Execute the commands today, at 9:30 PM.

```
$ at 12N fri week command.file
```

Execute the commands at noon, a week from next Friday.

```
$ at 2 PM apr 3 command.file
```

Execute the commands on April 3 at 2 PM.

Error Messages

```
$ at 1559 1600 1601 storedate
1600: No such file or directory
```

Second argument must be a file.

```
$ at 1800 storedates
at: cannot open input:  storedates
```

The source file **storedates** can't be read or doesn't exist.

```
$ at -x 1800 storedate
at: bad time format
```

The **at** command takes no character options.

Notes on at

The **at** utility executes one or more commands at a specific time without your direct supervision. The commands must first be stored in a file. You may use an editor or some other utility to create this file. We refer to this file as a "command file" or, in reference to the **at** program, as an "at-file."

To schedule the "command file" to be run, use the following format for the command line:

$$\$ \textbf{ at } time \;[\; day \;]\;[\; file \;]$$

Time is a one- to four-digit number with an optional **A**, **P**, **N**, or **M** to stand for AM, PM, noon or midnight, respectively. One- and two-digit numbers will be interpreted to be an hour, and three- and four-digit numbers represent hours and minutes. If no letters follow the digits, a 24-hour clock time will be assumed. The *day* can be a month name followed by a space then a day number, or it can be the name of a day of the week. Furthermore, if you specify **week** on the command line the command file will be scheduled for execution in seven days from today's date. The **at** command can recognize names of months and days which are conventionally abbreviated. Finally, *file* is the name of the command file where the command(s) are stored.

Tutorial

In the standard UNIX system, **at** programs are executed only at certain periodic intervals depending on how often a file called **/usr/lib/atrun** is executed. This may occur every ten minutes, every twenty minutes, or even every half hour depending on your particular system. However, if you schedule a file to be executed at some intermediate time then the system waits until the regularly scheduled execution of the **/usr/lib/atrun** file before executing your commands. You might compare this to catching a bus which only runs every half hour. If you miss one bus, you must wait until the next bus arrives on the half hour.

First we will investigate the granularity for executing the **/usr/lib/atrun** file. Invoke an editor to create a file named **storedate** which contains the command "date >>datefile". If you employ the **ed** editor, follow the directions in boldface in the following screen.

```
$ ed storedate
? storedate
a
date > >datefile
.
w
16
q
$ [ ]
```

Now verify that **storedate** contains the desired command by typing "cat storedate<CR>" and you will see the following display.

```
$ cat storedate
date > >datefile
$ □
```

Now enter the **at** commands shown in the following screen. You may wish to use a different starting hour of the day, but schedule **storedate** to run every ten minutes.

```
$ at 1500 storedate
$ at 1510 storedate
$ at 1520 storedate
$ at 1530 storedate
$ at 1540 storedate
$ at 1550 storedate
$ □
```

Wait until the hour has elapsed and print the contents of the file **datefile** with the **cat** command, typing "cat datefile<CR>". If you saw a result as shown in the following screen then you could conclude that the system runs the **/usr/lib/atrun** file every 20 minutes.

```
$ cat datefile
Sat Oct 17 15:00:09 PDT 1981
Sat Oct 17 15:21:26 PDT 1981
Sat Oct 17 15:40:08 PDT 1981
Sat Oct 17 16:00:16 PDT 1981
$ □
```

Now that you know when the "at-files" are actually examined you can design your processes to run in synchronization with the system.

Incidentally, the above example also demonstrates that a command file will be run at the next opportunity, should you miss one of the scheduled execution times.

It is interesting to explore the files which the system uses to implement the **at** command. First type "ls /usr/spool/at/*" to list all the files ready for execution. The shell will expand the "*" character to give a series of filenames of the form /usr/spool/at/*yy.ddd.hhhh.uu* where the activity is to be performed at hour *hhhh* of year day *ddd* of year *yy*. The *uu* is a unique identifying number. For the example above, typing "ls /usr/spool/at/*<CR>" produced the following display on our system.

```
$ ls /usr/spool/at/*
/usr/spool/at/81.289.1500.04
/usr/spool/at/81.289.1510.20
/usr/spool/at/81.289.1520.33
/usr/spool/at/81.289.1530.43
/usr/spool/at/81.289.1540.57
/usr/spool/at/81.289.1550.64
/usr/spool/at/lasttimedone
/usr/spool/at/past
$ □
```

Next, use **cat** to examine the file **/usr/spool/at/81.289.1500.04**. You can see the actual commands the system squirreled away to execute the simple request "date >>datefile".

```
$ cat  /usr/spool/at/81.289.1500.04
cd /cb/rathomas
umask 77
HOME='/cb/rathomas'
export HOME
PATH=':/usr/cc/bin:/usr/ucb/bin'
export PATH
SHELL='/bin/sh'
export SHELL
TERM='sd'
export TERM
exec /bin/sh  < <'. . .AT.EOF. . .'
date >> datefile
. . .AT.EOF. . .
$ □
```

Fortunately, you don't need to type all of this to use the **at** utility.

If you wish to execute a particular function once every 24 hours you can call the **at** program recursively. To illustrate, use an editor and append the line "at 0800 storedate" to the file **storedate**. After exiting your editor, list the file contents with **cat**.

```
$ cat storedate
date > >datefile
at 0800 storedate
$ □
```

Finally, type "at 0800 storedate<CR>" to get the first "at" started. At 8 AM the file containing the two lines shown in the last screen will be executed. The second line will cause this same file to be executed at 8 AM the next morning, and so on. You might use such a feature to execute a task such as a file backup operation or other maintenance duty once every day without your intervention after the initial startup.

Echo — Echo Arguments

This command echoes (repeats) its arguments, each separated by blanks, to the standard output (terminal).

$ **echo** [**-n**] [*arg*]. . .

Writes its arguments separated by blanks and ends in newline unless the
-n option is used.

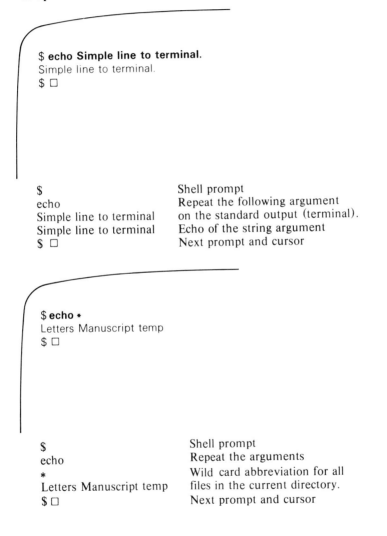

$ **echo Simple line to terminal.**
Simple line to terminal.
$ □

$	Shell prompt
echo	Repeat the following argument
Simple line to terminal	on the standard output (terminal).
Simple line to terminal	Echo of the string argument
$ □	Next prompt and cursor

$ **echo** *
Letters Manuscript temp
$ □

$	Shell prompt
echo	Repeat the arguments
*	Wild card abbreviation for all
Letters Manuscript temp	files in the current directory.
$ □	Next prompt and cursor

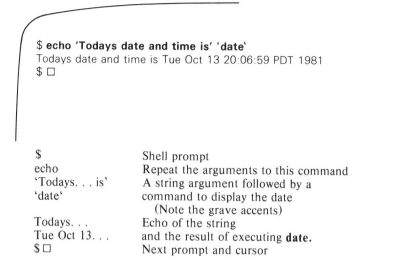

```
$ echo 'Todays date and time is' 'date'
Todays date and time is Tue Oct 13 20:06:59 PDT 1981
$ □
```

$	Shell prompt
echo	Repeat the arguments to this command
'Todays. . . is'	A string argument followed by a
'date'	command to display the date
	(Note the grave accents)
Todays. . .	Echo of the string
Tue Oct 13. . .	and the result of executing **date.**
$ □	Next prompt and cursor

Error Messages

There are no error messages given by the **echo** command. The shell may be unable to satisfy the request and issue an error message, though.

Notes on echo

When you type a command in the UNIX system a program called the shell interprets your requests. The shell expands all wild card abbreviations in the command you type and checks the resulting command line for correct syntax. If your command request is valid, the shell coordinates the system resources to execute your command.

When the **echo** program writes out its arguments, all wild card abbreviations and other special characters and constructions have been completely interpreted by the shell. This lets you "preview" the final form of a command line which the shell will execute prior to actual execution. This "preview" feature provided by the **echo** utility can be employed for diagnostic purposes.

For instance, let's say you type a command using the "*" wild card, which doesn't work as you had expected. Now if you type "echo" followed by the command line you presented to the shell (what was typed after the $ prompt) your terminal will display the expanded and interpreted form of the command which the shell objected to. By inspecting this expanded command format you may discover why the command didn't work as you had expected. If there is no expansion performed by the shell, the line displayed will be identical to what was typed in. Consider another example. You wish to use a command which could irreparably alter one or more files. You might wish to "preview" the form of the command which the shell will actually execute to see if everything looks correct before you ask the shell to execute the command.

The **echo** command line is indispensable in writing simple command lines and useful for placing one command in a file to be executed by the shell. It is also useful for writing strings of text to the terminal for diagnostic or other informational purposes. In these cases the **echo** command will expand its arguments to display the effects of command substitution, parameter substitution, interpretation of white space separators, expansion of filename wild cards, and the effects of various special characters used for quoting expressions.

Tutorial

Recall that a simple command is a sequence of words separated by blanks (a blank is a tab or a space character). The first word always specifies the name of the command to be executed. The remaining words on the command line are passed as arguments to the invoked command. The **echo** utility may be used to "preview" the unabbreviated form of the arguments which are passed to the invoked command.

In the simplest case all the argument words are simply composed of text strings. To demonstrate how text can be printed on your terminal by using the **echo** utility, type "echo This line is a string argument.<CR>".

```
$ echo This line is a string argument.
This line is a string argument.
$ □
```

An argument word can also be the standard output (result) of a command if the command is enclosed in grave accents (``). This is called *command substitution,* and the inner command is invoked before the outer command. For instance, type "echo 'Todays date and time is' `date`<CR>." Observe that the string in quotes is displayed as typed, while the command surrounded by grave accents is actually executed, its standard output interpreted, and the entire result displayed by the **echo** utility.

```
$ echo 'Todays date and time is' `date`
Todays date and time is Tue Oct 13 20:06:59 PDT 1981
$ ▢
```

A $ character can indicate a shell "variable" which has a particular value. You can assign values to shell variables and so can the system. You may use the **echo** command to display the value of a shell parameter. For example, for the Bourne Shell the parameter $HOME refers to the pathname for your login directory. Type "echo 'My login directory is ' $HOME<CR>" and you will see a display similar to the following screen.

```
$ echo 'My login directory is ' $HOME
My login directory is /usr/your-name
$ ▢
```

After the commands and parameters are substituted the shell scans the command for special characters which separate the word arguments. Usually the tab and space characters separate these arguments, but you can also specify other characters for this purpose.

After the commands and parameters are substituted and the blanks are interpreted, the shell will scan each command word for the *, ?, and [ ] characters. If one of these characters appears, the argument word as a whole is regarded as a "pattern" to be replaced with the alphabetically sorted filenames which match the pattern. The interpretations of these special characters are as follows:

*   Matches any string.

?   Matches any single character.

[. . .]   Matches any one of the enclosed characters. A pair of characters can be separated by "-" to match any character which occurs in ASCII value between the pair.

To illustrate filename substitution, create a directory named "Cprograms" by typing "mkdir Cprograms<CR>". Move to that directory with the command "cd Cprograms<CR>". Finally, create three "C" program files by using the **echo** command, redirecting the output to appropriate files as shown in the following screen. (The **mkdir** *make directory* and **cd** *change directories* commands are fully explained elsewhere in this chapter.)

```
$ mkdir Cprograms
$ cd Cprograms
$ echo This is program no. 1 >prog1.c
$ echo This is program no. 2 >prog2.c
$ echo This is program no. 3 >prog3.c
$ ls
prog1.c     prog2.c     prog3.c
$ □
```

The **ls** command was used in the above example to verify that the three files were created as we intended.

For the first example of filename substitution, type "echo *<CR>".

```
$ echo *
prog1.c   prog2.c   prog3.c
$ □
```

This shows all the filenames in your current directory (Cprograms) because the * character matches any filename string.

For your second example, type "echo prog?.c<CR>".

```
$ echo prog?.c
prog1.c   prog2.c   prog3.c
$ □
```

You get the same result as in the previous example because the ? was matched by **1**, **2**, and **3** in the filenames.

As a third example, type "echo prog[1-3].c<CR>" and you will again obtain the same result.

```
$ echo prog[1-3].c
prog1.c   prog2.c   prog3.c
$ □
```

For some variations type the commands shown in **boldface** in the following screen.

```
$ echo *.c
prog1.c   prog2.c   prog3.c
$ echo prog[2-4].c
prog2.c   prog3.c
$ echo prog???
prog1.c   prog2.c   prog3.c
$ □
```

Consider the case in which no match occurs. For every command you type you will immediately get another prompt, as shown in the following screen.

```
$ echo prog.*
$ echo prog[4-5].c
$ echo prog?c
$ □
```

Use the "preview" feature of the **echo** command to interpret the effects of quoting the characters which have special meaning to the shell. A list of these characters follows:

; & ( ) | < >   newline   space   tab

To remove the special significance these characters have to the shell, you may escape (or quote them) with the backslash \ . To illustrate, compare the displays obtained from typing "echo *<CR>" and "echo *<CR>".

```
$ echo *
prog1.c    prog2.c    prog3.c
$ echo \*
*
$ □
```

In the second case the asterisk acts like any other character (compare with the result of typing "echo a<CR>") because the backslash removes its special significance to the shell, as shown above.

All characters enclosed in single quotes (except a single quote) are displayed in quotes. No substitution of any kind is performed inside single quotes. Type: echo '*'<CR> and observe the display.

```
$ echo '*'
*
$ □
```

Finally, double quotes can be used to quote the special characters listed above, except in the case of *'command'* and $*variable* substitution. Note the difference in the displays from typing "echo $HOME<CR>", "echo \$HOME<CR>", "echo '$HOME'<CR>", and "echo "$HOME" <CR>."

```
$ echo $HOME
/usr/your-name
$ echo \$HOME
$HOME
$ echo '$HOME'
$HOME
$ echo "$HOME"
/usr/your-name
$ □
```

Kill — Terminate a Process

Use this command to terminate a background process.

$ kill *number. . .*

Terminates process *number*.

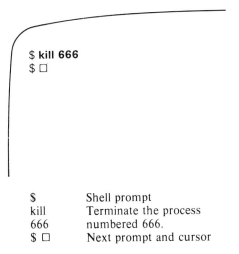

$	Shell prompt
kill	Terminate the process
666	numbered 666.
$ ☐	Next prompt and cursor

Error Messages

No argument specified.

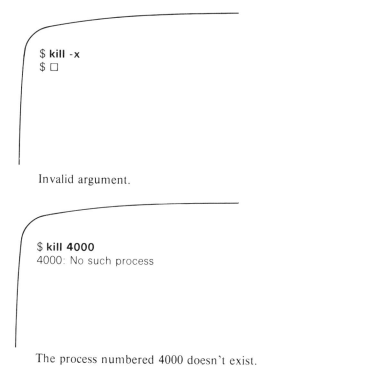

```
$ kill -x
$ □
```

Invalid argument.

```
$ kill 4000
4000: No such process
```

The process numbered 4000 doesn't exist.

Notes on kill

To initiate a concurrent background process use the **&** directive at the end of the command line. After you press the <CR>, the shell will reply with a number. This is the process number or process-id for the background process you just initiated. The process number is the only way to identify the process.

You cannot interrupt background processes by issuing an interrupt signal (pressing DEL or RUBOUT). Instead, you must direct the **kill** command to terminate the process using the following command form:

$ **kill** *number*

number is the process number for the background process you wish to terminate.

You may wish to terminate a background process if it seems to overload system resources or if you no longer need the process which you began executing in background.

Tutorial

First we will start a process in background which will take at least one minute to complete. A good example is to **sort** the 20,000+ word on-line spelling dictionary **/usr/dict/words** in reverse. Type "sort -r /usr/dict/words -o word.sort&<CR>" and note the process number displayed. (The **sort** command and its options are discussed in a separate section.)

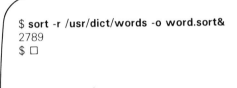

```
$ sort -r /usr/dict/words -o word.sort&
2789
$ □
```

The number on your display will be different. Make a note of your process number.

Now wait at least two minutes for the process to finish. Display the output file by typing "cat word.sort<CR>". You can abort the long display by pressing your terminal's delete key.

```
$ cat word.sort
zucchini
zounds
zoom
zoology
zoo
zone
[ Interrupt ]
$ □
```

Your display may differ depending on the entries in your on-line dictionary. [Interrupt] will not be displayed; we show it on the preceding screen to indicate when we generated the interrupt signal to abort the **cat** command.

If an error message or nothing was displayed, the sorting process had not finished. In that case type "ps *number*<CR>", where *number* is the process number you noted for your background sorting process. If you get the message "*number:* No such process" then either the sorting process was not initiated correctly or it terminated while you were requesting the process status. If this is the case retype "cat word.sort<CR>" to display the result.

After you initiate a background process you may decide to terminate before it finishes on its own accord. Two common reasons for this are that you started a process you later decided not to run, or the process you started seems to be taking "forever," indicating that the system is already heavily loaded. In this case you might decide to run the process at a later time.

To illustrate the **kill** command, first erase your output file by typing "rm word.sort<CR>". Initiate the same sorting process in background by typing "sort -r /usr/dict/words -o word.sort&<CR>" and again note the process number displayed by the system.

Now type "kill *number*<CR>", where *number* is the process number for the sorting routine you just started in background.

```
$ sort -r /usr/dict/words -o word.sort&
2890
$ kill 2890
$ □
```

Some versions of **kill** may reply with a message such as "2890: Terminated".

One way to verify that this process was terminated successfully is to wait at least two minutes from the time you began the sort, then type "cat word.sort<CR>".

```
$ cat word.sort
cat: can't open word.sort
$ □
```

You may observe the message "cat: can't open word.sort", indicating that the output file had not been created. Or another shell prompt may immediately appear, indicating that the file **word.sort** was created, but that the result of the sort was never stored in the file. If a display of the on-line spelling dictionary appears in reverse then you did not terminate the sort process.

Another way to verify that a process is running is to use the **ps** utility. Consider this example. First make sure that the output file is removed by typing "rm word.sort<CR>", then type "sort -r /usr/dict/words -o word.sort & <CR>" to start the sort again. Then type "ps<CR>". After a short delay a display similar to the following will appear.

```
$ sort -r /usr/dict/words -o word.sort&
3000
$ ps
PID              TTY              TIME CMD
3000             tty5             0:06 sort -r /usr/dict/words -o word.sort
2667             tty5             0:12 -sh
$ □
```

Look at the right-hand column of the **ps** program display, which may be labeled "CMD." The names of the various active processes associated with your terminal are shown (tty5 in this case). You should see a process entry for your shell (denoted by -sh if you are using the Bourne Shell or -csh if you are using the "C" shell), an entry for the sorting routine you just began in background, and perhaps an entry for the **ps** command itself.

Now kill the background process as you did before by typing "kill *number*<CR>". You should replace *number* with the actual process number for the sorting procedure. Then monitor the active processes again by typing "ps<CR>". You should not see an entry for the sort (sort -r /usr/dict/words -o word.sort).

```
$ sort -r /usr/dict/words -o word.sort &
3000
$ kill 3000
$ ps
PID                 TTY .               TIME CMD
2667                tty5                0:12 -sh
$ □
```

After issuing the **kill** directive you may or may not receive a message indicating that the process has been terminated. This is implementation-dependent.

Finally, check the contents of the output file **word.sort** by typing "cat word.sort<CR>" and note the response. The sort program places its intermediate results in a temporary file. Only after the sort is completed is the temporary file copied to your designated output file (**word.sort** in this case).

Tee — Pipe Fitting

The **tee** (for a "T" connection) command transfers data from the *standard input* to the *standard output* and diverts a copy into one or more files.

$ **tee** [**-i**] [**-a**] *file . . .*

Makes a copy of the data which is being transmitted from the standard input to the standard output in *files(s).*

Options:

-i   Ignore the command interrupt signal.

-a   Append the copy to the file instead of overwriting.

```
$ who | tee who.now | wc -l
   5
$ cat who.now
bodega              tty04           Oct   7 09:56
avante              tty13           Oct   7 19:33
rathomas            tty24           Oct   7 19:57
bodega              tty27           Oct   7 17:16
bodega              tty28           Oct   7 19:21
$ □
```

$	Shell prompt
who	The output of the **who** utility
|	is directed to the input of the
tee	**tee** branch utility which makes a
who.now	copy in the file **who.now** as the
|	output is directed to the
wc -l	utility for counting lines (number of on-line users).
5	Response to "wc -l" is 5 lines (for 5 on-line users).
cat who.now	Verify that the intermediate result
bodega tty04. . .	is stored in **who.now.**
$ □	Next prompt and cursor

```
$ pr temp | tee /dev/tty | lpr
Oct 11 11:49 1981   temp Page 1
Now is the time
for all good citizens
to come to the aid
of their country.

. . .
$ □
```

$	Shell prompt
pr	Formatted printing of
temp	the file **temp** is
|	directed to the **tee** branch utility
/dev/tty	for display on your terminal as the data
|	is being directed to
lpr	a queue for the line printer.
Oct 11 . . .	Display of output from **pr** on your
. . .	terminal on the way to the line printer.
$ □	Next prompt and cursor

Error Messages

This command is silent, producing no error messages.

Notes on tee

Use **tee** for sampling data at an intermediate point in a *pipeline* by storing the intermediate results in a file or diverting them to your terminal. Examples for both cases are presented above.

The **tee** utility diverts a copy of the data to the named *file*. If the file doesn't already exist, it is created. If the file does exist then the diverted information is copied to the file, overwriting anything in that file, unless the append option is employed. Use the **-a** (append) option when you wish to add the diverted data to the end of the specified *file*.

Use the **-i** (interrupt) option when it is necessary to ignore the command interrupt signal (usually generated by pressing the DEL or RUBOUT key).

If you wish the diverted output to appear on your terminal specify **/dev/tty** as the file. The **/dev/tty** is the generic name for your login terminal. Recall that all physical devices in the UNIX system are treated as files.

Tutorial

To use **tee** to store the intermediate output of a pipeline process, type the command line "who | tee who.now | wc -l<CR>". When the shell prompt returns, type "cat who.now<CR>". Your results will differ in content but should be similar in format to the following.

```
$ who | tee who.now | wc -l
   3
$ cat who.now
jlyates              tty5            Aug 27 13:28
rathomas            dz24            Aug 28 07:42
veronica            bx066           Aug 28 07:39
$ □
```

Now send the intermediate result directly to the terminal by typing the command "who | tee /dev/tty | wc -l<CR>".

```
$ who | tee /dev/tty/ | wc -l
jlyates                     tty5        Aug 27 13:28
rathomas                    dz24        Aug 28 07:42
veronica                    bx066       Aug 28 07:39
    3
$ □
```

The intermediate result (from **tee**) will be displayed before the result from **wc -l**. (**Wc** (word count) is fully described in a separate section.)

For the last example, type the command line shown in boldface in the following screen.

```
$ who | tee tmp | wc | cat - tmp
    5     25     184
bodega                      tty04       Oct  7 09:56
avante                      tty13       Oct  7 19:33
rathomas                    tty24       Oct  7 19:57
bodega                      tty27       Oct  7 17:16
jlyates                     tty28       Oct  7 19:21
$ □
```

Again, the results will differ in content but not in format.

The **tee** utility diverts a copy of the output of the **who** command to a temporary file named **tmp.** The output of the **who** command is further piped into the **wc** to give a count of lines, words, and characters. These results are directed to the standard input of the following **cat** command. The "-" after the **cat** command causes the display of its standard input (the results of the **wc** command) followed by the display of the **tmp** file.

Status Information

Date — Print or Set Current Date and Time

This command displays and records the date and time of day.

$ date

Displays the current time and date.

```
$ date
Fri Aug 14 09:27:20 PDT 1981
$ □
```

$	Shell prompt
Fri Aug 14	Current date
09:27:20 PDT 1981	and time when <CR> was pressed.
$ □	Next prompt and cursor

Error Messages

```
$ date -x
unrecognized option: x
Sat Sep 26 09:58:02 PDT 1981
```

The **date** command accepts no options.

```
$ date temp
date: bad conversion
```

Date tried to interpret **temp** as a time
for resetting the system clock.

Notes on date

Use this utility to display the current date and time of day. When you
press the <CR> after typing "date" the exact time to the second will be
displayed on your terminal.

Tutorial

To set your digital clock, type "date<CR>".

```
$ date
Fri Aug 14 09:27:20 PDT 1981
$ □
```

You can also use this utility to record the date and time of a particular
event. Perhaps you would like to record the times you log into the
system. Use an editor and append the commands "echo -n 'This login:
'; date" and "date >> login_times" to your **.profile** (or **.login** for "C"
shell) file. The **.profile** file is used to customize your environment upon
logging in, if you are using the Bourne Shell ($ prompt) customization.

The following screen shows how to enter these commands in a new **.profile** file.

```
$ ed .profile
? .profile
a
echo -n 'This login: '; date
date >> .login_times
.
w
45
q
$ □
```

The next time you log in, your terminal will print something like the following display.

```
UNIX SYSTEM BANNER
:login: your-name
password:
[ System messages ]
This login: Fri Aug 14   09:27:30 PDT 1981
$ □
```

You can print all your previous login times at any time by typing "cat .login_times<CR>".

Du — Disk Usage

The **du** utility is used to obtain cumulative information on your usage of disk space in 512-byte blocks. If a directory is named, blocks used for that and all subdirectories are given. With the appropriate option an entry for all files as well as directories will be generated.

$ **du** *dirname*

Displays the block count for each directory and the total for all directories starting with the directory *dirname*. The default case is the current directory (.).

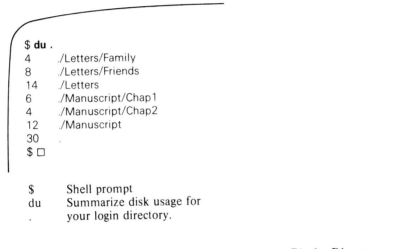

```
$ du .
4       ./Letters/Family
8       ./Letters/Friends
14      ./Letters
6       ./Manuscript/Chap1
4       ./Manuscript/Chap2
12      ./Manuscript
30      .
$ □
```

$	Shell prompt
du	Summarize disk usage for
.	your login directory.

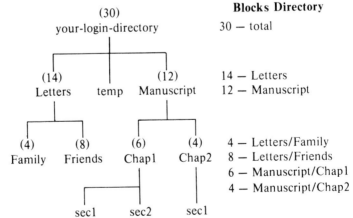

	Blocks Directory
(30) your-login-directory	30 — total
(14) Letters temp (12) Manuscript	14 — Letters 12 — Manuscript
(4) Family (8) Friends (6) Chap1 (4) Chap2	4 — Letters/Family 8 — Letters/Friends 6 — Manuscript/Chap1 4 — Manuscript/Chap2
sec1 sec2 sec1	

$ **du** [-s] [-a] *name* . . .

Summarizes the disk usage of one or more directories or filenames substituted for name according to the option specified (if any). Options may not be concatenated.

Options:

-s   Give only the total number of blocks for all files.

-a   Display an entry for each file as well.

```
$ du -s .
30
$ □
```

$	Shell prompt
du	Summarize disk usage
-s	as a grand total
.	for your login directory.
30	30 (512-byte) blocks
$ □	Next prompt and cursor

```
$ du -a .
2       ./Letters/Family/parents1
4       ./Letters/Family
2       ./Letters/Friends/john1
2       ./Letters/Friends/jane1
2       ./Letters/Friends/jane2
8       ./Letters/Friends
14      ./Letters
2       ./temp
2       ./Manuscript/Chap1/sec1
2       ./Manuscript/Chap1/sec2
6       ./Manuscript/Chap1
2       ./Manuscript/Chap2/sec1
4       ./Manuscript/Chap2
12      ./Manuscript
30
$ □
```

$	Shell prompt
du	Summarize disk usage
-a	for all files in
.	your login directory.

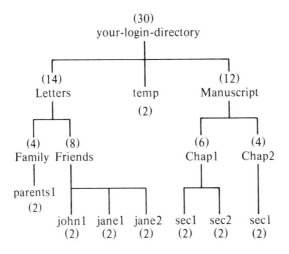

Blocks/Directory
30 blocks total

Subdirectories level 1:

Letters
Manuscript

Subdirectories level 2:

Letters/Family
Letters/Friends
Manuscript/Chap1
Manuscript/Chap2

Files:

Letters/Family/parents1
Letters/Friends/john1
Letters/Friends/jane1
Letters/Friends/jane2
Manuscript/Chap1/sec1
Manuscript/Chap1/sec2
Manuscript/Chap2/sec1

Error Messages

```
$ du Letter
--bad status < Letter >
```

Letter directory nonexistent.

```
$ du Manuscript
--cannot open < Manuscript >
```

No read permission for **Manuscript**.

```
$ du -d *
--bad status < -d >
```

-d is not a valid option.

```
$ du -as Manuscript
--bad status < -as >
```

Can't concatenate these options.

Notes on du

Use this utility to summarize the disk space you have occupied. It may be necessary for you to delete certain unwanted files and directories when space becomes an issue. Use this command to find the largest obsolete files and remove them to permit more effective allocation of disk space.

All directories beginning with the specified directory are searched recursively. That is, after the specified directory, all subdirectories of that directory are searched and the results are presented as indicated by the options, if any. If you want only the total number of blocks occupied, specify the **-s** (summary) option. The other option, **-a** (all), is mutually exclusive with **-s**, and will cause the listing of all files and their block sizes.

Tutorial

You will see how to summarize the disk usage in your various subdirectories in the examples which follow. Type "du Manuscript<CR>" and observe the display.

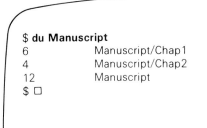

```
$ du Manuscript
6            Manuscript/Chap1
4            Manuscript/Chap2
12           Manuscript
$ □
```

If you wish to see the usage for every file in the **Manuscript** directory as well, type "du -a Manuscript<CR>".

```
$ du -a Manuscript
2            Manuscript/Chap1/sec1
2            Manuscript/Chap1/sec2
6            Manuscript/Chap1
2            Manuscript/Chap2/sec1
4            Manuscript/Chap2
12           Manuscript
$ □
```

If you wish to summarize the disk usage for all the files in your login directory, give the command "du -a *<CR>".

```
$ du -a *
2              Letters/Family/parents1
4              Letters/Family
2              Letters/Friends/john1
2              Letters/Friends/jane1
2              Letters/Friends/jane2
8              Letters/Friends
14             Letters
2              Manuscript/Chap1/sec1
2              Manuscript/Chap1/sec2
6              Manuscript/Chap1
2              Manuscript/Chap2/sec1
4              Manuscript/Chap2
12             Manuscript
2              temp
$ □
```

The **du** command gives information in blocks, as does the **ls** command with the **-s** (size) option.

Use this command to summarize the disk usage in other files on your system. Usually the system administrator is concerned with the amount of disk space occupied by various files, but you might find it interesting to "explore" your system using the **du** command. To do this specify directories such as /, **/usr**, **/bin**, or **/etc** with the **du** command.

File — Determine File Type

Use this command to help classify the type of file.

$ **file** *file* . . .

Attempts to classify *file*.

```
$ file temp
English text
$ □
```

$	Shell prompt
file	Determine the file type
temp	for the file **temp**.
English text	File type
$ □	Next prompt and cursor

```
$ file *
Letters: directory
Manuscript: directory
temp: English text
$ □
```

$	Shell prompt
file	Determine the file type
*	for all files in current directory.
Letters:	The first alphabetical entry is
directory	a directory.
Manuscript:	The second directory entry
directory	is also a directory.
temp:	The last directory entry
English text	is English text.
$ □	Next prompt and cursor

Error Messages

```
$ file temps
temps: cannot stat
```

The file **temps** can't be found.

```
$ file -x temp
-x: cannot stat
temp: English text
```

There are no options for **file** command.

```
$ file temp
temp: cannot open
```

The file **temp** can't be read.

Notes on file

The **file** utility program performs a series of tests on the specified file(s) in an attempt to classify it. This utility is especially useful if you are in a foreign directory and need a quick idea of the types of files in the directory.

If the file appears to be *ASCII* then the program examines the first block of the file and tries to guess its language. This program often makes mistakes. For instance, it sometimes suggests that command files are C programs.

The following is a partial list of the classifications which the **file** program may use to type a file:

empty   The file exists in the directory but contains nothing.

cannot open   The file is named in the directory but you do not have read permission.

directory	This file is a directory.
English text	This file contains alphabetical characters, numbers, and punctuation. More than 20% of the punctuation is followed by a space or newline.
ascii text	This differs from English text in that less than 20% of the punctuation is followed by a space or newline.
data	Everything else.

Tutorial

First try the **file** program on your home directory. Type "file *<CR>". If your directory is set up according to our conventions you should see something like the following display.

```
$ file *
Letters:  directory
Manuscript:  directory
temp:  English text
$ □
```

Use this command to explore the types of files in your UNIX installation. Change directories to the "root" by typing "cd / <CR>" and then list the directory contents by using the file command "file *<CR>". The display should contain all the files and their attributes. Choose a subdirectory of the "root" (choose **usr** for this example) and investigate that directory. First move to **usr** by typing "cd usr<CR>" and then give the form of the **file** command shown above. After investigating this directory, change to another subdirectory of the "root" (/**etc**, for example) with the command "cd /etc<CR>". (The **cd** (change directories) command is fully described in a separate section.)

By this time you should have a good idea of the types of files on your system. Display the contents of the files which appear to be worth further investigation, and see if **file** identified them correctly.

Ps — Process Status

This command is used to provide status information for currently active system processes.

$ **ps [alx]** [*namelist*]

Provides information about active processes, in particular those specified in *namelist*.

Options:

a	For all processes associated with a terminal.
l	Long listing format.
x	For all processes not associated with a terminal.

Long listing categories:

F   Flags associated with the process:
01: in core
02: system process
04: locked in core (physical I/O)
10: being swapped
20: being traced by another process

S   State of the process:
O: nonexistent
S: sleeping
W: waiting
R: running
I: intermediate
Z: terminated
T: stopped

UID	The user ID of the process owner.
PID	The process ID number.
PPID	The ID number for the parent process.

CPU	Process utilization for scheduling.
PRI	Priority of the process; high numbers are low priority.
NICE	Number used in priority computation.
ADDR	If resident in memory, the core address. Otherwise, the disk address.
WCHAN	The event for which the process is waiting or sleeping. If blank, the process is running.
TTY	The tty controlling the process.
TIME	The cumulative execution time for the process.

```
$ ps
PID        TTY        TIME CMD
2411       tty4       0:04 -sh
$ □
```

$	Shell prompt
ps	Provide status information for your own processes
2411	Process ID for the process
tty4	associated with tty4 terminal.
0:04	Accumulated CPU time
-sh	Process (Bourne Shell)
$ □	Next prompt and cursor

```
$ ps alx
 F  S    UID   PID  PPID CPU PRI NICE ADDR SZ WCHAN  TTY      TIME CMD
 3  S      0     0     0  52   0   20  5447  2  10252  ?      280:32 swapper
 1  S      0     1     0   4  30   20 10746 17  65620  ?        0:39 /etc/init
 1  S      0    37     1   0  40   20  6126  5 140000  ?        0:28 /etc/updat
 1  S      1    44     1   0  40   20 14336 22 140000  ?        0:08 /etc/cron
 0  S  11345  2561  1980   0  28   20  3011 41 122772 tty2     0:08 ed mar.p
 1  S      0   137     1   0  28   20 15355  7 133306 console  0:00 -4
 1  R      5  2707  2411  40  52   20 20727 34        tty4     0:09 ps alx
 1  S  10213  2411     1   0  30   20  5500 12  70650 tty4     0:04 -sh
 0  S  11327   149     1   0  30   20  4220 35  71076 tty1     0:06 -sh
 0  S  11345  1980     1   0  30   20  4113 35  71172 tty2     0:05 -sh
$ □
```

$	Shell prompt
ps	Provide status information for
a	all processes,
l	listing them in long format
x	whether or not associated with a terminal.
[Display]	See above
$ □	Next prompt and cursor

Error Messages

The error messages depend on your system's implementation for this command.

Notes on ps

You may occasionally need to list information about processes running on your system. For instance, you may need a status report on commands running in background. You can also find out what processes other users are running with this program. Use this command to display status information for system processes not associated with a terminal (commonly referred to as *daemons*).

Tutorial

Type "ps<CR>" and view all the active processes associated with your terminal. You will see a display similar to the following screen.

```
$ ps
PID        TTY      TIME CMD
3874       tty4     0:06 -sh
$ □
```

Since the **ps** command is implementation-dependent, your format may differ. Also, you may see an entry for the process which requested this information (the -ps process itself).

If you need only status information about a particular process associated with your terminal, you can specify one or more process numbers
as your *namelist*. Continuing with the example used above, to view the
entry for the shell (-sh), you would type "ps *namelist*<CR>" where
namelist is the process number for your current shell process (3874 in
this example).

```
$ ps 3874
3874        tty4        0:06 -sh
$ □
```

Let's begin a process in background and then look at all your current
processes. A good example is sorting the 20,000+ word on-line spelling
dictionary in reverse. To initiate this, type "sort -r /usr/dict/words -o
word.sort&<CR>". The number displayed is the process number for
the background sort. (The **sort** command is fully described in a separate
section.)

```
$ sort -r /usr/dict/words -o word.sort&
4202
$ □
```

Now type "ps<CR>" and you will see a display similar to the previous one except for an additional entry for the background sort
(labeled -sort /usr/dict/sort -o word.sort).

```
$ ps
PID        TTY        TIME CMD
3874       tty4       0:06 -sh
4202       tty4       0:04 sort -r /usr/dict/words -o word.sort
$ □
```

So far we have requested the short form listing, which tells you the process ID number, associated terminal number, cumulative execution time, and an approximation of the command line which began the process. Use the l option to obtain an extended listing. Type "ps l<CR>".

```
$ ps l
 F  S   UID    PID  PPID CPU PRI  NICE  ADDR  SZ WCHAN   TTY    TIME CMD
 1  S 10213   3874     1   0  30    20  5500  12 70706   tty4   0:06 -sh
 1  R 10213   4202  3874  51  53    20 41502  80          tty4   0:25 sort -r /u...
$ □
```

Compare the information in this listing with the description for the categories given above. Note that the sorting process is running (R under the S heading) and that it has as its parent PPID (3874), the shell which created it.

You can also look at processes not necessarily associated with your terminal by specifing the a (all) option. Concatenate this with the long option by typing "ps al<CR>".

```
$ ps al
 F  S   UID    PID  PPID CPU PRI  NICE  ADDR  SZ WCHAN   TTY    TIME CMD
 0  S 11345   2561  1980   0  28    20  3011  41 122772  tty2   0:08 ed mar.p
 1  S     0    137     1   0  28    20 15355   7 133306  console 0:00 -4
 1  R     5   4250  3874  40  52    20 20727  34          tty4   0:09 ps al
 1  S 10213   3874     1   0  30    20  5500  12 70650   tty4   0:04 -sh
 0  S 11327    149     1   0  30    20   420  35 71076   tty1   0:06 -sh
 0  S 11345   1980     1   0  30    20  4113  35 71172   tty2   0:05 -sh
$ □
```

Of course, the actual processes will be different for your system. Here you see that **tty1**, **tty2**, and **tty4** have the Bourne Shell (-sh) associated with them. In addition, **tty2** is running **ed** to edit a file named **mar.p**, and **tty4** is running **ps al**, which is the process that generated this listing.

You can look at all the system processes not associated with a terminal by specifying the **x** option. Concatenate this with the long option as well. Type "ps lx<CR>".

```
$ ps lx
   F  S    UID   PID  PPID CPU  PRI  NICE  ADDR   SZ  WCHAN    TTY      TIME CMD
   3  S     0     0     0  52    0    20   5447    2  10252    ?       280 32 swapper
   1  S     0     1     0   4   30    20  10746   17  65620    ?       0 39 /etc/init
   1  S     0    37     1   0   40    20   6126    5  140000   ?       0 28 /etc/updat
   1  S     1    44     1   0   40    20  14336   22 1400000   ?       0 08 /etc/cron
$ □
```

The **swapper** has the highest priority (PRI = 0) and has accumulated 280 minutes and 32 seconds CPU time so far since the system has been up and running. Another interesting process is **/etc/cron** which is the cron "daemon." We "caught it in the act" above.

You can combine all three options to obtain a long listing for all the system processes by typing "ps alx<CR>".

```
$ ps alx
   F  S    UID   PID  PPID CPU  PRI  NICE  ADDR   SZ  WCHAN    TTY      TIME CMD
   3  S     0     0     0  52    0    20   5447    2  10252    ?       280 32 swapper
   1  S     0     1     0   4   30    20  10746   17  65620    ?       0 39 /etc/init
   1  S     0    37     1   0   40    20   6126    5  140000   ?       0 28 /etc/updat
   1  S     1    44     1   0   40    20  14336   22  140000   ?       0 08 /etc/cron
   0  S  11327  2561  1980   0   28    20   3011   41 122772    tty2     0 08 ed mar.p
   1  S     0   137     1   0   28    20  15355    7 133306    console  0 00 - 4
   1  R     5  4254  3874  40   52    20  20727   34            tty4     0 09 ps alx
   1  S  10213  3874     1   0   30    20   5500   12  70650    tty4     0 04 -sh
   0  S  11327   149     1   0   30    20   4220   35  71076    tty1     0 06 -sh
   0  S  11345  1980     1   0   30    20   4113   35  71172    tty2     0 05 -sh
$ □
```

Pwd — Print Working Directory

This command prints the pathname of your working directory.

$ pwd

Displays the full pathname of your current directory.

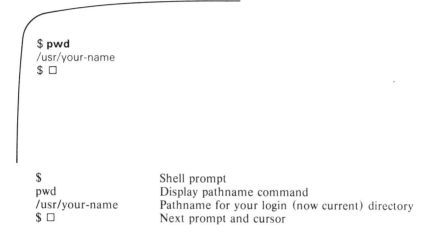

```
$ pwd
/usr/your-name
$ □
```

$	Shell prompt
pwd	Display pathname command
/usr/your-name	Pathname for your login (now current) directory
$ □	Next prompt and cursor

Error Messages

Pwd ignores the remainder of the command line. There are no error messages with this command.

Notes on pwd

The current (or working) directory is the directory in which you are currently working. This command displays the full pathname, starting at the root and proceeding through any intermediate directories until it reaches the current directory. This utility is quite handy if you forget where you are in the file system. You only have immediate access to any files or directories in the current directory unless you specify full pathnames.

Tutorial

Type "pwd<CR>".

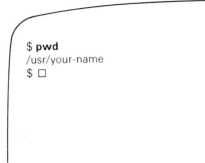

```
$ pwd
/usr/your-name
$ □
```

In this example, you are currently in the directory **your-name**, which is in the directory **usr**, which is in the root directory designated as /.

Stty — Set Terminal Options

This command is used to set up the I/O options for a new terminal or to change these options. This command with no arguments reports the current settings for your terminal.

$ **stty** [*option*] . . .

Sets or displays status of your current output terminal I/O options.

Options strings:

even	Allow even parity.
-even	Disallow even parity.
odd	Allow odd parity.
-odd	Disallow odd parity.
raw	Raw mode (no erase, kill, interrupt, quit, EOT)
-raw	Negate raw mode.
cbreak	Read each character as received.
-cbreak	Read entire line at one time when terminator is received.
nl	Accept only newlines to end line.

-nl	Allow carriage return for newline, output <CR><LF>.
echo	Echo back typed characters.
-echo	Do not echo characters.
lcase	Map upper case to lower case.
-lcase	Do not map case
tabs	Preserve tabs.
-tabs	Replace tabs by spaces
ek	Reset erase and kill characters to # and @, respectively.
erase *c*	Set erase character to *c*.
kill *c*	Set kill character to *c*.
cr0 cr1 cr2 cr3	Carriage return delay.
n10 n11 n12 n13	Newline delay.
tab0 tab1 tab2 tab3	Tab delay.
ff0 ff1	Form feed delay.
bs0 bs1	Backspace delay.
tty33	Mode for Teletype 33.
tty37	Mode for Teletype 37.
vt05	Mode for DEC VT05.
tn300	Mode for GE TermiNet 300.
ti700	Mode for TI 700
tek	Mode for Tektronix 4014.
hup	Hang up dataphone on last close.
-hup	Do not hang up dataphone on last close.
0	Hang up phone immediately.
50 75 110 134 150 **200 300 600 1200** **1800 2400 4800 9600**	Set baud rate.

```
$ stty
speed 300 baud
erase = '#'; kill = '@'
even odd -nl echo -tabs
$ ☐
```

$	Shell prompt
stty	Display current terminal options
speed 300 baud	Computer terminal transmission rate
erase = '#'	The character-erase character is #
kill = '@'	The line-kill character is @
even odd	Both even and odd parity are enabled
-nl	<CR> terminates a line
echo	Characters are echoed back to terminal
-tabs	Tabs are replaced by spaces
$ ☐	Next prompt and cursor

```
$ stty 1200 > /dev/tty5
$ ☐
```

$	Shell prompt
stty	Set the baud rate
1200	to 1200 for the device,
/dev/tty5	a hard-copy mechanical line printer.
$ ☐	Next prompt and cursor

Error Messages

```
$ stty +echo
unknown mode: +echo
```

Enable options are not preceded by a +.

```
$ stty file
unknown mode:file
```

This is not a valid option.

```
$ stty 1200 >/dev/tty5
/dev/tty5:cannot create
```

/dev/tty5 is not writable.

Notes on stty

Use **stty** to tailor your UNIX system to connect with your terminal device. The terminal device can be any character I/O device which can be driven by your UNIX system. This includes CRT terminals, keyboards, modems, hard-copy draft, and letter-quality printers. Because all low-speed asynchronous communication devices share the same general interface, you achieve significant independence from the particular hardware used.

When you log into the UNIX system a terminal device file is assigned as your input and output file. It plays a special role as the *control* terminal for your commands; it handles the quit and interrupt signals.

Your terminal generally operates in full-duplex mode. This means you only see a display of a character you type after the system has "echoed" it back to you. Occasionally, this echo feature is temporarily turned off (for instance, while you enter your password).

You may type characters at any time, even while output from another process is occurring. The characters are stored in a 256-byte system input buffer. The system will "remember" all the characters you type, unless this buffer overflows, which is rare. The buffer could overflow if you were to type for a long time before your program read its standard input. When this limit is reached the system discards all the saved characters without warning.

Normally your terminal input is processed one line at a time. The program which reads your keyboard input is suspended until you finish typing the entire line and press the line termination character, usually a carriage return or newline or line feed character (cooked mode). You can, however, set your terminal protocol so that each character is passed to the program as it is typed without waiting for the line terminator (cbreak mode). See the Tutorial for this command for an explanation of "cooked" and "cbreak" modes.

Erase and kill processing is normally performed during input. In the default case, the special character # erases the last character typed. It cannot erase beyond the beginning of the line. The @ character kills the entire line. You can reassign the erase and kill characters using the **stty** utility. To convey a standard non-special character meaning, you must precede # and @ with the backslash (\) escape character. The \ character will not be included in the input unless you precede it with another \ character (that is, \\ will enter one \).

The **stty** command can map all upper-case letters into the corresponding lower-case letters. In this case you can input an upper-case letter by escaping it with the \ character. In this mode, the following escape sequences are generated on output and accepted on input:

For	Use
`	\`
|	\!
~	\^
{	\(
}	\)

This mode is useful if you have an older terminal which is capable of generating only upper-case letters. You can input the characters shown shown under the "For" column (above) by keying in the corresponding escape sequences in the "Use" column.

Certain ASCII characters have a special meaning in the UNIX system. They are not usually passed to the reading program except in "raw" mode (defined in the following section), where they lose their special significance:

EOT   End-of-file character (control-D). When received, all the characters waiting to be read are passed to the program. Then the EOT is discarded. When typed at the beginning of a line, EOT acts as the end-of-file indication.

DEL   The rubout character (octal 177) generates an *interrupt* signal which is sent to all processes associated with your terminal. Normally each process will terminate unless other arrangements have been made.

FS   Control- \ (control-shift-L) generates the *quit* signal which generally acts as an *interrupt* signal unless other arrangements are made. In addition, a memory core image file will be generated which can be used later for diagnostic purposes.

DC3   Control-S will suspend all terminal output until something is typed in. A second **DC3** character can be used to restart output. On some systems control-Q is used to restart output.

Tutorial

Type "stty<CR>" to display the current settings for your terminal options. You will see a display similar to the following.

```
$ stty
speed 300 baud
erase = '#'; kill = '@'
even odd, -nl echo -tabs
$ □
```

These options are interpreted as follows:

- The baud rate (character transmission speed) is 300 (approximately 30 characters per second).
- The character-erase character is #.
- The line-kill character is @.
- Both even and odd parity are on.
- The carriage return key is mapped in and out as the newline terminator.
- The characters are echoed back to the terminal.
- Tabs are replaced by the equivalent number of spaces in the output display.

There are three basic modes for terminal I/O: raw, cbreak, and cooked. You will generally operate in "cooked" mode (the opposite of "raw"), which means that programs read input one line at a time, and character erase, line kill, end-of-file, interrupt, and quit characters operate as described above. In "raw" mode, input is passed to a program one character at a time. Erase, kill, end-of-file, interrupt, and quit characters have no special significance in raw mode. Also, all delays are turned off and characters are not echoed back to the terminal. You will not generally be dealing with raw mode input.

The cbreak mode is a kind of "half-cooked" mode. Programs receive each character as it is typed. Quit and interrupt characters are functional, and output delays, upper- to lower-case translation, echo, and parity work normally. However, there are no erase or kill characters and no special treatment of the backslash \ or **EOT** character in cbreak mode.

Generally you would only put your terminal in raw mode if you were programming a very special character input routine which required that most of the system's I/O processing be turned off. If such a program "blows up," you may find afterwards that your terminal does not respond to your input. You can try giving the command "stty -raw echo <newline><CR>" to learn if the terminal was somehow put in raw or no-echo mode.

For a more practical application, let's invoke the "half-cooked," or cbreak, mode. Type "stty cbreak<CR>" followed by the command line "tr a-z A-Z<CR>". Now slowly type a few letters and notice that the letters are translated one by one to upper-case rather than a line at a time after the carriage return or newline line terminator was typed.

```
$ stty cbreak
$ tr a-z A-Z
tTrRaAnNsSlLaAtTiInNgG
[ Interrupt ]
$ □
```

We pressed the rubout key to generate an interrupt signal (denoted by [Interrupt]) to terminate the translation program. Type "stty -cbreak<CR>" to return to normal (cooked) mode.

The function of the **nl** option can be seen by specifying the mode change "stty nl<CR>". The carriage return will no longer terminate the line. Instead you must use the newline (or line feed) character for this purpose. Now type "date<CR>" and note that the current date and time is not displayed until you type a newline. If your keyboard doesn't have a line feed key, type the equivalent control-J instead. Now switch to return mode by typing "stty -nl^J".

Momentarily turn off your terminal echo by typing "stty -echo <CR>". Carefully type "date<CR>". You will not see the letters "d" "a" "t" "e" as you type them, but after you press the carriage return you will see the output from the **date** program. Now turn on the echo again by typing "stty echo<CR>".

You can speed up your terminal display a little if you preserve tabs. To do this your terminal must respond to a tab character (control-I) by moving the cursor to the next tab stop. Press a control-I and see if this is the case. If so, type "stty tabs<CR>" then press the TAB key several times. The cursor seemingly "jumps" from tab stop to tab stop. Now type "stty -tabs<CR>" and then press the TAB key several more times. This time the cursor moves between tab stops in a series of one-column increments corresponding to each space character which is now output to simulate the tab.

To reset your character-erase character to a percent sign (%) type "stty erase %<CR>". Now type "datr%e<CR>" and note that the shell found the **date** program and executed it.

```
$ stty erase %
$ datr%e
Mon Oct 19 17:39:24 PDT 1981
$ □
```

Now reset your line-kill character to "+" by typing "stty kill +<CR>", then type "datte+". The cursor jumps to the beginning of the next line. Finish the line, typing "date<CR>" and again notice that the shell found **date** and ran it correctly.

```
$ stty kill +
$ datte+
date
Mon Oct 19 17:39:54 PDT 1981
$ □
```

You can conveniently reset both the character erase and line kill back to the default values (# and @) by typing "stty ek<CR>". Verify this by typing "stty<CR>" to see the current terminal I/O option.

```
$ stty ek
$ stty
speed 300 baud
erase = '#'; kill = '@'
even odd -nl echo -tabs
$ □
```

You may find, especially with hard-copy mechanical terminals, that characters are "lost" at high transmission speeds (baud rates). The **stty** utility lets you create delays after the carriage return, newline, tab, form feed, and backspace characters. These delays in resuming character transmission allow the mechanical components time to position themselves so that they can continue printing the characters correctly. Characters can be lost while the print head returns to the left margin because it has to travel the width of the page. A delay after the carriage return (cr1 or cr2) will ensure that you do not lose any characters at the beginning of the next line.

Combinations of the various I/O options for some commonly used terminals have been preset. For example, if you are installing a Texas Instruments Silent 700 thermal printing terminal you simply need to type "stty ti700<CR>" and all the appropriate options will be set for you.

Sort — Sort or Merge Files

Use this command to sort one or more files on a line-by-line basis. If the files are already sorted they can be merged with this command.

$ **sort** *name* . . .

Sorts the file *name* using the entire line as the key.

```
$ who >who.now
$ cat who.now
bodega              tty04          Oct   7 09:56
avant               tty13          Oct   7 19:33
rathomas            tty24          Oct   7 19:57
bodega              tty27          Oct   7 17:16
jlyates             tty28          Oct   7 19:21
$ sort who.now
avante              tty13          Oct   7 19:33
bodega              tty04          Oct   7 09:56
bodega              tty27          Oct   7 17:16
jlyates             tty28          Oct   7 19:21
rathomas            tty24          Oct   7 19:57
```

$	Shell prompt
who	List current on-line users,
>who.now	storing result in file **who.now**.
cat who.now	Display contents of **who.now**
bodega	Users listed, their terminal
	and date and time of login
. . .	ordered by terminal designation.
sort who.now	Sort the file **who.now** using entire
avante tty13. . .	line as sort key, which essentially
bodega tty04. . .	orders the **who** output by login name.
bodega tty27. . .	
. . .	
$ ☐	Next prompt and cursor

$ sort -mubdfinrtx [+*pos*] [*-pos*] [-o *nameout*] *name*

Sort lines of file *name* together into the file *nameout* modified by the options specifying the key fields with +*pos* and *-pos*.

Options:

- **-m** Merge the specified files.

- **-u** Eliminate duplicate lines in sorted output.

- **-b** Ignore leading blanks and tabs in comparisons.

- **-d** Dictionary order: only letters, digits, and blanks count.

- **-f** Ignore distinction between upper and lower case.

-i   Ignore characters outside ASCII range 040-0176 in non-numeric comparisons. Control characters are in the ASCII range 000-037. The "upper" ASCII character set is above 0176 octal.

-n   Sort on first numeric field.

-r   Reverse order of sort.

-c   Check if sorted already.

-o *nameout*   Save output in *nameout* (can be same as *name*).

Sort operates on the entire line or on fields within the line. A field is a non-empty, non-blank string separated from other strings by blanks. If the **-t***x* option is specified the fields are separated by the character *x*.

Sort keys are specified using the notation +*pos1* -*pos2*, which limits the sort key to a field beginning with *pos1* and ending just before *pos2*. The first field is called **+0**. Each *pos1* and *pos2* can be expressed as *m.n* where *m* is the number of fields to skip from the beginning of the line and *n* is the number of characters to skip further. Each field designator *m.n* can be followed by one or more of the options **bdfinr**. A missing *.n* means *.0* and a missing -*pos2* means the end of the line.

When there is more than one sort key field, later keys are compared only after all earlier keys compare equal. Whole lines that otherwise compare equal are ordered with all bytes significant.

```
$ sort -br +1 who.now
jlyates       tty28       Oct   7 19:21
bodega        tty27       Oct   7 17:16
rathomas      tty24       Oct   7 19:57
avante        tty13       Oct   7 19:33
bodega        tty04       Oct   7 09:56
```

$	Shell prompt
sort	Sort the file **who.now**
-br	in reverse order, ignoring leading blanks,
+1	skipping the first field to order by the
jlyates tty28. . .	terminal designation in the second column.
bodega tty27. . .	
. . .	
$ □	Next prompt and cursor

Note: you can also specify the command as **sort +1br who.now**.

Error Messages

```
$ sort temp2
sort: can't open temp2
```

The file **temp2** can't be read.

```
$ sort odd.numbers -o tempout
sort: can't create tempout
```

The file **tempout** exists and is not writable.

```
$ sort -c odd.numbers
sort: disorder:1
```

Display of first disordered entry.

Notes on sort

The **sort** command is a very capable and fairly efficient program for sorting and merging files. The wide range of options and the ability to precisely select key sorting fields makes this an outstanding utility for the UNIX system environment.

A *field* is a collection of adjacent characters which are not blanks. Both tab and space characters are considered to be blanks in this discussion. One field can be separated from the next by blanks, tabs, or other specially designated field separators. For example, a personal name can be thought of as having three fields: the first name, middle name, and last name, separated by a blank. Unless you specify the **-b** option with **sort**, the leading blanks of a field are considered part of that field in the comparison performed by this program.

Tutorial

Employ an editor to enter the list of names shown in the next screen in the file named **namelist**.

```
$ cat namelist
John A. Smith
John Q. Public
Jane R. Public
John R. Public
$ □
```

The fields in the previous screen are designated left to right as 0 (first name), 1 (middle initial), and 2 (surname). If you use **sort** to order this list without specifying any options the utility will sort by characters in first names, then middle initials, and finally last names to give the following display.

```
$ sort namelist
Jane R. Public
John A. Smith
John Q. Public
John R. Public
$ □
```

To order such a list by last name, first name, and middle initial, skip the first two fields and use the third field as the key field.

```
$ sort +2b namelist
Jane R. Public
John Q. Public
John R. Public
John A. Smith
$ □
```

+2b means skip the first two fields and ignore the preceding blanks of the third field. In this case the "b" can be left off since all third field entries have the same number of preceding blanks; however, it is probably a good idea to get into the habit of using the **b** option. You can specify one of the options **bdfinr** after any of the key field designators. In our example, when the third field entry compared equal, the list was further ordered in the remaining fields.

Use your editor again to add phone numbers to this list of names.

```
$ cat namelist
John A. Smith        415-642-3228
John Q. Public       212-961-0052
Jane R. Public       415-335-4672
John R. Public       415-787-6000
$ □
```

To sort this list by last name, ignoring the phone numbers, you should specify the command line "sort +2b -3 namelist<CR>". This skips the first two fields and ignores any field after the third.

```
$ sort + 2b -3 namelist
Jane R. Public          415-335-4672
John Q. Public          212-961-0052
John R. Public          415-787-6000
John A. Smith           415-642-3228
$ □
```

To sort by the phone numbers you would skip the first three fields. To skip the area code you can specify the sort key in the format *m.n*, so the command line becomes "sort +3.4 namelist<CR>".

```
$ sort +3.4 namelist
Jane R. Public          415-335-4672
John A. Smith           415-642-3228
John R. Public          415-787-6000
John Q. Public          212-961-0052
$ □
```

In this case specifying the field format as "+3.4b" is not necessary, since the ".4" counts characters which are not blanks.

Alternatively, you can achieve the same result by specifying the field separator to be a dash, then skipping the first field (the area code).

```
$ sort -t- +1 namelist
Jane R. Public          415-335-4672
John A. Smith           415-642-3228
John R. Public          415-787-6000
John Q. Public          212-961-0052
$ □
```

The "-t-" option divides each line into three fields; the first field starts at the beginning of each line and extends to the first "-". The second field extends from after the first "-" to the second "-", and so on.

Enter the following two lists of numbers with an editor. Store the lists in the files indicated by the argument to the appropriate **cat** command in the following screen.

```
$ cat even.numbers
2
8
6
10
4
12
$ cat odd.numbers
7
9
1
3
5
11
$ □
```

First we will try to merge these files without sorting them. Type the command "sort -m odd.numbers even.numbers<CR>" and observe the result.

```
$ sort -m odd.numbers even.numbers
2
7
8
6
10
4
12
9
1
3
5
11
$ □
```

Now sort each of the number lists, storing the result in a file with the same name as the original source file.

```
$ sort -n odd.numbers -o odd.numbers
$ cat odd.numbers
1
3
5
7
9
11
$ sort -n even.numbers -o even.numbers
$ cat even.numbers
2
4
6
8
10
12
$ □
```

You must specify the **-n** option to sort the numbers by numeric value rather than by ASCII collating sequence.

Now the two lists of numbers can be correctly merged into one file (named **all.numbers**).

```
$ sort -mn odd.numbers   even.numbers   -o all.numbers
$ cat all.numbers
1
2
3
4
5
6
7
8
9
10
11
12
$ □
```

Use the **-u** option to remove duplicates during the sort. For example, use the following form of the **tr** command to place every word in the file **temp** on a line by itself, directing the result to the file **temp.wordlist**.

```
$ cat temp | tr -cs A-Za-z '\012' >temp.wordlist
$ cat temp.wordlist
Now
is
the
time
for
all
good
citizens
to
come
to
the
aid
of
their
country
$ □
```

Now type the command ''sort -u +0f temp.wordlist<CR>'' and observe the display.

```
$ sort -u +0f temp.wordlist
aid
all
citizens
come
country
for
good
is
Now
of
the
their
time
to
$ □
```

Using the **-f** option, the **sort** utility treats upper case as lower case.

Using the combined options **-um** with one sorted input file will give a repeatable unique result even from differing lines whose keys are identical. To illustrate, use your editor to create a file, **dates**, containing the following text.

```
$ cat dates
Aug 24
Jan 03
Jan 10
Mar 05
Mar 07
Nov 28
Sep 02
Sep 13
$ □
```

Now type the command "sort -um +0 -l dates<CR>" to create a unique representation of these dates with the key field (1) containing several duplicates (Jan, Mar, and Sep).

```
$ sort -um +0 -l dates
Aug 24
Jan 03
Mar 05
Nov 28
Sep 02
$ □
```

To verify, compare results obtained by typing "sort -u +0 -l dates<CR>".

```
$ sort -u +0 -l dates
Aug 24
Jan 10
Mar 05
Nov 28
Sep 13
$ □
```

In this screen Sep 13, and not the first entry Sep 02, was displayed. The **-um** option combination always uses the earliest appearing entry in a list of duplicates.

Tty — Get Terminal Name

This command displays your current terminal name.

$ tty

Displays the pathname of your login terminal.

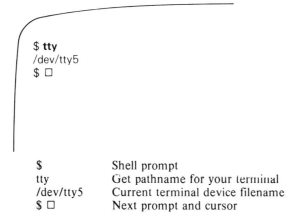

```
$ tty
/dev/tty5
$ □
```

$	Shell prompt
tty	Get pathname for your terminal
/dev/tty5	Current terminal device filename
$ □	Next prompt and cursor

Error Messages

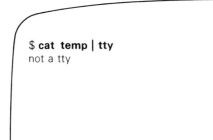

```
$ cat  temp | tty
not a tty
```

The standard input is not a terminal.

Notes on tty

When you log into the UNIX system you use a particular terminal from which you control all your processes. The UNIX system knows each device by a unique filename, and using this filename you can refer to your terminal or someone else's terminal. By default, standard input, standard output, and standard error files will be associated initially with your terminal. When you need to refer to your terminal designation you can use the **tty** command to find out what your terminal is called.

Tutorial

Type "tty<CR>" to see your terminal designation.

```
$ tty
/dev/tty5
$ □
```

You can display more information about your terminal now that you know its name. For instance, type "ls -l *ttyname*<CR>", where *ttyname* is the pathname for your terminal reported by **tty**.

```
$ ls -l /dev/tty5
crw--w--w-  l  your-name 22, 28  Oct19  17:56  /dev/tty5
```

The character "c" to the left of the permission modes indicates that your terminal is a special character file. Also observe that you have read and write permission for your terminal but that other users have write but not read permission. This is so other users can use the **write** command for direct inter-terminal communication yet cannot "peek" at what you are doing. (The permission modes are discussed in the **ls** command section.)

Who — Who Is on the System

This command lists the login name, terminal name, and time of logging in for every current user on the UNIX system.

$ who

Provides a list of all current users on the system sorted in alphabetical order by terminal designation.

```
$ who
veronica     bx066    Aug 27 13:28
rathomas     dz24     Aug 28 07:42
jlyates      tty5     Aug 28 07:39
$ □
```

$	Shell prompt
who	Who is on the system?
veronica	User **veronica**
bx066	on bussiplexer port number **bx066**
Aug 27 13:28	logged on **Aug 27 1:28 PM**.
rathomas	User **rathomas**
dz24	on direct dial-up port number **dz24**
Aug 28 07:42	logged on **Aug 28 7:42 AM**.
jlyates	User login **jlyates**
tty5	on teletype device number **tty5**
Aug 28 07:39	logged on **Aug 28 7:39 AM**.
$ □	Next prompt and cursor

$ who am i

Displays how you are logged in. Any two arguments will do the same thing, since **who** only looks for an argument count of two.

```
$ who am i
rathomas      dz24    Aug 28 07:42
$ □
```

$	Shell prompt
who am i	Identify self
rathomas	Login name **rathomas**
dz24	on port **dz24**
Aug 28 07:42	since 7:42 AM Aug 28 1981.
$ □	Next prompt and cursor

Error Messages

```
$ who -x
who: cannot open utmp
```

Invalid option.

Notes on who

In a multi-user environment the more users currently using the system, the slower the system's response to your commands. Use the **who** command to see how heavily the system is loaded. Use this command before employing the **write** command to verify that the recipient is currently logged into the system and to see what terminal name is associated with him/her. You can also verify the recipient's correct login name with **who**.

If you use two separate arguments after the **who** command, as in **who am i** or **who are you**, the system responds with your login name. This is useful if you forget your login name or in what directory you started.

Tutorial

Type the command "who<CR>" to see who is currently logged into your UNIX system. Your login name should appear on this list as well. Try using the **write** command to send a brief message to one of the other users currently logged in.

Now type "who am i<CR>". The system will respond with your login name, terminal or connection port, and time of login.

When the system response to your requests becomes very sluggish, you might type "who | wc -l<CR>". Recall that the output of the **who** command consists of one line per user, so piping it to the word count (**wc**) program just prints the number of current users without displaying the entire list.

Text Processing

Crypt — Encode/Decode Information

This command is used to encrypt and decrypt files for security purposes. **Crypt** reads from the *standard input,* or keyboard, and writes on the *standard output,* or terminal.

$ **crypt** [*key*]

Encodes or decodes using the same *key.*

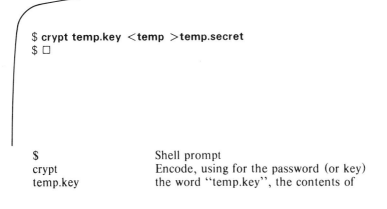

```
$ crypt temp.key <temp >temp.secret
$ □
```

$	Shell prompt
crypt	Encode, using for the password (or key)
temp.key	the word "temp.key", the contents of

<temp	the file **temp,** writing out the
>temp.secret	result to the file **temp.secret**.
$ ▢	Next prompt and cursor

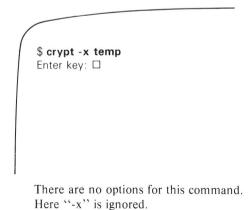

```
$ crypt temp.key <temp.secret >temp
$ ▢
```

$	Shell prompt
crypt	Decode using the same password
temp.key	that was used for encoding
<temp.secret	the file **temp.secret**, storing
>temp	the result as **temp**.
$ ▢	Next prompt and cursor

Error Messages

The **crypt** command doesn't provide error messages. However, you can
state a command line with **crypt** which can be considered an error condition.

```
$ crypt -x temp
Enter key: ▢
```

There are no options for this command.
Here "-x" is ignored.

```
$ crypt -x  <temp
[ Gibberish ]
$ □
```

The "option" is taken for the key.

```
$ crypt key  <temps
can't open temps
```

Shell can't read **temps**.

Notes on crypt

Although the **crypt** program is not the most powerful encryption scheme known, it is certainly adequate for most purposes. Crypto-analysis would probably require so much effort, both in human and machine time, that it would not be practical.

The best way to ensure security is to select a complex password or key. It is advisable to use a combination of letters and numbers rather than a simple dictionary entry.

The **ed** editor is the only other UNIX system command which can handle encrypted files. Otherwise you might employ **crypt** to decode the file, and "pipe" the results into some other text processing programs, and finally "encrypt" (or encode) the result again at the end of the pipeline. In this way the time that the document appears unencrypted (in human-readable form) is minimized.

Western Electric Company is careful to deny any warranty concerning this program or the results of using this program.

Tutorial

This tutorial outlines the steps required to create an encrypted document with the **ed** editor and to use the **crypt** utility to decode the text momentarily in order to use one or more UNIX system utilities, and finally to encode the document again for storage in non-readable form.

First invoke **ed** to edit the file called **namelist** by typing "ed namelist<CR>". The editor will respond with a question mark followed by the specified filename. Enter the encryption mode by typing "x<CR>" and **ed** will respond with a request for a key (or password). Now type in a password. For example, type "name.key<CR>".

```
$ ed namelist
? namelist
x
Entering encrypting mode!
Key:
□
```

For security reasons you will not see the password you typed echoed back to your terminal from the system.

While the editor is in encryption mode, the read (**r**), edit (**e**), and write (**w**) commands will encrypt and decrypt the text with the key you just specified.

Next, enter append mode by typing "a<CR>" and enter the short list of names shown in the following screen.

```
a
Johnson
White
Smith
Anderson
Zolman
.
□
```

Display the contents of the edit buffer with the command "1,$
p<CR>".

```
1,$p
Johnson
White
Smith
Anderson
Zolman
□
```

The contents of the edit buffer are readable (unencrypted) when the
editor is in encryption mode. Now write the contents of the edit buffer
to disk by typing "w<CR>" and exit **ed** with the command "q<CR>".

After returning to the shell ($ prompt) use the **cat** command to list
the contents of **namelist.** You will observe the encrypted text as a display of gibberish characters.

```
$ cat namelist
ELZ^Gxw^GT^AO/~xIW^C/OYI^UKIOUKOYE10t#dlb ^N
$ □
```

Your display may differ, depending on your terminal's characteristics.

You can always use **ed** in the encryption mode to read and modify encoded text (such as the file **namelist**). You may wish to use other UNIX system commands to manipulate the text without having a copy of the text in decoded form stored on your file system. First decrypt the text with the **crypt** program, "pipe" it through the desired sequence of utilities, then encrypt the file again for security storage. Since both the **ed** editor and the **crypt** program use the same encryption algorithm, encrypted data files are interchangeable for these two programs.

Continuing our example, we will use the **sort** program to order the list of names in the file **namelist**. (The **sort** command is fully explained in a separate section.) First consider what happens if you attempt to sort the encoded **namelist** file. Type "sort namelist -o namelist.sort<CR>".

```
$ sort namelist -o namelist.sort
$ □
$ cat namelist.sort
$ □
```

The file **namelist.sort** was empty. You can verify with **wc** as well, as shown in the following screen.

```
$ wc namelist.sort
0    0    0 namelist.sort
$ □
```

Because of the encrypted garbage characters and misplaced newlines, the **sort** utility will not sort the encrypted version of **namelist**.

To sort the file use **crypt** to decrypt **namelist,** ''pipe'' the output to the input of the **sort** command, ''pipe'' the sorted output to the input of **crypt** for encoding, and store the result as the file **namelist.sort**.

```
$ crypt name.key <namelist | sort | crypt name.key >namelist.sort
$ □
```

To visualize the result, invoke **ed** in encryption mode, using the **-x** option to read in **namelist.sort**.

```
$ ed -x namelist.sort
Key:
36
□
```

After you enter the password ''name.key'', **ed** reads in the file and displays the number of characters read (36 in this example). To look at the edit buffer type ''1,$ p<CR>'' and see that the list of names was sorted by the pipelines of commands given above.

```
1,$p
Anderson
Johnson
Smith
White
Zolman
$ □
```

Now exit **ed** by typing "q<CR>". To restore your file system, remove the extra files used in this tutorial with the command "rm namelist*<CR>".

Grep — Search a File for a Pattern

Grep, short for Globally find Regular Expressions and Print, can be used to find a specified string in one file, or in several files simultaneously.

$ **grep** *options pattern file. . .*

Displays all lines of *file . . .* which contain *pattern.*

Options:

-v	Variant: all lines but those matching are displayed.
-c	Print only the number of matching lines.
-l	Only the name(s) of files which contain the indicated pattern are displayed.
-n	Precedes each line displayed by the source file line number.
-h	Suppress display of filename headers in output. Filename header is only displayed when more than one file was specified.
y	Lower-case letters in the pattern will match upper-case letters in the input.
-e *pattern*	Used in case *pattern* begins with "-".

```
$ grep the temp
Now is the time
to come to the aid
of their country.
$ □
```

```
$                         Shell prompt
grep                      Find all lines
the                       which contain "the"
temp                      in the file temp.
Now is . . .              Display of lines containing "the" . . .
to come . . .
of their . . .
$ □                       Next prompt and cursor
```

```
$ grep -v the temp
for all good citizens
$ □
```

All lines *not* containing "the" are displayed.

```
$ grep -c the temp
3
$ □
```

Only the count of the number of lines is displayed.

```
$ grep now temp
$ □
```

No output because "now" is not the same as "Now".

```
$ grep -y now temp
Now is the time
$ □
```

With this option, **grep** ignores upper/lower-case distinction.

Error Messages

```
$ grep -x the temp
grep: unknown flag
```

Not a known option.

```
$ grep temp the
grep: can't open the
```

You reversed *pattern* and *file*.

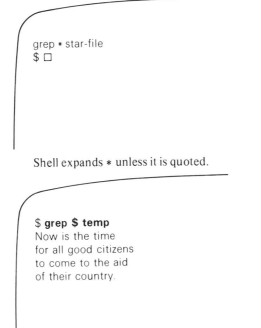

grep * star-file
$ □

Shell expands * unless it is quoted.

$ **grep $ temp**
Now is the time
for all good citizens
to come to the aid
of their country.

$ matches every end-of-line.

Notes on grep

If no files are specified with the **grep** command, input text will be taken from the keyboard until an end-of-file (control-D) is typed. Lines matched by **grep** are normally copies to standard output (your terminal). Frequently **grep** is employed as a filter program in a command pipeline.

You will appreciate the usefulness of this command when you have to search more than one file for a pattern. For a single file an editor program can perform the pattern search. But since an editor looks at each file separately, **grep** performs multiple-file searches more effectively.

Tutorial

For the first example, type ''grep the temp<CR>'' and observe the display.

```
$ grep the temp
Now is the time
to come to the aid
of their country.
$ □
```

Note that the last line matched because "the" is a part of "their". If you want to avoid this, use single or double quotes and include a leading and a trailing blank. Now type "grep 'the ' temp<CR>".

```
$ grep 'the ' temp
Now is the time
to come to the aid
$ □
```

The leading or trailing blank has to be modified if the *pattern* is the first or last word of a sentence.

Use the **-v** (variant) option to display all lines which do not match the pattern. For example, type "grep -v the temp".

```
$ grep -v the temp
for all good citizens
$ □
```

The number option (**-n**) is useful to quickly locate the line(s) in the file where the match occurred for using an editor. To number the lines which match the pattern, type "grep -n the temp<CR>".

```
$ grep -n the temp
1:Now is the time
3:to come to the aid
4:of their country.
$ □
```

If only a count of the lines which match the pattern is needed, type "grep -c the temp<CR>".

```
$ grep -c the temp
3
$ □
```

Sometimes the pattern match may fail because of lower/upper-case distinction. To avoid missing such a match, use the **-y** option. To illustrate, use the pattern "now" with and without this option, as shown in the following display.

```
$ grep -y now temp
Now is the time
$ grep now temp
$ □
```

In the first case there was a match between "now" and "Now" because there was no case distinction with the **-y** option. In the second case there was no match since "now" and "Now" are not identical.

Use the -l option when you need to search several files which contain many occurrences of the pattern. In this case only the name(s) of files which contain the indicated pattern are displayed. This option alone does not provide the location within the file(s) containing the pattern.

Consider that your current directory contains several business letters named **letter1**, **letter2**, and **letter3**. Which letter of the three was sent to Acme Computers? To find out, type "grep -l "Acme Computers" letter?<CR>" and the filename where the match occurred is the letter to Acme Computers. This is a quick way to obtain information.

Spell — Find Spelling Errors

Use this command to find spelling errors in your documents. An on-line dictionary, **/usr/dict/words**, is used.

$ **spell** [*option*]. . . [*file*]. . .

Finds spelling errors in *file* as defined by one or more options. The standard output of **spell** consists of words not included in the on-line spelling dictionary.

Options:

-v   Print all words not literally in the dictionary.

-b   Use the British spelling dictionary (**/usr/dict/hlistb**).

-x   Print every plausible stem.

For the examples in this command summary, create a short document named **doc** which contains the one line "UNIX is a graate computerrific operating system.".

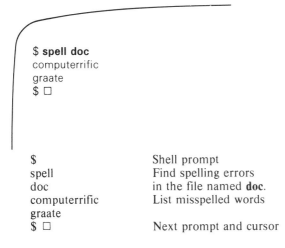

```
$ spell doc
computerrific
graate
$ □
```

$	Shell prompt
spell	Find spelling errors
doc	in the file named **doc**.
computerrific	List misspelled words
graate	
$ □	Next prompt and cursor

Error Messages

The particular error messages displayed will depend on your system's implementation of these spelling programs.

Notes on spell

The **spell** program provides the user with the basic tools for checking document spelling. In the default case, the 20,000 + word on-line spelling dictionary, **/usr/dict/words**, is used in the spelling check. Actually a condensed form of this same list of words is employed by **spell**. The output of the **spell** program will be a list of words which do not appear in **/usr/dict/words**. These words could be listed for three reasons: 1) they are misspelled and are in the dictionary (correctly spelled), 2) they are spelled correctly but are not in the dictionary, or 3) they are misspelled and not in the dictionary. We will deal with the first two cases in this discussion. The **spell** program is implementation-dependent. See your system administrator for your system documentation.

Tutorial

Use an editor to create a simple document named **doc** which contains the one line "UNIX is a graate computerrific operating system.". This is outlined in the next screen for **ed.**

```
$ ed doc
? doc
a
UNIX is a graate computerrific operating system.
.
w
49
q
$ □
```

Then run a spelling check against the on-line dictionary by typing "spell doc<CR>" and observe the results.

```
$ spell doc
computerrific
graate
$ □
```

This shows that the words "computerrific" and "graate" are not in **/usr/dict/words**. Actually the equivalent hashed dictionary **/usr/dict/hlista** is used.

Our next step is to correct the misspelled words. For this example, if you use **ed** follow the directions in the screen display below.

```
$ ed doc
49
s/graate/great/p
UNIX is a great computerrific operating system.
w
48
q
$ □
```

Now run the spelling program again, typing ''spell doc >doc.spell<CR>'' to collect the output in a file named **doc.spell.** Display the contents of the output file for verification.

```
$ spell doc  >doc.spell
$ cat doc.spell
computerrific
$ □
```

On some systems, **spell** will internally log all its output lists (along with your login name, terminal, and date) to the spelling history file **/usr/dict/spellhist.** Your system administrator may update the public dictionary. You can access this information yourself by employing **grep.** You would type a command in the following form:

$ **grep -n** *your-name* **/usr/dict/spellhist**

Here *your-name* is your login name. To find the line number(s) in **/usr/dict/spellhist** where your spelling history data is stored use the following command:

$ **tail** +*n*

Here *n* is the line number corresponding to the history data you are seeking.

Uniq — Remove Repeated Lines in a Sorted File

This command is used to collapse or count redundant adjacent lines in a file, yielding a file with a unique collection of lines.

$ **uniq** [**-udc** [+*n*] [*-m*]] [*input*] [*output*]

Removes repeated adjacent lines in *input* file when copying to *output* file.

Options:

-u   Display only the lines which are *not* repeated in the file named *input*.

-d   Display only the lines which are repeated in the file *input*.

-c   Precede each line displayed by the number of times it occurred.

-*m*   Ignore the first *m* fields and any blanks before each. A field is defined as a series of non-space, non-tab characters which are separated from one another by spaces and tabs.

+*n*   Ignore the first *n* characters along with any blanks before each in the comparisons.

For the examples which follow, the file **temp2** is created from **temp** by the following command line:

tr -cs A-Za-z '\012' >temp2<CR>

This reformats the **temp** file to place every word on a line by itself. (A separate section describes the **tr** (translate) command and all its options.)

```
$ uniq temp2
Now
is
the
time
for
all
good
citizens
to
come
to
the
aid
of
their
country
$ □
```

$	Shell prompt
uniq	Remove all duplicate lines (words here) which are adjacent and display result on terminal.
Now	The output is the same as the input file
is	since no two words which are
the	repeated were adjacent.
time	
. . .	
country	
$ □	Next prompt and cursor

```
$ sort temp2 -o temp2.sort
$ uniq -c temp2.sort
   1 Now
   1 aid
   1 all
   1 citizens
   1 come
   1 country
   1 for
   1 good
   1 is
   1 of
   2 the
   1 their
   1 time
   2 to
$ □
```

$	Shell prompt
uniq	Remove all duplicate lines (words here)
-c	which are adjacent and display the count of repeat number for the file **temp2.sort**.
1 Now	Since the file **temp2** was sorted, all
1 aid	duplicate lines (actually words here)
1 all	were removed.
. . .	
$ □	Next prompt and cursor

Error Messages

```
$ uniq temps
cannot open temps
```

The file **temps** cannot be read.

```
$ uniq temp2.sort temp2.sort.o
cannot create temp2.sort.o
```

The file **temp2.sort.o** cannot be written to.

Notes on uniq

The **uniq** program reads the input file, comparing adjacent lines. In the default case (no options are entered), the second and succeeding copies of repeated lines are removed. The remainder is written to the output file. Repeated lines have to be adjacent to be found. Use the **sort** utility to arrange the input file so all repeated lines will be adjacent. (The **sort** utility is fully discussed in a separate section.)

If you specify the **-u** (unique) option, only the lines not repeated in the input file are displayed. The **-d** (duplicate) option causes only repeated lines to be displayed. The **-c** (count) option precedes each line with the number of times it occurred. You can skip m fields then skip n characters before the comparison by specifying -m +n options.

Tutorial

For the following examples, reformat the **temp** file to create the file **temp2** which contains one word per line by typing "tr -cs A-Za-z '\012' <temp > temp2<CR>".

```
$ tr -cs A-Za-z '\012' <temp >temp2; cat temp2
Now
is
the
time
for
all
good
citizens
to
come
to
the
aid
of
their
country
$ □
```

Use the **uniq** program to remove all duplicate words in the file **temp2** by typing "uniq temp2<CR>".

```
$ uniq temp2
Now
is
the
time
for
all
good
citizens
to
come
to
the
aid
of
their
country
$ □
```

The repeated words "the" and "to" were not removed. Words must be adjacent in order for **uniq** to remove them. Use the **sort** program to order the contents of **temp2.** Now type "sort temp2 -o temp2.sort; cat temp2.sort<CR>" and verify the result.

```
$ sort temp2 -o temp2.sort; cat temp2.sort
Now
aid
all
citizens
come
country
for
good
is
of
the
the
their
time
to
to
$ □
```

Apply the **uniq** command to remove the duplicate words which are now on adjacent lines. Type "uniq temp2.sort<CR>" and observe the result.

```
$ uniq temp2.sort
Now
aid
all
citizens
come
country
for
good
is
of
the
their
time
to
$ □
```

To count the number of times the lines (words here) were repeated in the file **temp2.sort** use the **-c** option. Type "uniq -c temp2.sort<CR>" and you will see the counts as well.

```
$ uniq -c temp2.sort
  1 Now
  1 aid
  1 all
  1 citizens
  1 come
  1 country
  1 for
  1 good
  1 is
  1 of
  2 the
  1 their
  1 time
  2 to
$ □
```

The **-u** option reports all the lines not repeated in the original file. For this example, type "uniq -u temp2.sort<CR>".

```
$ uniq -u temp2.sort
Now
aid
all
citizens
come
country
for
good
is
of
their
time
$ □
```

On the other hand, if you wish to report only the lines which were repeated in the original file use the **-d** option. Type "uniq -d temp2.sort<CR>".

```
$ uniq -d temp2.sort
the
to
$ □
```

If you attempt to use the **-c** option with either the **-u** or **-d** option you will obtain a report of the repeat count, but both of the other options will be ignored.

If the original file contains more than one field (column) of information you may wish **uniq** to ignore one or more fields before the comparison for duplicates is made. To illustrate, use an editor and enter the following short list of names in the file named **namelist.**

```
$ cat namelist
John Q. Public
Judy N. Public
Jean A. Smith
Jim L. Smith
```

First apply the **uniq** command without skipping any fields by typing "uniq namelist<CR>".

```
$ uniq namelist
John Q. Public
Judy N. Public
Jean A. Smith
Jim L. Smith
$ □
```

No lines were removed because all the lines are different.

To ignore the first two fields (columns here) and any blanks before each entry during the comparison, type "uniq -2 namelist<CR>". The **uniq** command chooses the first entry from each family as a representative.

```
$ uniq -2 namelist
John Q. Public
Jean A. Smith
$ □
```

If you need to skip several characters further in the field (but not the entire field), you need to specify an additional option in the form +*n*, where *n* is the number of additional characters to skip. To illustrate, use your editor again and add the following invoice numbers and dates to the end of the appropriate lines as shown here.

```
$ cat namelist
John Q. Public     Inv.443:Jan10
Judy N. Public     Inv.533:Jan10
Jean A. Smith      Inv.495:Jan10
Jim L. Smith       Inv.605:Jan11
```

Now say that you wish to collapse all adjacent entries which were invoiced on the same date. Since the last field contains the invoice number as well as the date, you must skip to the last field and ignore the first eight characters of that field in order to compare the lines solely on the basis of the date entry. To do this type "uniq -3 +8 namelist<CR>".

```
$ uniq -3 +8 namelist
John Q. Public       Inv.443:Jan10
Jim L. Smith         Inv.605:Jan11
$ □
```

Wc — Word Count

This command counts lines, words, and characters in one or more files.

$ **wc** *filename*

Counts lines, words, and characters for the file *filename*.

```
$ wc temp
      4     16      75 temp
$ □
```

$	Shell prompt
wc	Word count for
temp	the file name **temp**.
4	Number of lines
16	Number of words
75	Number of characters
temp	Filename counted
$ □	Next prompt and cursor

$ wc *file. . .*

Counts lines, words, and characters for the files indicated on the command lines and displays a combined count.

```
$ wc Chap1 Chap2
      10      45      210 Chap1
      12      50      189 Chap2
      22      95      399 total
$ □
```

$	Shell prompt
wc	Count for the files
Chap1 Chap2	**Chap1** and **Chap2**.
10 45 210 Chap1	10 lines, 45 words, 210 characters
12 50 189 Chap2	12 lines, 50 words, 189 characters
22 95 399 total	22 lines, 95 words, 399 characters in all
$ □	Next prompt and cursor

$ wc<CR>

Counts the lines, words, and characters in text entered from the keyboard until a ^D is typed.

```
$ wc
This is a line of text.
And this another.
[^D]2      9      42
$ □
```

$	Shell prompt
wc	Count for the text
This is . . .	entered from
And this . . .	the keyboard
[^D]	until a ^D is typed (not shown on screen).
2 9 42	2 lines, 9 words, and 42 characters
$ []	Next prompt and cursor

$ **wc** [**-lwc**] *filename* . . .

Counts only the number of lines, words, or characters in *filename* as specified in the options.

Options:

-l   Count the number of lines in a file.

-w   Count the number of words in a file.

-c   Count the number of characters in a file.

The options can be concatenated, (e.g., **-lc**).

```
$ wc -l temp
    4 temp
$ □
```

$	Shell prompt
wc	Count the number of
-l	lines in the file
temp	named **temp**.
4	The **wc** program says there are 4 lines
temp	in the file **temp**.
$ □	Next prompt and cursor

```
$ wc -lc prog.c
   132    3752 prog.c
$ □
```

$	Shell prompt
wc	Count the number of
-lc	lines and characters in
prog.c	the ''C'' source program file **prog.c**.
132	132 lines of source code,
3752	comprising 3752 characters (or bytes) in
prog.c	the file **prog.c**.
$ □	Next prompt and cursor

Error Messages

```
$ wc -x temp
temp
```

Invalid option; gives no counts.

```
$ wc -lx temp
      4 temp
```

Only valid option (-l) gives a count.

```
$ wc +l temp
wc: can't open +l
      4     16
      4     16
```

Wc considered +l a file.

Notes on wc

The command **wc** counts the lines, words, or characters in one or more files which you specify in the command line. If no file is named **wc** counts the standard input (the text you have input) from the keyboard.

A line is separated from the next line by a newline character "\n". In the UNIX system a word is a string of characters delimited, or separated, by spaces, tabs, or newlines. Three options limit the count to either lines, words, or characters. Type the correct option to specify the count. You can specify lines, words, or characters by typing **l, w,** or **c,** respectively.

Tutorial

For the simplest case type "wc temp<CR>".

```
$ wc temp
     4      16      75 temp
$ □
```

There are four lines, 16 words, and 75 characters in the file **temp**. Use this basic command form on other files in your file system.

If you want counts on more than one file, simply add the desired files to the command line. Wild card abbreviations for the filenames will also work. For example, type "wc Manuscript/Chap1/sec?<CR>" to enumerate the counts for the files **Manuscript/Chap1/sec1** and **Manuscript/Chap1/sec2**.

```
$ wc Manuscript/Chap1/sec?
  5    45    269 Manuscript/Chap1/sec1
  5    45    264 Manuscript/Chap1/sec2
 10    90    533 total
$ □
```

Type "wc -l /usr/dict/words<CR>" to get the number of lines in the on-line spelling dictionary. This will also be the number of words since each line of that file contains only one word. Verify that fact by typing "wc -lw /usr/dict/words<CR>".

```
$ wc -l /usr/dict/words
   24001 /usr/dict/words
$ wc -lw /usr/dict/words
   24001     24001     /usr/dict/words
$ □
```

This last example shows how certain numerical information can be obtained indirectly by using **wc.** You may also use **wc** to obtain the number of user terminals currently on-line. The **who** program prints one line per logged-in terminal, so **wc -l** can be used to count the number of active terminals by "piping" the output of **who** into the input of **wc.**

```
$ who | wc -l
   3
$ who
michael     dz07     Oct   1 17:26
tripi       dz14     Oct   1 16:07
rathomas    dz24     Oct   1 18:01
$ □
```

Miscellaneous

Cal — Print Calendar

Use this command to print a calendar for a specified year or month.

$ **cal** *year*

Displays the calendar for the *year*.

```
$ cal 1982
                                              1982
               Jan                             Feb                                 Mar
   S   M  Tu   W  Th   F   S         S   M  Tu   W  Th   F   S         S   M  Tu   W  Th   F   S
                  1   2               1   2   3   4   5   6                  1   2   3   4   5   6
   3   4   5   6   7   8   9         7   8   9  10  11  12  13         7   8   9  10  11  12  13
  10  11  12  13  14  15  16        14  15  16  17  18  19  20        14  15  16  17  18  19  20
  17  18  19  20  21  22  23        21  22  23  24  25  26  27        21  22  23  24  25  26  27
  24  25  26  27  28  29  30        28                               28  29  30  31
  31

               Apr                             May                                 Jun
   S   M  Tu   W  Th   F   S         S   M  Tu   W  Th   F   S         S   M  Tu   W  Th   F   S
                  1   2   3                               1                  1   2   3   4   5
   4   5   6   7   8   9  10         2   3   4   5   6   7   8         6   7   8   9  10  11  12
  11  12  13  14  15  16  17         9  10  11  12  13  14  15        13  14  15  16  17  18  19
  18  19  20  21  22  23  24        16  17  18  19  20  21  22        20  21  22  23  24  25  26
  25  26  27  28  29  30           23  24  25  26  27  28  29        27  28  29  30
                                   30  31

               Jul                             Aug                                 Sep
   S   M  Tu   W  Th   F   S         S   M  Tu   W  Th   F   S         S   M  Tu   W  Th   F   S
                  1   2   3         1   2   3   4   5   6   7                      1   2   3   4
   4   5   6   7   8   9  10        8   9  10  11  12  13  14         5   6   7   8   9  10  11
  11  12  13  14  15  16  17        15  16  17  18  19  20  21        12  13  14  15  16  17  18
  18  19  20  21  22  23  24        22  23  24  25  26  27  28        19  20  21  22  23  24  25
  25  26  27  28  29  30  31        29  30  31                       26  27  28  29  30

               Oct                             Nov                                 Dec
   S   M  Tu   W  Th   F   S         S   M  Tu   W  Th   F   S         S   M  Tu   W  Th   F   S
                          1   2          1   2   3   4   5   6                      1   2   3   4
   3   4   5   6   7   8   9         7   8   9  10  11  12  13         5   6   7   8   9  10  11
  10  11  12  13  14  15  16        14  15  16  17  18  19  20        12  13  14  15  16  17  18
  17  18  19  20  21  22  23        21  22  23  24  25  26  27        19  20  21  22  23  24  25
  24  25  26  27  28  29  30        28  29  30                       26  27  28  29  30  31
  31

$ □
```

$	Shell prompt
cal	Display the calendar
1982	for 1982.
[Display]	Display of formatted calendar
$ □	Next prompt and cursor

$ **cal** *month-number year*

Displays the calendar for the *month-number,* an integer between 1 and 12, of the *year,* an integer between 1 and 9999.

```
$ cal 1 1983
           January 1983
   S   M  Tu   W  Th   F   S
                               1
   2   3   4   5   6   7   8
   9  10  11  12  13  14  15
  16  17  18  19  20  21  22
  23  24  25  26  27  28  29
  30  31
$ □
```

$	Shell prompt
cal	Display the calendar
1	for the first month
1983	of 1983.
[Display]	Display for January 1983
$ □	Next prompt and cursor

Error Messages

```
$ cal 0 1983
Bad argument
```

0 is not a valid *month-number.*

```
$ cal 1 0
Bad argument
```

0 is not a valid *year.*

Notes on cal

The **cal** command prints a nicely formatted calendar for any year from 1 to 9999 inclusive. If you precede the year with a numeral from 1 to 12, corresponding to a month of the year, then the calendar for that month of the specified year is printed.

Tutorial

Print the calendar for your birthyear and display it on your local line printer with the command "cal *birthyear* | lpr<CR>".

Display the calendar for January '82. Did you get the correct year?

THE UNIX SYSTEM AND OFFICE AUTOMATION

Chapter 5

THE UNIX SYSTEM AND OFFICE AUTOMATION

AMERICA'S SHIFT FROM AN INDUSTRIAL to an informational economy has been well documented over the last ten years. Business and government operations increasingly depend on the systems employed to gather, process, analyze, and disseminate information. This growing demand for increased information necessitates the arrival of the automated office.

Every office is an information system. We use data to make decisions, and we generate more data internally and externally in order to administer and account for those decisions. Traditionally, pencils, paper, typewriters, and telephones have been used to transmit information. In the future, automated office equipment will increase productivity by increasing the speed and efficiency of office functions. It will increase the volume of data handled, connect data sources and operations, permit timely analysis of data, and permit better forecasts and planning.

The automated office is not simply a room full of machines. It is an environment in which employees use interconnected electronic equipment to perform the organization's administrative, managerial, and analytical functions.

The change to automated offices is evolutionary; most businesses will use a building block approach to introduce new office automation equipment, as they determine what functions are best automated.

Automated office equipment must fit functionally, organizationally, physically, and economically into an existing office organization. There are many positive reasons for implementing office automation.

Typically, a company that changes from typewriters to word processing can more than double productivity. However, producing paperwork faster and in greater quantities is not necessarily better. Forcing new equipment and new procedures to replace established practices can be dangerous. The successful introduction of office automation requires convincing fellow workers of its viability and integrating it into the company with minimal problems.

The implementation of automated office products in large companies will take from seven to ten years, and high-volume sales of more complex automated office products will not occur until the late 1980s. While the office of the future will be filled with an amazing diversity of sophisticated communications, word processing, and storage equipment, the systems will still be dependent upon us, the people who use them. We can adapt slowly to change, but an instant, profound change in our office work may affect day-to-day operations significantly for many months or years.

In the office of the future, equipment which once operated independently will be linked in networks. Digital Equipment Corporation, Intel Corporation, and Xerox Corporation have joined together to develop a local communications network (Ethernet) that will permit equipment from different manufacturers to communicate within the same building. Ethernet uses a coaxial cable similar to that of a cable television. Other companies, including Wang, AT&T, IBM, Datapoint, and BBN, all have their own concepts. Consequently, a major shakeout will occur in the market while standards are determined.

The heart of most large telephone systems is the PBX (private branch exchange). Tomorrow's PBX may well be the center of the modern office, integrating networks of CRT terminals and office equipment where data processing, word processing, electronic mail, facsimile transmission, and voice transmission are connected with one cable. Voice/data communication is evolving, allowing voice and data to simultaneously use telephone wiring for communication.

There are four aspects of office automation: administrative automation, data processing, data base administration, and telecommunications. These four disciplines must be combined for efficient performance in an integrated office system. Local networks will eventually allow these functions to communicate back and forth.

On a larger scale, future automated offices will operate through networks of PBX or other voice-controlled systems. Work stations, either limited terminals or complete microcomputer systems, will fulfill word processing and data base applications. Facsimile devices (FAX) will transmit graphic images as well as typed text. Mass storage devices will store an electronic office's records, partially replacing filing cabinets filled with records on paper. The machines will be connected together in local networks and tied into larger networks to connect several branches of a corporation or access external information exchanges.

Soon CRT terminals will become as common as desk telephones. Large companies now use clustered work stations for word processing and data entry. Desk-top computers will provide management with access to central data processing functions. No longer estranged from the data processing department, management will supplement hard copy reports by directly accessing data bases, sending electronic mail, and running financial modeling programs to support rapid analysis of the company's activities.

As work stations are increasingly adopted, new functions will be added. Data entry, once limited to writing or typing, will be supplemented by methods such as voice data entry and OCR (optical character recognition). Most important, the terminals will be connected to local networks of voice and data transmission, shared files, and disk storage.

Electronic Mail

A standard definition of electronic mail is still under development, but it is generally considered to be the electronic delivery of messages that would otherwise be transmitted through the postal system or local interoffice mail facilities. Interest in electronic mail is stimulated by the inadequacies of the postal services today and the need to increase speed and efficiency in interoffice communications.

Electronic mail provides the speed and convenience of phone calls with the option of retaining a copy of the message. At about 50 cents per message, electronic mail costs more than a postage stamp, but its speed and efficiency make it preferable to traditional mail services in many situations. A large number of firms plan to install electronic mail systems within two years. Electronic mail terminals will be on the desks of employees of these corporations, paving the way for more advanced functions, such as data base manipulation or analysis.

Data Base Management Systems

Data base management systems have traditionally been used by mainframe computer operators to produce rough analytical reports for managers. In the automated office, employees will use machines networked into the mainframe computer, requiring a different data base management system. Few companies have implemented distributed data bases in offices. Data base management systems continue to be used for writing reports and not for on-line analytical inquiries, which senior executives could do themselves.

Users of data base management systems agree that several characteristics of today's data bases need to be changed. Command languages similar to English must be used to support many people without extensive training in the access and use of a data base. Multitasking, that is, the ability of several people to update and work with the same file at the same time, is crucial in distributed processing. Data security must be maintained, limiting personnel to data appropriate to their functions only.

Data base systems for microcomputers are much simpler than those for mainframes or distributed systems. Most data base programs on 8-bit microcomputers are file managers. More complex 16-bit systems can use relational data bases adapted for them from the minicomputer world. These products will require more installation, and multi-user capabilities will make their file manipulations and access procedures more complex. Connecting these microcomputers — now containing the same relational data base systems as many computers — to other computers will result in new security and protection mechanisms being formulated. These mechanisms will allow the minicomputer to control access to its larger data files, while the microcomputer analyzes and performs data entry functions.

Color Graphics and "What-If" Analysis

Financial and sales projections, when supplemented with color graphics, stimulate immediate understanding of the material presented. According to psychological studies, color-coded graphs are not only more aesthetically pleasing than black-and-white graphs, but they can also be perceived more efficiently.

Technological advancements have reduced the time needed to perform calculations for "what-if" analysis. Electronic spread sheets are used in many offices. But these "what-if" programs display the data in rows and columns that require further interpretation. The statistical relationships are used to make important decisions that can potentially involve large sums of money. It is important for timely and accurate analysis that data be presented in as clear a fashion as possible.

A major drawback in using business graphics has been the difficulty of implementation. Graphics software has assumed the users are technically sophisticated, but this is changing. A study by Gnostic Concepts, Inc., a market research firm based in Menlo Park, California, documented a high demand for packaged color business graphics programs for micro- or minicomputers. The study found more than 80 projects under development which were designed to make color business graphics software easier to use.

Another factor limiting color graphics in management has been the cost of devices that print the color image displayed on the screen. Hard-copy printouts are available in several forms today. Cameras are used to photograph an image on the CRT for transfer into slides or overhead projection foils. Color printers are also available. Currently, hard-copy output of color graphics must be centralized within one relatively expensive printer, but the increasing demand for color graphics reproduction will eventually decrease the price of color graphics printers. Multiple-color ink jet printers may soon be available for as little as $2,000.

Text Processing

More sophisticated word processing systems include programs to verify accurate spelling and diction, and will add paper-handling devices to increase printing speed and facilitate processing. For example, these systems will stuff letters into envelopes and print customized forms. Optical character recognition (OCR) devices will be used to input printed data to a computer. These OCR devices read a printed page of text and convert it into binary data. Voice entry will be used (we will be able to talk to a computer and dictate instructions for editing rather than typing at a keyboard). Very small and inexpensive text processing machines will become available. Liquid crystal displays will be used to decrease cost and size.

Facsimile Devices (FAX)

Facsimile transmission has been popular for the last few years, but has been used in limited applications because of its cost. Facsimile transmission sends photographs and documents from one FAX machine to another over conventional telephone lines. The use of facsimile is natural for an office where these functions are routinely needed. Facsimile techniques will also affect the way we design photocopying and printing machines in the future. Eventually, facsimile devices may be included in our desk-top work station unit.

The key to an integrated electronic office is the electronic storage of data. As we have file cabinets full of paper today, we will have mass storage devices full of data in the future. Mass storage costs are decreasing rapidly; Winchester disks and bubble memories will be integral parts of every desk-top computer. This data storage will be supplemented at the minicomputer and mainframe levels of local networks. In the most inexpensive configurations, data will be stored on floppy disks. However, with Winchester disks and other storage becoming less expensive, the greater capacity provided will make desk-top computers very popular, even in the most basic work station environment.

Successful Computer Networking

Considered the harbinger of future networks, the Arpanet packet-switching system developed by Bolt, Beranek, and Newman of Cambridge, Massachusetts has been installed in several dozen locations and supports thousands of people on dozens of interconnected computers. Electronic mail, a focal point of the system, is used extensively for communications among programmers and office personnel.

The product, Info Mail, is designed to operate with existing computers, terminals, and networks. Info Mail simulates a desk-top system with "in and out" boxes, and includes multi-level filing systems. Other networks also answer the need for connecting different brands and types of computers and terminals together in both local and remote networks.

Two of the largest networks, Tymnet and GTE Telenet, offer electronic mail service in their packet-switch national networks. Tymnet's service, called OnTyme II, will handle different terminal types and models, including teletypewriters. Most of these systems allow each user to have an individual electronic mailbox, which can receive "mail" from any other computer or terminal on the system. Messages can also print out automatically at end user's terminals.

The UNIX System in the Automated Office

The UNIX operating system supports office automation. Many conventional operating systems are limited to the central processing units for which they were developed. The UNIX operating system, however, can be transported easily from office work stations to minicomputers, microcomputers, and mainframe computers, and can control typesetting machines, photocopiers, and many other kinds of equipment.

This transportability now introduces competition for computer manufacturers who have historically bound their customers to a single brand of equipment, using proprietary operating systems and communications protocols. The UNIX operating system allows communication among many brands of equipment, which will be an absolute necessity in the automated office of the future, where no single manufacturer can supply all the required hardware and software.

The UNIX system supports a revolution in the way all office personnel interact with computers. It signals a dramatic shift in the role of the software user. The end user learns a single operating system to control multiple operations on multiple machines, from manipulating text files on desk-top microcomputers to accessing mainframe computers with huge data bases representing many thousands of records. The same UNIX system commands that perform administrative functions, such as text processing, are used by system administrators and programmers to maintain and enhance the system.

Almost daily, users of the UNIX system are taking advantage of the design of the system to add applications and make sophisticated changes. The UNIX system is designed to be easily customized to a particular company's needs. Many of the improvements made in UNIX system installations are incorporated into the operating system at other sites, or into new releases by Western Electric so that the system is constantly improving.

Many users of operating systems consistently complain about the clumsy structure of the programs. These systems often contain massive interrelated programs with long histories of fixes and changes. The resulting jumble of commands becomes increasingly difficult to understand, and reflects the interdependent impact of modifying the system. In contrast, the UNIX operating system is a set of small, separate modules, many of which could be deleted from the system without affecting the operation of the others. Therefore, the UNIX system allows you to use only the part needed. The system contains many flexible tools that you can learn to use as your needs grow.

The UNIX operating system today contains the networking and telecommunications software necessary to tie together many brands and types of machines. Vendors of equipment related to the UNIX system are developing the hardware and software connectors that they need to tie into the network.

It is often possible to completely avoid programming when developing a new use for the UNIX system. Many times a combination of UNIX commands can do the job. We can combine several UNIX commands to handle simple tasks that occur in an office workday using pipes and shell "scripts."

In UNIX system installations, general and special purpose programs that can convert data from a file or program into a different form are being written in greater and greater numbers. If a new program is necessary, it can be written as a shell procedure instead of a C program. This consists of typing names of commands with specific arguments, and requires a minimal investment of time and effort. Therefore, programs that might be used only a few times can be economically developed with existing tools.

Because the UNIX operating system can be placed on a microcomputer as well as a mainframe, a common language becomes available to all of us, the language of the UNIX operating system tools.

Using the Powers of the UNIX System Tools

One of the greatest powers of the UNIX operating system is its capacity to be customized to accommodate everyone's particular needs. Since the UNIX operating system is in separate modules (or tools) the most popular tools are enhanced and strengthened while the weaker procedures die out.

The unique file structure of the UNIX operating system allows programs, documents, data, and so forth to be stored in the UNIX file system and to be protected either by the file mechanism or more elaborate software. Much of the drudgery involved in file and program manipulation and maintenance is bypassed by the UNIX system. Tools exist in the system that automate many common programming tasks and tie them into single-command sequences. The UNIX system minimizes the number of techniques needed to organize and maintain a library of files. This minimal style is one of the aspects most appreciated by UNIX system users.

The tool aspect of the UNIX system has a wide range of applications. Combinations of existing small and reliable commands in the system can be designed into different structures, rather than having to construct larger, unproven ones. The UNIX system helps us meet our individual needs and configure the system to our own purposes without having to learn programming or the requirements for producing new software.

Although the UNIX operating system comes to us as a set of tools, the system is easily individualized, both within a total installation for a number of users in an office, and at our own work stations. Programmers working for our companies may make changes that affect programs most frequently used throughout the company. But we can also individually write, shift, or change programs that we want to use ourselves. This chameleon feature of the operating system means that no one is stuck with a system that doesn't work.

The UNIX operating system was not written to be a general product that would fit everyone, but as a product designed to be customized. It offers the many tools needed to perform this task easily. This is radically different from many operating systems and programming philosophies. In most cases, a very general program is available and that program is difficult to change. When multiple users operate on a program, the impact of changing one part of a program (particularly if parts of the program feed into others) is staggering. A whole new selection of bugs and mistakes can be created by changing one line of code in a section of a program.

For this reason, many programs (accounting systems in particular) become large and inflexible monsters that cannot be changed and shifted to the changing needs of the office. The UNIX operating system builds software in modular pieces, many of which can be removed from the system and rebuilt without causing side effects. By following simple design procedures, a system designer can use a computer to produce programs customized to the needs of the office today and be assured that these programs can be easily replaced and upgraded to meet the needs of the office in years to come.

Learning to use the UNIX system in performing your office duties will give you great power for the relatively few commands typed. Many companies offer programs for the UNIX system that already perform office tasks. However, you will not implement the powers of the system if you do not use any of the commands yourself. If you learn the concepts behind the programming that your company buys, you can apply them to packaged software and can customize the system to your needs. Also, we found it much easier to learn to use software packages when we understood something about the system.

On the UNIX operating system, many tools are available that allow non-specialists to define and process data. Although these tools were originally intended for the development of programs, they are very useful in a wide variety of application programs as well. By using tools, we are able to gain access to facilities that we do not have to understand in detail. We can construct programs by using available tools and pieces. Typing several commmands in succession results in what would otherwise require advanced programming knowledge and a long period of time to produce.

Using the UNIX system tools introduces the following programming features:

- The results are produced quickly

- Results are likely to function without bugs

- The program remains flexible and adaptable and can be
  easily changed without affecting performance

- The process is usually portable to another machine without
  any change

- The use of tools encourages a natural modularity of programming
  which is easier to maintain

- We can use tools created by experts and access complicated programs without having to understand the details involved.

Since complex tools written in languages unique to the UNIX system are built from simple and single-function components, programmers continue to create new tools to enhance those that exist. This stimulates growth of the UNIX system, rather than reinvention or redundancy. In addition, since each tool is an independent program, those tools that are not useful are weeded out, while those that are successful become more flexible and multifaceted as additions are made to their functions.

The current UNIX system has evolved through a process not unlike natural selection. The UNIX system received by end users is modified immediately to their specific needs. Each UNIX system at an end user location takes on the characteristics of that company's needs.

There are three types of information flow in an organization. These are

- Operations (the actual production of goods and services)
- Control (the monitoring of operational and administrative activity)
- Administrative (communication of decisions and plans, and information relevant to their execution).

Administrative functions, encompassing the creation, control storage, transmission, recall, and delivery of paperwork throughout an organization, can be handled with the UNIX operating system. We can use electronic mail to communicate information that previously would have been typed on paper and passed from hand to hand. Processing this information will be greatly speeded up by programs in the UNIX system that modify, compute, extend, or recombine these documents in ways that are too time-consuming to do by hand.

The UNIX operating system has more than the tools to perform these functions. The degree to which people like operating systems and the way in which a computer interacts with them will determine the success of an automated office. The UNIX operating system is ranked highly by many users for its functionality and manageability.

Administrative Functions And the UNIX System

Administrative functions performed in an office include the following:

1. Document processing
   - Creation
   - Editing/review
   - Storage and retrieval
   - Distribution

2. Document production
   - Printing/typing
   - Phototypesetting
   - Composition
   - Graphics creation
   - Mass reproduction

3. Message processing
   - Creation
   - Distribution
   - Storage/retrieval

4. Time management
   - Calendars
   - Time conflict analysis
   - Ticklers and reminders

5. Conferencing
   - Voice only
   - Data only
   - Voice/data
   - Voice/video

6. Calculating/computing
   - Expense accounts
   - Decision analysis support

- Financial analysis
- Return on investment analysis
- Strategic modeling

7. Inquiry
   - Internal status information
   - Simple reports
   - List access
   - Phone directory
   - External information services

Electronic Mail in the UNIX System

Internal documents within a company are frequently needed within a few hours after generation. Interoffice mail in large corporations takes much longer, implying that handling through internal mail slows information flow. Messages sent through electronic mail have a much faster speed of receipt and a much lower cost of production. After implementing computer systems with desk-top work stations for each office worker, electronic mail supersedes hand-carriage of messages and documents. It permits immediate and simultaneous on-line access by a number of people to the same message upon transmission.

With the UNIX operating system, you can talk to another user of the system with the write command, send electronic mail if he is not on-line, access any computer networked into your system (in some installations there are as many as seven to ten computers networked into a huge system), and perform many other functions. You can write a letter, send the letter to be printed on a typesetting unit, and send that output automatically to a photocopying machine that makes 500 copies of it. This can all be done from your desk, without moving from one unit to another.

Filing in the UNIX System

The UNIX operating system handles everything we do with files. In the typical UNIX system installation, each user (with individual terminals or work stations) has several hundred personal files within a directory. These files can be documents, programs, or subdirectories. In this way, different types of information can be categorized and stored within a tree-type directory system. Each person's own directory can be made selectively accessible to other people by changing parts of the personal directory system. This means that you can allow someone else to use the mailing list that you're responsible for, while keeping them out of other records.

When you move out of your own directory and decide to work on a large data base (say, the accounting records of your company), the same techniques and tools used to manage your own files are utilized. The UNIX system commands do not differentiate between large and small files; because the system is modular and tool-oriented, this is not necessary.

EVALUATING AND ACCESSING THE SYSTEM

Chapter 6

EVALUATING AND ACCESSING THE SYSTEM

SURVEYS HAVE BEEN CONDUCTED to determine how well the UNIX system functions in various business applications. The following features were rated highest: hierarchical file system, transportability of application software, flexibility for customized programming, and the variety of text processing and file manipulating programs. UNIX software has been customized for diverse environments, including banks, law firms, medical offices, and research institutions. In this chapter we will see how the UNIX system functions in commercial and industrial environments, and explore opportunities for UNIX system access and education.

Commercial Applications

Customizing the UNIX system for every function of every department could diminish the cost effectiveness gained by computerizing a company's operations. Potential UNIX system users should consider application packages as economical alternatives to a totally customized system. Application programs developed in specific installations are being packaged for a broader market.

Software vendors offer packages that simplify text editing, data base manipulation, and accounting, and include optional features. Some computer and software vendors have enhanced the UNIX system by adding menus and prompts. Appropriate system command options are chosen to support specific applications, and options that are not relevant to a particular application are deleted from the software. These features permit you to select a specific task from a menu of possible tasks, or to creatively combine UNIX system commands to perform new functions. The best programs add your newly created functions to the menu, creating a self-customizing system. Ask application program vendors which features they have implemented.

Document Preparation

Word processors and text processing software accelerate the process of writing and editing documents. Once we retyped an entire page to correct a single error; now we can move the cursor to retype, delete, move, or otherwise alter the text on the screen before printing it out on paper.

By speeding up the physical manipulation of words on paper, we have more time to be clear and precise with the text. Documents can be written and prepared more systematically. Word processing programs produce professional-quality documents; they can justify the right-hand margin, create columns and tables, and perform other tasks formerly too time-consuming for all but the most important documents.

The text processing programs in the UNIX operating system include editing and text formatting. Editing programs allow you to enter text and manipulate it on the screen. Inserting text-formatting commands into the edited text specifies the printed format.

In the UNIX system, the **ed** text editor inputs text, and the NROFF and TROFF text processors prepare the text for printout.

Since **ed** was designed to edit computer program listings, its commands are best suited to manipulate lines of data, rather than blocks of text. In addition **ed** was developed for systems which generate hard-copy output, rather than a CRT display. It lacks many standard features offered by commercially available text editing programs. Appendix A lists several vendors of systems based on the UNIX system which offer alternate text editing programs.

The UNIX system includes the following text processing programs:

- ROFF prepares files for high-speed, low-quality line printers;

- NROFF prepares files for low-speed, letter-quality printers; and

- TROFF prepares files for phototypesetting.

In the ROFF family of print formatters, command lines are interspersed in the text file. You cannot determine line and page composition until the text formatter processes the text file. If you require formatting changes, you must edit the original text file and pass it through the formatter. This slow and cumbersome process compares poorly with many word processing programs available today.

The ROFF series can send text to several types of printers, including typesetters and photocopy/printing equipment. UNIX systems currently print out text on at least 40 different brands of "hard-copy" devices. However, adapting the ROFF programs to specific printers requires the skill of a professional programmer.

Accounting Systems

The UNIX system contains accounting programs only for charging system users. While it can record login and logout times and send bills, it does not provide full accounting services for businesses.

Appendix A lists several accounting programs written for the UNIX system. They generally include payroll, accounts receivable and payable, and general ledger functions. Additional modules may include job costing, order entry, and report generation. Some vendors offer customized accounting programs for specific businesses.

Accounting packages developed to be compatible with the UNIX operating system are generally multi-user and multi-tasking. They include many features not available in accounting programs developed for microcomputers, which are generally single-user systems. Multi-user systems allow multiple users to work in the same program or data file. For example, if your company uses five order-entry clerks, each clerk can sit at a different terminal, accessing the same data base and using the same inventory program. The computer system will separate the inputs.

In multi-tasking, the computer simultaneously performs multiple tasks. One person calculates payroll, another creates a mail list, and a third edits text. Minicomputers have traditionally supported multi-user/ multi-tasking functions, but until recently microcomputers processed multiple entries and tasks too slowly to be practical.

Many accounting programs available for the UNIX system were originally written under different operating systems, and may offer limited interaction with the UNIX system. While this interaction is not absolutely necessary, the UNIX system commands do offer useful text and file manipulations. Using the UNIX system commands, you can manipulate whole files to reorganize accounting data. This function must be used carefully; an experienced programmer's direction will save you from destroying essential files.

Most of the commercial UNIX system installations were made on minicomputers. In-house programmers wrote or customized accounting software specifically for a company's needs. In contrast, the inexpensive microcomputer installations employ "canned" accounting software written to run under the UNIX operating system.

If your business uses a single-user microcomputer system, you can convert to a multi-user/multi-tasking system with the UNIX operating system. Starting with only one or two terminals, you can indefinitely expand the system. Multi-tasking is more efficient than installing several single-user systems. Multiple single-user computer systems do not share files efficiently. For example, several people may work with the accounting or inventory programs, requiring maintenance of several different copies of data files, and daily updates to a master file. The potential for error is obvious; consider the mayhem caused by the destruction of one user's data for a single day, multiplied by the number of system users. The UNIX system allows several people to simultaneously access the same file, and it manages file updating to include each user's input. This is much less confusing and time-consuming than single-user methods. For accounting and inventory applications, a network running under the UNIX operating system is more efficient than single-user systems, and costs about the same.

A data base program is similar to a filing cabinet full of information. A data base program combines this source of information with a superior filing and indexing system. The UNIX system commands include portions of a data base system. Appendix A lists several vendors who have already implemented data base systems. As with accounting software, minicomputer data base programs can be transported to the UNIX system, either for mini- or microcomputers.

Industrial Applications

Within the Bell System, the UNIX system is used to manage administrative and telecommunications tasks, forecast expansion requirements, and design programs to support long-range plans.

MERT (Multi-Environment Real Time), a variant of the UNIX system, permits computers to respond quickly to signals from telephone, laboratory, or other industrial equipment. MERT allows the UNIX system to connect with other, special-purpose operating systems for concurrent operations.

In the AT&T Long Lines network management of the Bell System, the UNIX system handles a multitude of simultaneous telephone messages. The UNIX file system permits rapid storage and access of information from a toll network of telephone lines. UNIX software efficiently controls telephone traffic during peak load periods.

In computer-aided design, the UNIX system utility programs allow the designer to draw circuit schematics on a graphics terminal and to automatically check for errors. An interactive graphics system for designing a circuit board includes the following programs:

- Draw — creates and modifies circuit drawings;
- Check — tests consistency of a circuit;
- Place — locates electronic components on a circuit board;
- Wrap — generates circuit wiring data.

These programs determine the required electronic connections for a given design, and generate the computer instructions for a machine to fabricate those connections.

The UNIX operating system features fulfill most requirements for industrial applications. The reliability and security of the file system are adequate for the limited number of users and the dedicated applications. Software transportability between operating systems is important during development of new industrial processes. The source code control system and Programmer's Workbench provide self-documentation for process programs. The UNIX system utility programs that perform data analysis are extensively utilized in building and maintaining industrial control programs. The UNIX system is compatible with utility programs that interface with analog-to-digital converters and scientific instruments.

Software Development

Many programmers favor the UNIX software development environment. The Programmer's Workbench supports using the UNIX system as the host system for large software development projects. Programs intended for many different computers can be developed and edited interactively on the UNIX system and then telecommunicated to the user's computer system. Tests are sent to the target machine and the results are transmitted back to the UNIX system for evaluation.

The Programmer's Workbench (PWB) assigns all development projects to the applicable part of the program. PWB stores a complete record of changes made to the program as it develops, and can rebuild the program at any point for exclusive study. It permits programmers to write a program and transport it to several different computers, even computers with different kinds of CPUs. For example, software developers can simultaneously write software to run on each of the different 16-bit microcomputers. This eliminates writing the same program several times, and supports the development of superior, economical software.

Gaining Access: Purchase, Time-Sharing, and Education

Now it is time to contact computer system vendors for specific product information. We recommend you speak with several vendors who support the UNIX system. Appendix A lists a number of these vendors.

The transportability of the UNIX system makes it an attractive package to consider; it largely eliminates your dependence on one brand of hardware. Non-standard systems based on the UNIX operating system present another consideration. In some cases, the lower cost or special features of such products may be an important consideration. Until recently, a multi-user UNIX system was quite expensive. The cost of a single work station of a PDP-11 with the UNIX system was about $12,060. The cost of the total system, about $120,000, precluded a very small business from purchasing this system. New microcomputers running under the UNIX system have a much lower cost per work station for equivalent power; a 16-bit microcomputer running under the UNIX system can support a maximum of six to ten users. Prices for these computers are generally higher than for 8-bit machines using a Z80 or 8080 microprocessor. Several variants of the CP/M® operating system have incorporated key elements of the UNIX system. These operating systems do not implement all of the UNIX system commands and features, but they provide some introduction to the UNIX system.

The tables in Appendix A list microcomputers that use operating systems based on the UNIX system. Average price per work station is above $10,000, but projections suggest rapid decreases. Bell Laboratories does not support end users using the UNIX system. We advise you to purchase or work with UNIX software that is supported by a licensed vendor. Further, we suggest you find the most stable source of long-term support possible. You are probably buying the UNIX system for several reasons, but an important one is the system's flexibility. You will want the assistance of a qualified and available vendor to make changes and additions as you learn to use the system. This does not preclude looking for a small or relatively new firm to support your system. Choose your vendor carefully. You will be associated with that vendor for a long time.

Consider buying the UNIX system from Western Electric only if you plan to change it extensively and you have the budget to do so. You can't buy UNIX software from Western Electric unless you buy the source code, an expensive proposition. Even in many large UNIX system installations, the programmers don't have source code. Binary licenses are sold only through licensed vendors who own the source code to UNIX software.

If your computer system will be dedicated to a single function, and you don't intend to modify the software, choose a vendor who has experience with your particular application, rather than experience with supporting the UNIX system.

We have used the UNIX system for text processing, accounting, file manipulation, and other office-related functions. We have frequently received support from UNIX system vendors. Most of our experience with the UNIX system has been through time-sharing educational systems, and we have contacted the system programmer on several occasions to ask questions. Our associates have expressed the same type of interactive relationship with the vendors of their UNIX system.

Here are two ways to gain access to the UNIX system:

- Interact with time-sharing networks running under the UNIX system, either commercial or educational

- Purchase individual computers running under the UNIX system or under software that is based on the UNIX system.

The resources directory in Chapter 7 describes UNIX system vendors and sources of time-sharing systems. The UNIX operating system is available on about 90% of the computer science department computers in the United States, and some permit access to their systems.

Commercial time-sharing vendors charge more than educational institutions for access, but offer better time-sharing priority. For example, the University of California at Berkeley prioritizes users by seniority and other classifications. Non-university users receive a lower priority when they sign onto the system and encounter difficulties in accessing the system during high-use hours. Universities restrict account privileges, and it is unlikely that many non-university accounts will use university facilities.

We verified the material in this book by using the UNIX system facility at the University of California at Berkeley. Our experience with the system was excellent. The combination of on-line support and telephone conversations with programmers was quite beneficial and accelerated our learning process. However, it is unlikely the University of California at Berkeley and its counterparts around the country can support the number of new UNIX system users (more than 200,000) expected in the next few years. We recommend that you explore alternative methods of learning the UNIX system.

Another potential source of access to the UNIX system is through the company for which you work. If your company owns a mini- or mainframe computer, chances are that the data processing managers can purchase the UNIX system for the in-house machine.

We learned a great deal about the UNIX system by attending user group meetings and by reading user group newsletters. These reasonably priced services are listed in Chapter 7. Meeting the people in the groups can provide you with access to some form of the UNIX system, or the opportunity to look over the shoulder of a UNIX system user at work.

User group meetings are held in different locations by several groups. The **usenix group** includes mainly educators and professionals programming in a research area of the UNIX operating system. While some vendors attend the conference, it is known for its academic orientation, and technical papers are presented.

In contrast, the **/usr/group** is dominated by vendors of the UNIX system and products based on the UNIX system. This group meets two or three times a year and is based in Stanford, California. The group is headed by Bob Marsh, former president of Onyx Systems and current president of Plexus Computers. The group meetings stress business opportunities in the UNIX system environment. A committee interacts with Bell Laboratories and Western Electric, and other committees are standardizing UNIX system changes, publishing a newsletter, and offering educational seminars.

Uni-Ops, another UNIX system users group, publishes a newsletter called "Pipes and Filters." Based in Walnut Creek, California, the organization publishes a directory of information on the operating system and periodically offers conferences oriented to beginners as well as experienced users.

There are also training courses available on the UNIX operating system. Several companies offer one or two day seminars on both the UNIX system and the C language.

Several papers listed in the Bibliography (Appendix E) were written at Bell Laboratories specifically for beginners, and provide excellent reference material for working with the specific programs they document.

Bell Laboratories provides source license purchasers with access to numerous technical papers written by Bell Laboratories researchers. These papers are available from Bell Laboratories for about $100, or from several educational UNIX system institutions. The University of California at Berkeley, for example, sells papers from Bell Laboratories and has supplemented these with papers written specifically for the Berkeley system. Other large university systems have supplemented the Bell Laboratories documentation with similar papers.

THE UNIX SYSTEM RESOURCES

Chapter 7

THE UNIX SYSTEM RESOURCES

WHEN YOU DECIDE TO PURCHASE A
system based on the UNIX system, or to enhance your computer by
adding the UNIX system, you will be faced with a number of questions
about available products. This chapter describes products related to the
UNIX system to help you determine which best suit your needs.

Portions of the information about the following companies have been
reprinted in this chapter with permission of InfoPro Systems: Western
Electric Company; Computer Consoles, Inc.; Cromemco, Inc.; Lifeboat
Associates; System Kontakt, Inc.; The Code Works; Ron Cain; The Soft-
ware Toolworks; tiny-c Associates; BDS C User's Group; Bell Laboratories;
DJR Associates; and RLG Corporation.

The Tables

The 12 tables in Appendix A list specific computers, operating systems,
and related products. The first two tables summarize vendors of the
UNIX system and similar operating systems. The third table describes
languages available in the UNIX operating system. Tables A-4, A-5,
A-6, and A-7 describe various applications packages, related to both
business and programming.

Table A-1 identifies the range of computers available to you. If you
want a relatively inexpensive system, consider the 16-bit microcomputers. You will eventually have as many as 100 vendors from which to
choose. If you need a larger system, consider the minicomputers and
mainframe computers described.

The UNIX system is complicated to maintain. Choose your computer vendors based upon their abilities to support the operating system. The hardware manufacturers are listed with vendors who sell hardware plus the UNIX operating system in a combined office automation package. The vendor of the supporting UNIX system is also listed. For example, Onyx Computer uses a UNIX system V7, which is supported by Interactive Systems Incorporated. Some computer companies specialize in systems for many users, while others specialize in computers limited to eight system users. Choice of your computer depends upon your needs.

The manufacturers' addresses and telephone numbers are included in this chapter, along with a description of the company and any areas of specialization.

Application Programs

A wide variety of application programs are available for computers on the UNIX system, and more are being written or converted every month. Today, not enough business application packages are available, but this situation is changing rapidly; the lists that follow will be only a subset of the products available within a year. Some vendors offer the CP/M operating system as a procedure running under the UNIX system. While we believe this underutilizes the power of the UNIX system, simply translating data files introduces you to valuable capabilities of the multi-user system.

Large companies and university personnel wrote most of the programs available for the system. Few were written by hobbyists. For this reason, software based on the UNIX system is more complex and comprehensive than programs written for personal microcomputers. Much of the UNIX software we describe was developed for the PDP-11 computer and is priced higher than most microcomputer programs. The addition of multi-user, multi-access options with software packages increases the price. A more complicated program has a higher price, both because the system took longer to write and because it requires more support. In general, you will pay more for software based on the UNIX system than for software designed for similar microcomputer applications.

Computer manufacturers also sell application programs. Some of these programs were generated in-house, while others were acquired from outside sources.

Educational Sources

Table A-8 lists vendors who offer classes on the UNIX system. Topics include the following:

- Introduction to UNIX and System III for programmers
- Introduction to UNIX and System III for users
- Introduction to UNIX and System III operations (for data center personnel)
- Advanced UNIX techniques
- UNIX Workbench using SCCS
- Text processing
- The C language
- Special seminars on specific UNIX System languages and facilities (for example, FORTRAN 77, YACC, Shell, Pascal, BASIC).

UNIX System Licensees

This section describes UNIX system licensees who sell and support the UNIX system Version 7 and System III. Most have enhanced the software, packaged it for several different computers, and given it a proprietary name. We differentiate system licensees as computer manufacturers or systems houses, since the former sell UNIX software and computers separately, while the latter sell complete systems.

This section provides a complete listing of the UNIX system software available from Western Electric. Since software purchased directly from Western Electric is unsupported, we recommend you purchase UNIX software from a source licensee. Western Electric will soon offer support to government and military facilities which purchase the UNIX system. Educational or nonprofit institutions can purchase UNIX software from Western Electric at a very low price, but it is unsupported.

Electronic Information Systems

364 Pepper Ridge Road
Stamford, Connecticut 06905
(203) 329-7030

This company sells UNIX system V7 under the name EUNIS. They enhanced V7, and offer system development tools in C.

Interactive Systems Corporation
1212 7th Street
Santa Monica, California 90401
(213) 450-8363

> Interactive, the oldest commercial supplier of systems based on the UNIX system, offers several applications software packages, including text editing, screen editing, and communications facilities. Basically, these enhance or modify Version 7 software. Several mini- and mainframe computer vendors have contracted Interactive Systems to put the UNIX system on their computers. Interactive Systems has transported the UNIX system and the Programmer's Workbench utilities to the DEC VAX computer and Onyx microcomputer. They have System III.

Microsoft
400 108th Avenue, N.E.
Suite 200
Bellevue, Washington 98004
(206) 454-1315

> Microsoft sells and supports the XENIX operating system, a 16-bit microprocessor adaptation of the UNIX system Version 7 and System III. The XENIX system has been configured for the Intel 8086, Zilog Z8000, and Motorola 68000 microprocessors, and is available on several different computer systems. Write Microsoft to obtain "A Functional Description of the XENIX Operating System."

UniSoft Corporation
2405 4th Street
Berkeley, California 94710
(415) 644-1230

> UniSoft has ported UNIX Software to a number of 68000 hardware configurations, including the recently announced Dual Systems Control Corporation S100 Bus system.

Western Electric Company
Bell Systems Software, P.O. Box 25000
Greensboro, North Carolina 27420
(919) 697-6530

> Contact this address for marketing and licensing information on the

UNIX system and related products. They will send a full information package on their software.

Western Electric sells the UNIX system as an unsupported product. It is advisable to consider purchasing the UNIX system from a company which offers enhanced support and applications packages. However, inexpensive educational licenses are available from Western Electric. Schools, universities, and nonprofit research organizations should apply to this address for an educational license.

Software from Western Electric:

UNIX System III system program. The UNIX system System III is a multi-programmed, time-sharing operating system that effectively converts the DEC PDP-11/34, 40, 45, 70 into a small-scale computer center supporting as many as 40 users.

    Hardware requirements: DEC PDP-11/34, 40, 45, 70, VAX 780

    Programming language: C Language, Fortran 77

UNIX/V7 system program. The UNIX Time Sharing System, Seventh Edition, is a multi-programmed, time-sharing operating system that runs on a DEC PDP-11/45 or 11/70. It converts into a small-scale computer center supporting as many as 40 users.

    Hardware requirements: DEC PDP-11/45, 70

    Programming languages: C Language, FORTRAN 77

UNIX/32V system program. The UNIX/32V system is a multi-programmed time-sharing operating system designed for the DEC-VAX-11/780 hardware. The UNIX/32V system is an enhanced version of the UNIX/V7 operating system, and functions in medium- to large-scale computer centers supporting as many as 40 users.

    Hardware requirements: DEC-VAX-11/780

    Programming languages: C Language, FORTRAN 77

PWB/UNIX Programmer's Workbench. The Programmer's Workbench (PWB/UNIX) is a specialized computing facility dedicated to satisfying the needs of developers of computer programs. Just as there are "front-end" and "back-end" computers, the PWB could be called a "human-end" computer. It improves productivity by efficient specialization. The PWB is an expanded version of the UNIX operating system for DEC PDP series minicomputers.

Hardware requirements: DEC PDP-11/45 and 70

Programming language: C Language

Magic graphics program. MAGIC (Machine Aided Graphics for Illustration and Composition) is an interactive computer graphics software package used for the preparation, editing, production, and storage of line pictorials, diagrams, and other technical documentation.

Programming language: Assembly code (both system configurations)

ROFF utility program. ROFF is a publications formatting program that offers unusual freedom in document style.

Hardware requirements: Honeywell 600/6000

Programming language: BCPL

Phototypesetter Version 7 utility program. Phototypesetter — Version 7 is a typesetting package which includes text formatting and utility mathematical equation processing. The Phototypesetter's language has been designed to be easily learned by people who know neither mathematics nor typesetting.

Hardware requirements: DEC PDP-11/40, 45 (runs under the UNIX Time-Sharing Operating System)

Programming languages: TROFF, EQN

The Wollongong Group
1135A San Antonio Road
Palo Alto, California 03
(415) 962-9224

The Wollongong Group has placed the UNIX system on Perkin-Elmer's 32-bit minicomputers. Wollongong supports Version 7 and the Version 7 Programmer's Workbench, and will soon offer the system on other minicomputers.

Wollongong provides educational training during the software installation phase. On-site classes provide training, ranging from introductory level for management end users to advanced classes for supporting programmers.

Computer Manufacturers and Systems Houses
Selling Computers with the UNIX System⎯⎯⎯⎯⎯⎯

Systems houses purchase computers from computer manufacturers, add services and software, and sell complete integrated systems. Computer manufacturers perform some or all of the same services, or sell hardware separate from software. Computer manufacturers and systems houses selling products related to UNIX system V6 and V7 are shown in Table A-2 of Appendix A.

Amdahl Corporation
1250 East Arques Avenue
Sunnyvale, California 94086
(408) 746-6000

Amdahl sells UNIX system V7 as an option on their IBM-compatible mainframe computers. A fully configured system ranges in price from several hundred thousand dollars to more than a million dollars.

BBN Computer
33 Moulton Street
Cambridge, Massachusetts 02238
(617) 491-1850

BBN Computer is a division of a company specializing in data communications. The company's computer, called "The C Machine," optimizes software development in the C language under the UNIX system. The product can support 15 users, and includes software tools. Available network control software connects the C Machine to any network using BBN packet switching processors including ArpaNET, a product of BBN. The computer can be used as a node on a Digital Equipment Corporation VAX computer.

CM Technologies, Inc.
525 University Avenue
Palo Alto, California 94301
(415) 326-9150

The Series 16 Multiprocessor System runs under Digital Research's CP/M operating system. A 68000-only version of the computer is designed to run under Microsoft's XENIX and is scheduled for 1982 release.

Codata Systems Corporation

285 North Wolfe Road
Sunnyvale, California 94086
(408) 735-1744

Codata's CTS-200/6 and CTS-300/6 systems are Z8000- or 68000-based desk-top units. They are configured with dual minifloppies, CRT display, and microWinchesters. The operating system is UNIX system V7.

Computer Consoles

1000 Potomac Street, N.W.
Suite 401
Washington, DC 20007
(202) 965-6655

This company sells office automation systems with the UNIX operating system. They recently purchased RLG Corporation. Their product is called the Office Power System.

Data Resources, Inc.

29 Hartwell Avenue
Lexington, Massachusetts 02173
(617) 861-0165

Data Resources sells a work station with the UNIX system V7 and the capacity for networking. The work station is targeted to financial analysts, strategic planners, and economists. The product, Drilink, is designed exclusively for economic financial analysis and planning, and utilizes Data Resources' procedures and data sets.

The Drilink machine is based on the Z8000 microprocessor, and includes a Winchester disk drive. The system can run four graphics terminals, printers, plotters, and communications, allowing it to access data from large computers and from the Data Resources central computer facility.

Digital Equipment Corporation

146 Main Street
Maynard, Massachusetts 01754
(617) 897-5111

Digital Equipment Corporation (DEC) manufactures the line of minicomputers on which Bell Laboratories developed UNIX software.

Today, at least 15,000 DEC computers run the UNIX operating system. The product lines include the PDP-11 and VAX systems, and range in price from $40,000 to more than $500,000, depending on the configuration. Some UNIX systems on DEC equipment support 100 users or more. Some programmers dream of owning their own VAX system, but it is not a typical personal computer. These machines are large, powerful, and expensive when fully configured.

DEC does not officially support or sell the UNIX system, but software packages are included in their "External Applications Software Library." They check out and provide these packages, but do not offer a warranty on them.

Dual Systems Control Corporation

720 Channing Way
Berkeley, California 94710
(415) 549-3854

This company targets their 68000-based microcomputer with UNIX system V7 to instrumentation and process control applications.

Fortune Systems Corporation

1501 Industrial Road
San Carlos, California 94070
(415) 595-8444

Fortune sells the 32:16 UNIX-based microcomputer. It has a 68000 microprocessor CPU and from 128 to 512K of memory. Disk storage ranges from 2 MB (floppies) to 10 MB (Winchester). The 32:16 operates in single or multiuser mode.

Fortune sells word processing for the 32:16 that emulates a very popular word processor. Accounting packages are also available. Fortune's UNIX system is based on System III with enhancements.

MicroDaSys, Inc.

1541 South Manhattan Place
Los Angeles, California 90019
(213) 731-1475

MicroDaSys offers the XENIX operating system for a 68000-based microcomputer with a 6809 microprocessor for memory management. MicroDaSys is developing a virtual memory version of XENIX, called VENIX.

Onyx Systems, Incorporated

73 East Trimble Road
San Jose, California 95131
(408) 946-6330

> Onyx manufactures a Z8000-based computer system with the UNIX operating system. The UNIX software is supported by Interactive Systems Corporation. Onyx offered one of the first microcomputers which runs on an operating system based on the UNIX system, and more than 600 machines have been installed.

Perkin-Elmer Corporation

Computers Systems Division
2 Crescent Place
Oceanport, New Jersey 07757
(201) 229-6800

> Perkin-Elmer manufactures a 32-bit superminicomputer with the UNIX system V7 operating system, supported by Wollongong Group and called Edition VII.

Plexus Computers, Inc.

2230 Martin Avenue
Santa Clara, California 95050
(408) 988-1755

> Plexus Computers sells two Z8000-based computers with the UNIX system. It uses multiple microprocessors and custom features to optimize UNIX system features. The systems will support 5 to 15 users and include as many as 580 MB of Winchester disk storage and 1 MB of main memory. The systems include a standard format nine-track tape unit on the P/40 for easy program transfer or streaming tape on the smaller unit, the P/25.

uniq computer corporation

28 South Water Street
Batavia, Illinois 60510
(312) 879-1566

> Uniq sells the UNIX operating system on Digital Equipment Corporation hardware as a complete system. The company offers newsletters, software modifications, patches, and other support services. The com-

pany also offers consulting services for software development.

Wicat Systems
P.O. Box 539
1875 South State Street
Orem, Utah 84057
(801) 224-6400

> Wicat Systems offers two systems based on the UNIX operating system: the System 100 and System 150. The System 150 includes a 10-MB Winchester drive, 5¼ inch floppy backup, 2-RS-232 serial ports, the Wicat operating system, and the UNIX V7 operating system. The System 150 can support four users. The System 100 has a 20-MB Winchester drive, a 17-MB tape cartridge backup, and can support 20 users.

Zilog
10340 Bubb Road
Cupertino, California 95014
(408) 446-4666

> Zilog offers a Z8000-based system, the System 8000 or Z-Lab 8000, with their supported version of UNIX V7, ZEUS. The machine will support as many as 12 users, and includes optional disk storage up to 80 MB.

Vendors of Systems Based on the UNIX System

> Because of the high cost of Western Electric's operating system source code, and the interest of other companies in adapting the concepts of the UNIX operating system to their own proprietary products, a number of operating systems based on the UNIX system have been developed. Some were developed by software companies, and are intended for a variety of hardware systems. Some were developed by computer manufacturers, and are unique to their brand. This section details UNIX software vendors, and the following section describes computer manufacturers offering computer systems based on the UNIX system. These sections are summarized in Tables A-3 and A-4 of Appendix A.

Mark Williams Company
1430 W. Wrightwood Avenue
Chicago, Illinois 60614
(312) 472-6659

> Mark Williams Company sells COHERENT, an operating system based on the UNIX system. Written in C, COHERENT contains many UNIX system features and is available for the DEC PDP-11. In the future it will support machines containing the 8086, Z8000, and 68000 microprocessors.

Whitesmiths, Limited
1780 Broadway, Suite 601
New York, New York 10019
(212) 799-1200

> Whitesmiths offers several software packages, including IDRIS, an operating system based on the UNIX system. IDRIS is a separate system, not just an adaptation of the UNIX system. It lies between a very simple operating system for microcomputers and UNIX system Version 7. A multiprocessing system, IDRIS offers additional functions to smaller computers.
>
> Whitesmiths also offers a C compiler, a C cross-compiler, a Pascal compiler, and a Pascal cross-compiler. Whitesmiths offers software for the PDP-11, 68000, 8080, Z80, and other processors. A catalog is available from the company.

Manufacturers Offering Systems
Based on the UNIX System

Charles River Data Systems, Inc.
4 Tech Circle
Natick, Massachusetts 01760
(617) 655-1800

> Charles River Data Systems offers an operating system based on the UNIX system, written in C, on their 68000-based microcomputer. Compatible with the UNIX operating system, it includes extensions.

Chromatics, Inc.
2558 Mountain Industrial Boulevard
Tucker, Georgia 30084
(404) 493-7000

> The CGC 7900 desk-top computer, based on the 68000 microprocessor, uses Whitesmiths' IDRIS operating system. The color CRT and other system features support color graphics applications.

Computhink
965 West Maude Avenue
Sunnyvale, California 94086
(408) 245-4033

> Computhink's 68000-based Eagle 32 computer runs under Whitesmiths' IDRIS.

Cromemco, Inc.
280 Bernardo Avenue
Mountain View, California 94043
(415) 964-7400

> Cromemco offers CROMIX, an inexpensive operating system based on the UNIX system, for its microcomputer. To the user, CROMIX looks similar to the UNIX system and includes many similar functions. A separate bank of memory (64K) is required for each user on the system, and one for the system itself.

Ithaca Intersystems Incorporated
P.O. Box 91
Ithaca, NY 14850
(607) 257-0190

> Ithaca Intersystems offers a Z8000-based microcomputer with Mark Williams Company's COHERENT, an operating system based on the UNIX system. The machine allows up to 128K per user and a selection of disk storage sizes.

Morrow Designs
5221 Central Avenue
Richmond, California 94804
(415) 524-2101

> Morrow Designs offers a Z80-based system with their own operating system, M/OS, which is based on the UNIX operating system.

Communications with UNIX Software

> Several vendors offer unique network packages with the UNIX system, many of which are proprietary. Companies are introducing products rapidly, and this is a partial list of available UNIX system networking facilities. Communications with UNIX software are shown in Table E-5 of Appendix E.

Sytek, Inc.
1153 Bordeaux Drive
Sunnyvale, California 94086
(408) 734-9000

> Sytek offers a local network called "LocalNet," a local data communications system that connects intelligent and "dumb" terminals. LocalNet provides a data communications interface with the UNIX operating system.

3COM Corporation
1390 Shorebird Way
Mountain View, California 94043
(415) 961-9602

> Bob Metcalfe, a developer of the Ethernet network standard, started 3COM Corporation. 3COM's UNET software provides Ethernet-compatible communication among computers running the UNIX operating system. UNET transfers files, connects remote terminals, and carries electronic mail. 3COM Corporation has a mutual marketing agreement with Microsoft.

Software Catalogs

Several companies offer catalogs of software related to the UNIX system. They are detailed in this section, and compared in Table A-6 of Appendix A.

Intelligent Decisions, Inc.
6424 Myrtlewood Drive
Cupertino, California 95014
(408) 996-2399

This company offers a catalog of software tools, university-developed products, and public domain software that operates in the UNIX system or allows you to emulate the UNIX system under other operating systems. Published twice a year, the catalog describes the UNIX software available from universities and tells how to get it.

Lifeboat Associates
1651 Third Avenue
New York, New York 10028
(212) 860-0300

Lifeboat Associates distributes software worldwide, including tiny-c, BDSC, and the Whitesmiths compiler, on all CP/M disk formats.

Accounting Software

Presented here is a subset of currently available applications packages for the UNIX operating system, including accounting, data base, text processing, and utilities. This list is expanding greatly, and will be much larger within six months. Table A-7 in Appendix A compares the packages discussed here.

American Business Systems, Inc.

439 Littleton Road
Westford, Massachusetts 01886
(617) 486-3509

American Business Systems, known for their accounting software for the Oasis and CP/M operating systems, now offers a series of accounting modules for the UNIX system. Written in COBOL, the software runs on Z8000-based computers and is available on the Onyx C8002. The programs are available in single-user, single-tasking form. Multitasking, multi-user versions are scheduled for future release.

Cybernetics, Incorporated

8041 Newman Avenue, Suite 208
Huntington Beach, California 92647
(714) 848-1922

Cybernetics sells accounting packages written in COBOL that operate in the UNIX system.

Open Systems

430 Oak Grove
Suite 409
Minneapolis, Minnesota 55403
(612) 870-3515

Open Systems offers a set of accounting programs written in RM-COBOL. The products run on the Onyx 8002 computer with the UNIX operating system. Programs include accounts receivable, accounts payable, general ledger, inventory, payroll, and job costing. The software has been installed in many small- to medium-sized businesses which make $500,000 to $30 million a year in sales. The package includes a built-in report generator, and a source code program. The software runs largely independent of the UNIX system and does not utilize the features of the UNIX operating system in its implementation.

Data Base Programs

Britton Lee, Inc.

90 Albright Way

Los Gatos, California 95030

(408) 378-7000

> Britton Lee offers the System 500, a back-end processor for data base applications. It implements a B-tree-index RDBUS without loading the host CPU. It runs on the PDP-11/70 with the UNIX operating system.

Logical Software, Inc.

1218 Massachusetts Avenue

Cambridge, Massachusetts 02138

(617) 864-0137

> Logical Software offers LOGIX, a relational data base management system for the UNIX system and similar systems.

Pacific Software Manufacturing Company

2608 8th Street

Berkeley, California 94710

(415) 540-5000

> Pacific Software offers Sequitur, a relational data base for the UNIX system. It includes integral text editing and report generation facilities.

Rhodnius Inc.

P. O. Box 1, Station D

Scarborough, Ontario, Canada M1R4Y7

(416) 922-1743

> Rhodnius offers a relational data base management system called Mistress. It includes a superset of a query language, and a host-language interface. The company continues to enhance and develop its product.

The data base runs on PDP-11 and LSI-11 computers under the UNIX operating system.

Utilities

Human Computing Resources Corporation
10 St. Mary Street
Toronto, Ontario, Canada M4Y1PG
(416) 922-1937

Human Computing Resources offers the XENIX operating system on PDP-11 hardware and a number of utility programs, including MAP, MAP-300, and RT-EMT. These utility tools support programmers working in the UNIX operating system or transporting to different machines. HCR also offers text overlay conversion tools to install the UNIX system on small machines.

Interactive Systems Corporation
1212 7th Street
Santa Monica, California 90401
(213) 450-8363

Interactive Systems offers its version of Programmer's Workbench, networking electronic mail and remote communications programs for the UNIX operating system.

System Kontakt Inc.
6 Preston Court
Bedford, Massachusetts 07130
(617) 275-2333

System Kontakt offers macro cross-assemblers, simulators, linkers, and Pascal compilers for 8- and 16-bit microprocessors. Available software runs on the UNIX and DEC operating systems, although a $1,400 surcharge is levied if the product is purchased for the UNIX operating system.

Text Processing

Interactive Systems Corporation
1212 7th Street
Santa Monica, California 90401
(213) 450-8363

> Interactive Systems offers enhanced text processing for the UNIX operating system, including a special terminal that enhances operation of the software.

Mark of the Unicorn
P.O. Box 423
Arlington, Massachusetts 02174
(617) 489-1387

> Mark of the Unicorn offers Amethyst, a user-reconfigurable word processing package written in BDS C. An editor called Mince is based on mainframe editing software and includes split-screen and cross-document editing. A formatter called Scribble uses macro-commands for functions such as beginning a new chapter and creating a footnote. Scribble automatically numbers chapters and sections, creates a table of contents, and revises these as the document changes.

Technical Type and Composition
6443 Lardon Road
Salem, Oregon 97303
(503) 371-8655

> This company offers phototypesetting programs for the UNIX system; 160 faces in 250 fonts are available, and custom fonts can be manufactured. The programs can work directly from tp files with -t codes; from nroff or troff files, adding kerning, ligatures, and hyphenation (includes a 120K-word dictionary); or from sources other than the UNIX system. Media include a nine-track tape; RX01, 3740, RL01, and PM11 disks; and OCR B.

The C Language for Microcomputers

Numerous C compilers are available today, on computers that use the CP/M operating system as well as the UNIX operating system. If you own a microcomputer, and are considering replacing CP/M with the UNIX system, you might first test out the C language by purchasing one of those products. For that reason, we include information on C compilers for CP/M-based machines as well as machines based on the UNIX system. The products described here are compared in Table A-8 in Appendix A.

Alcyon Corporation

8474 Commerce Avenue
San Diego, California 92121
(714) 578-0860

Alcyon Corporation is developing a system based on the UNIX system for a 68000-based computer. Alcyon currently offers a PDP-11 to 68000 C-compiler and related utilities.

The Code Works

5266 Hollister Avenue
Suite 224
Santa Barbara, California 93111
(805) 683-1585

The Code Works offers a product called Small-C for the CP/M operating system. The software is $15 for disk plus documentation. It is a partial implementation of the C compiler.

Computer Innovations

75 Pine Street
Lincroft, New Jersey 07738
(201) 530-0995

A C compiler for CP/M 86 is available from this company. It requires 64K of memory.

Relational Software Inc.
3000 Sand Hill Road
Menlo Park, California 94025
(415) 854-7350

> Relational Software offers a C compiler for the IBM 370, 4300, and Series 30 computers. This company will offer or support the UNIX system on the same machines. They offer a data base program as well.

Ron Cain
811 11th Avenue
Redwood City, California 94063
(415) 321-2041

> Ron Cain's small-c compiler, which was published in "Doctor Dobb's Journal," supports a small subset of the language. The subset is distributed by Lifeboat Associates.

The Software Toolworks
14478 Glorietta Drive
Sherman Oaks, California 91423
(213) 986-4885

> The Software Toolworks offers the small-c compiler, and also sells macroassemblers, a text formatter, a full-screen editor, a LISP interpreter, and some games, all written in C. Many are specifically written for Heathkit machines.

Supersoft Associates
P.O. Box 1628
Champaign, Illinois 61820
(217) 359-2112

> Supersoft Associates offers a C compiler that supports most of UNIX system V7 standard C. It is a two-pass compiler, and comes with source code to the I/O libraries. It runs in the CP/M operating system.

tiny-c associates
P.O. Box 269
Holmdel, New Jersey 07733
(201) 671-2296

> Tiny-c associates offers a very small subset of C. It is a low-cost educational tool for those starting to explore the C language. It is an

interpreter that also provides an environment for fast program development. The newest tiny-c product is a compiler. It has more features of the full language, and supports I/O redirection. Tiny-c is available in source code version, and in formats for many machines.

Languages for the UNIX System

Many languages are available for the UNIX system. We describe a subset of the languages available from independent vendors. Some companies only offer languages when you purchase their computer hardware. Table A-9 of Appendix A compares these products.

Human Computing Resources Corporation
10 St. Mary Street
Toronto, Ontario, Canada M4Y1PG
(416) 922-1937

Human Computing Resources offers HCR/BASIC for the UNIX operating system with the PDP-11 computer, and offers MAPL, a preprocessor language for the PDP-11, as well.

Interactive Systems Corporation
1212 7th Street
Santa Monica, California 90401
(213) 450-8363

Interactive Systems offers FORTRAN and other languages for the UNIX operating system on the PDP-11 and Onyx computers.

Micro Focus Incorporated
1601 Civic Center Drive
Santa Clara, California 95050
(408) 248-3982

Micro Focus offers CIS COBOL for the CP/M and UNIX operating systems. They also offer a report generator package.

Ryan McFarland Corporation
609 Deep Valley Drive
Rolling Hills Estates, California 90274
(213) 541-4828

Ryan McFarland Corporation offers RMCOBOL for the UNIX operating system. A popular version of COBOL, it has been used by many accounting software vendors for their packages. Their customers are mostly OEMs and computer manufacturers.

System Kontakt Inc.
6 Preston Court
Bedford, Massachusetts 07130
(617) 275-2333

System Kontakt offers Pascal for the UNIX operating system.

Newsletters, User Groups, and Educational Facilities

Amethyst Users Group
P.O. Box 8173
University Station
Austin, Texas 78712
(512) 441-9466

This group is for users of a proprietary text processing and formatting system that is written in C and runs under the UNIX system. A monthly newsletter promotes software exchanges. Membership rates include the newsletter: US $6 per year, $8 outside North America. The group consists mostly of programmers.

Australian UNIX Users Group

c/o Peter Ivanov
Computer Science
Electric Engineering
University of New South Wales
P.O. Box 1
Kensington 2033
Australia

> This is a general user group that offers a bimonthly newsletter.

BDS C Users Group

c/o Robert Ward
409 East Kansas
Yates Center, Kansas 66783
(316) 625-3554

> Robert Ward is the coordinator for disseminating programs of interest
> to users of the BDS C compiler and other C material available on the
> CP/M operating system. A bimonthly newsletter is published.

Bell Laboratories

600 Mountain Avenue
Murray Hill, New Jersey 07974
(201) 582-3000

> Bell Laboratories is the home of the UNIX system and the C language,
> but this is not where you buy UNIX software. UNIX software may be
> purchased from Western Electric. The founders of the operating
> system — Brian Kernighan, Ken Thompson, and Dennis Ritchie — and
> other Bell Telephone staff members associated with the operating
> system can be contacted at this address.

Canadian UNIX SIG

c/o Human Computing Resources Corporation
10 Saint Mary Street
Toronto, Ontario
Canada M4Y 1P9

> This is a general user group offering a newsletter, software exchanges,
> and meetings. It is affiliated with Decus.

European UNIX User Group
Administrative: c/o R.A. Mason
Computer Engineering
Heriot-Watt University
Mountbatten Building
31-35 Grassmarket
Edinburgh EH1 2HT
Scotland

Newsletter: c/o Jim McKie, UNIX Support Officer
Edinburgh Regional Computing Centre
c/o EdCAAD
20 Chambers Street
Edinburgh
Scotland

> This is a general user group that provides quarterly newsletters, software exchanges, and conferences. Membership is restricted to institutions and presently requires the UNIX system source license. The group developed from the UK group which had been affiliated with Decus. The newsletter exceeds 100 pages per issue.

Gnostic Concepts, Inc.
2710 Sand Hill Road
Menlo Park, California 94025
(415) 854-4672

> Gnostic Concepts' UNIX System Information Service is a continuing program of market research on the UNIX operating system. The yearly fee is $18,000 and includes six reports, telephone inquiry privileges, and a one-day presentation. Gnostic Concepts also offers custom and multi-client market research on the UNIX system and other areas of the electronics industry. The authors of this book manage Gnostic Concepts' UNIX System Information Service.

InfoPro Systems
P. O. Box 33
East Hanover, New Jersey 07936
(201) 625-2925

> InfoPro Systems publishes a monthly newsletter entitled "UNIQUE: Your Independent UNIX and C Advisor." The newsleter is oriented toward both

new and experienced users of the UNIX system. "UNIQUE" covers UNIX and UNIX-like computer hardware, software written in C (and other languages that run on UNIX), and related services offered by consulting and educational firms and user groups. Coverage includes pricing, technical details, and product analysis.

The staff does periodic evaluation of software and hardware submitted by manufacturers for this purpose. Feature articles, industry news and rumors, and tutorials on UNIX-related subjects are presented. As a matter of editorial policy, commercial advertising is not accepted. The Uni-Ops official newsletter, "Pipes and Filters," is also included as part of "UNIQUE."

Instrumentation Interface Incorporated
P. O. Box 22411
San Francisco, California 94122
(415) 664-6401

Jean Yates and Rebecca Thomas, the authors of this book, are Instrumentation Interface. We welcome your comments and suggestions. We also write manuals for computers and software and manage the UNIX Information Service for Gnostic Concepts.

Software Tools Users Group
1259 El Camino Real, O242
Menlo Park, California 94025

Dedicated to the concepts in Kernighan and Plauger's book, *Software Tools,* this group offers a quarterly newsletter, software exchanges, and semi-annual conferences. Currently, membership is free. The group grew from a nucleus of users at Lawrence Berkeley Laboratory.

University of California at Berkeley
Department of Computing Services
215 Evans Hall
Berkeley, California 94720

The University of California at Berkeley maintains one of the largest UNIX system facilities in the world. It includes a network of six DEC PDP-11/70 computers and one VAX computer. The computing services group offers time-sharing into the UNIX system for educational or research purposes. Non-students cannot obtain access to the Berkeley computer, but a subscription to the computing services newsletter is useful. The newsletter provides both specific information for the Berkeley campus community and general information on the UNIX system. It lists a series of frequently offered introductory courses. The University offers documentation through its library, and copies of many of the Bell Laboratories articles can be purchased from the Computing Services Center. In addition, the University offers reference cards for specific programs.

Urban Software Corporation
19 West 34th Street
New York, New York 10001
(212) 947-3811

A C-based software vendor, Urban Software occasionally publishes a free newsletter. It contains numerous articles of interest to prospective UNIX system microcomputer users.

Usenix Association
Box 8, The Rockefeller University
12330 York Avenue
New York, New York 10021
(212) 360-1182

This organization is the oldest UNIX system user group. It is oriented toward educational and research environments. USENIX conducts two conferences each year and mails a periodic newsletter to its members. Much of the material available from USENIX is specific to the PDP-11.

/usr/group
P. O. Box 8570
Stanford, California 94305-0221
(408) 988-1755

This UNIX system user group is oriented toward vendors of products related to the UNIX system. They offer a periodic newsletter, "CommUNIX™ations," and conferences.

Walter Zintz's Uni-Ops
P.O. Box 5182
Walnut Creek, California 94596
(415) 933-8564

Uni-Ops is a user group for beginners and experienced users of the UNIX system and related products. Membership in Uni-Ops includes subscription to its newsletter, "Pipes and Filters." The company also offers a mailing list program for the UNIX system, and periodic meetings and tutorials.

Seminars

DJR Associates
340 East 66th Street
New York, New York 10021
(212) 421-3700

> In the New York area, DJR runs training courses covering the UNIX system, the C language, and related subjects.

International Technical Seminars
2000 Center Street
Suite 1036
Berkeley, California 94704
(415) 621-6415

> International Technical Seminars offers documentation, reference cards, and presentations on the UNIX system and related topics.

Plum Hall, Inc.
303 Forest Drive
Edison, New Jersey 08817
(201) 572-1017

> Plum Hall offers an Operating System Workshop dealing both with the UNIX system and IDRIS, Whitesmiths' version of the UNIX system. Whitesmiths Ltd. cooperates with Plum Hall on the introductory level workshop, which presupposes no previous experience with the UNIX system or computers. An advanced course on the C language is also offered by Plum Hall.

Structured Methods Incorporated
7 West 18th Street
New York, NY 10011
(212) 741-7720

> Structured Methods gives seminars on UNIX software and the C language in New York and other large cities.

Technical Consulting _____

The Perchwell Corporation
56 Cliffside Trail
Denville, New Jersey 07834
(201) 625-1797

> The Perchwell Corporation provides management and technical consulting services for firms becoming actively involved with the UNIX operating system. Custom studies, in-house training, technology forecasts, software guidance, and advice on product planning and positioning are made available to companies competing in the UNIX marketplace.

Time-Sharing _____

International Data Services, Inc.
1020 Stewart Drive
Sunnyvale, California 94086
(408) 738-3368

> International Data Services offers time-sharing on its PDP-11/70 for local users. IDS also offers consulting and training services.

Marketing Information Institute, Inc.
861 Sixth Avenue, Suite 510
San Diego, California 92101
(714) 231-8939

> Marketing Information Institute offers a PDP-11/45 minicomputer with floating point, 128K of memory, 160M hard disk, three phone ports, RS 232C, 300/1200 baud modems, 800 bpi tape, card reader, and dot matrix and daisy wheel printers. The system runs under UNIX system V7.

RLG Corporation
1760 Reston Avenue
Reston, Virginia 22090
(703) 471-6860

> RLG offers UNIX system time-sharing as a commercial product. RLG also offers data base management, an office automation system called OPUS, various screen editors, and graphics programs. The company also conducts training courses.

APPENDICES

TABLES OF
UNIX SYSTEM RESOURCES

Appendix A

TABLE A-1: UNIX System Licensees

Operating System Name †	Supplier	Computer	CPU
EUNIX	Electronic Info Systems, Inc.	PDP-11	*
IS/1	Interactive Systems, Inc.	PDP-11 line Onyx	* Z8000
XENIX	Microsoft Corp.	Codata, Altos Others	Z8000 8086 68000
UNIX V7	UniSoft		68000
UNIX V7	Western Electric Corp.	PDP-11, VAX	*
UNIX V7	Wollongong Group, Inc.	All Perkin-Elmer 32-bit systems	*

† Many vendors call *their* supported version of Version 7 of the UNIX system by a special trade name. The products listed here are still licensed from Western Electric.

* Proprietary

TABLE A-2: Computer Manufacturers and System Houses
Selling Computers with the UNIX System

Hardware Manufacturer	Hardware System	CPU	Software Support	Software	System Vendor
Amdahl	VM/370	*	Amdahl	UTS	Amdahl
BBN Computer	C Machine	*	BBN	UNIX	BBN
CM Technologies	CMS-16DS2 CMS-16XNX	68000	Microsoft	XENIX	CM Technologies
Codata Systems Corp.	CTS-200/6 CTS-300/6	Z8000 68000	Microsoft	XENIX	Codata Systems Corp.
Data Resources Inc.	Drilink	Z8000	Data Resources Inc.	UNIX V7	Data Resources Inc.
DEC	PDP-11	*	Uniq Computer Corp.	UNIX	Uniq Computer Corp.
	PDP-11	*	Interactive Systems	ID/5	Interactive Systems
	PDP-11	*	Computer Consoles Inc.	UNIX Inc.	Computer Consoles Inc.
	PDP-11	*	Human Computing Resources Inc.	XENIX	Human Computing Resources Inc.
Dual Systems	68KS-7 68KS-8	68000	Dual Systems	UNIX V7 Systems	Dual
MicroDaSys	68K Miniframe	68000	Microsoft MicroDaSys	XENIX VENIX	MicroDaSys
Onyx	C8002	Z8000	Interactive	IS/1	Interactive Systems, Onyx
Perkin-Elmer	32-bit machines	*	Wollongong	UNIX	Perkin-Elmer
Plexus	P/40	Z8000	Plexus	UNIX V7	Plexus
Wicat Systems	150 & 100	68000	Interactive	UNIX	Wicat Systems
Zilog	System 8000	Z8000	Zilog	ZEUS	Zilog
* Proprietary					

TABLE A-3: Operating Systems Similar to the UNIX System ††

System Name	Manufacturer	Computer	CPU	Comments
Unica	Knowlogy	CP/M	Z80	Adds UNIX systems features to CP/M
Coherent	Mark Williams Company	PDP-ll	*	Available on 16-bit micro-processors
OS-1	Software Labs	CP/M systems	Z80	Single user
Marc	Vortex Technology	CP/M systems	Z80	Written in BDS-C
IDRIS	Whitesmiths Ltd.	68000 PDP-11	68000 *	Multi-user

†† These operating systems have characteristics of the UNIX system from Western Electric, but are different programs. The vendors pay no royalties to Western Electric, and their products are not supported by or related to vendors selling the UNIX system under another name (like XENIX or ZEUS).

* Proprietary

TABLE A-4: Computer Systems with Operating Systems Similar to the UNIX System

Hardware Manufacturer	Hardware System	CPU	Software Support	Software	System Vendor
Charles River Data Systems (CRDS)	CRDS	68000	CRDS	JOS	CRDS
Chromatics	CGC 7900	68000	Whitesmiths	IDRIS	Chromatics
Computhink	Eagle 32	68000	Whitesmiths	IDRIS	Computhink
Cromemco	System One	Z80	Cromemco	Cromix	Cromemco
Ithaca Intersystems Inc.	DPS 8000	Z8000	Mark Williams Co.	Coherent	Ithaca Intersystems Inc.
Morrow Designs	Decision 1 Designs	Z80	Morrow Designs	M/OS	Morrow

TABLE A-5: Communications with UNIX Software

Product Name	Developer	Operating System	CPU	Comments
FTP	Interactive	IS/1	PDP-11	File transfer between systems
Connect	Interactive	IS/1	PDP-11	Terminal to port connecting software
Local Net	Sytek	UNIX V7	various	Data communication interface for intelligent and dumb terminal to UNIX system
UNET	3COM	UNIX V7	various	Ethernet-compatible Communications for computers using UNIX system; file transfer, electronic mail

TABLE A-6: Catalogs of Software

Vendor	Product	Notes
Intelligent Decisions Inc.	Catalog of software tools	Specialize in public domain products, university-developed software
Lifeboat Associates	Software Catalog	CP/M and XENIX-related software; Sell several C compilers

TABLE A-7: Application Programs for the UNIX Operating System

	Product Name	Developer	Operating System	CPU	Comments
Accounting	GL, AR, AP Payroll	American Business Systems Inc.	UNIX	Z8000	Other microprocessor versions under development
	GL, AR, AP Payroll	Cybernetics Inc.	UNIX	PDP-11, Z8000	
	GL, AR, AP Payroll, Job costing	Open Systems	UNIX	Z8000, PDP-11	Includes source code, report generator
Data Base	IDM 500	Britton Lee Inc.	UNIX	PDP-11/70	Hardware/software combination of RDBMS and backend processor
	Logix	Logical Software Inc.	UNIX		Relational data base
	SEQUITUR	Pacific Software	UNIX	PDP-11, Onyx	Relational
	MISTRESS	Rhodnius, Inc.	UNIX	PDP-11	Relational data base
Medical	MED-IX	Medical Micro-Systems, Inc.	CP/M UNIX	Z8000	
Utilities	MAP	HCRC	UNIX	PDP-11	Converts CSPI SNAP-11 software to UNIX software, in C and FORTRAN
	MAP-300 driver	HCRC	UNIX V6		Interfaces MAP hardware to UNIX operating system
	RT/EMT	HCRC	UNIX	PDP-11	Allows RT-11 software development under UNIX operating system

TABLE A-7: Application Programs for the UNIX Operating System (Continued)

	Product Name	Developer	Operating System	CPU	Comments
Utilities (Continued)	Text overlay conversion tools	HCRC	UNIX	PDP-11	Assists in installing UNIX software on small machines and V6-to-V7 conversions
	IS/1 Workbench	Interactive	IS/1	PDP-11	PWB supported by Interactive Systems
	INnet network mail	Interactive	IS/1	PDP-11	Electronic mail between networked computers
	INmail	Interactive	IS/1	PDP-11 VAX	Electronic mail for a single system
	INremote/ HASP	Interactive	IS/1	System 360, 370	Remote job entry for IBM machines
	Various	System Kontakt Inc.	CP/M UNIX	Z80 Z8000	Cross assemblers and compilers
	Tools	The Toolsmith	CP/M	Z80	CP/M software tools
Text Editing and Print Formatting	INtext II	Interactive	IS/1	PDP-11	Terminal configured for INed and INword
	INed Editor	Interactive	IS/1	PDP-11	Text editor (screen-oriented)
	INword WP	Interactive	IS/1	PDP-11	Text formatter for printing
	INcompose	Interactive	IS/1	PDP-11	Text formatter for typesetting
	Amethyst	Mark of the Unicorn	CP/M	Z80	Text editor for CP/M written in C
	Phototype-setting	Technical Type & Composition	UNIX		Typesetting of TROFF files

TABLE A-8: The C Language

Language	Developer	Operating System	CPUs	Comments
C Compiler	Alcyon Corporation	UNIX	PDP-11 68000	Cross-compiler PDP-11 to 68000
small C	The Code Works	CP/M	Z80	Partial implementation
C compiler	Computer Innovations	CP/M 86	8086	
C Compiler	Interactive	IS/1	PDP-11, VAX	PDP-11 to Z8000 Cross-compiler
C Compiler	Relational Software Inc.	UNIX	IBM 370, 4300, Series 30	Data base program also
C compiler	Ron Cain	CP/M	Z80	Partial
small C	The Software Toolworks	CP/M	Z80	Heathkit-specific
C Compiler	Supersoft Associates	CP/M	Z80	
C Compiler	tiny-c associates	CP/M	Z80	Subset of C

TABLE A-9: Languages Available for the UNIX Operating System

	Language	Developer	System	Operating CPU	Comments
COBOL	Micro-COBOL	Micro Focus Ltd.	UNIX	PDP-11	
	COBOL	Ryan McFarland Corp.	UNIX	PDP-11	Z8000
BASIC	HCR/BASIC	HCRC	UNIX	PDP-11	
FORTRAN	FORTRAN	Interactive	IS/1	PDP-11	Code-compatible with C compiler
MAP Preprocessor Language	MAPL	HCRC	RT-11	'PDP-11	Interface MAP array processor to FORTRAN, C, or Pascal
Pascal	Pascal	System Kontakt	misc.	misc.	Pascal compilers for many machines

TABLE A-10: Newsletters, User Groups and Educational Materials
for the UNIX System

Company	Product	Comments
Amethyst Users Group	Newsletter and software exchange	
BDS C Users Group	Newsletter, programs	
Canadian UNIX Sig	Market research	UNIX system information service
Gnostic Concepts		
Human Computing Resources Corp.		
Heriot-Watt University, Scotland	European UNIX User Group	
Interface, Inc.	Manuals, books, consulting	
InfoPro Systems	UNIX Software list	Also have occasional newsletter
Lawrence Berkeley Labs	Software tools user group	
University of California at Berkeley	Introductory courses	Limited space for non-students
University of New South Wales	Australian UNIX Users Group	
Urban Software Corporation	Newsletter	
Usenix Association	User group	Technically oriented
/usr/group	User group	Newsletter
Walter Zintz' Uni-Ops	User group	Newsletter, seminars

TABLE A-11: Seminars

Company	Product	Comments
DJR Associates	Seminars	The UNIX system and C language
International Technical Seminars	Seminars, documentation	
Plum Hall Inc.	Seminars	C language and UNIX system
Structured Methods, Inc.	Seminars	5-day seminar on C language; 2-day seminar on UNIX system

TABLE A-12: Commercial Time-Sharing Access to the UNIX System

Company	Location	Operating System	Comments
International Data Services	Sunnyvale, CA	UNIX V7	PDP-11 or Onyx computers
Jeff Schreibman Consulting	Berkeley, CA	UNIX V7	Offers Z8000 and 68000 cross-compilers
RLG Corp.	Washington, DC	UNIX V6	Minimum monthly fee of $100.00
Marketing Information Institute	San Diego, CA	UNIX V7	Local only
Various universities across the United States have time-sharing available for educational purposes. Check with your local college for information. In general, only students qualify.			

A SUMMARY OF THE
UNIX SYSTEM VERSION 7

Appendix B

Basic Software

Basic software includes the time-sharing operating system with utilities, a machine language assembler, and a compiler for the programming language C — enough software to write and run new applications and to maintain or modify the UNIX system itself.

Operating System

UNIX The basic resident code on which everything else depends. Supports the system calls, and maintains the file system. A general description of the UNIX system design philosophy and system facilities appeared in *Communications of the ACM,* July 1974. A more extensive survey is in the *Bell System Technical Journal* for July-August 1978. Capabilities include the following:

- Reentrant code of user processes
- Separate instruction and data spaces
- "Group" access permissions for cooperative projects, with overlapping memberships
- Alarm-clock timeouts
- Timer-interrupt sampling and interprocess monitoring for debugging and measurement
- Multiplexed I/O for machine-to-machine communication.

DEVICES   All I/O is logically synchronous. I/O devices are simply files in the file system. Normally, invisible buffering makes all physical record structure and device characteristics transparent, and exploits the hardware's ability to do overlapped I/O. Unbuffered physical record I/O is available for unusual applications. Drivers for these devices are available; others can be easily written. The devices are

- Asynchronous interfaces: DH11, DL11. Support for most common ASCII terminals

- Synchronous interface: DP11

- Automatic calling unit interface: DN11

- Line printer: LP11

- Magnetic tape: TU10 and TU16

- DECtape: TC11

- Fixed head disk: RS11, RS03 and RS04

- Pack-type disk: RP03, RP04, RP06; minimum-latency seek scheduling

- Cartridge-type disk: RK05, one or more physical devices per logical device

- Null device

- Physical memory of PDP-11, or mapped memory in resident system

- Phototypesetter: Graphic Systems System/1 through DR11C.

BOOT   Procedures to get the UNIX system started.

MKCONF   Tailor device-dependent system code to hardware configuration. As distributed, the UNIX system can be brought up directly on any acceptable CPU with any acceptable disk, any sufficient amount of core, and either clock. Other changes, such as optimal assignment of directories to devices, inclusion of floating point simulator, or installation of device names in file system, can then be made at leisure.

User Access Control

LOGIN Sign on as a new user.

Verify password and establish user's individual and group (project) identity

- Adapt to characteristics of terminal
- Establish working directory
- Announce presence of mail (from MAIL)
- Publish message of the day
- Execute user-specified profile
- Start command interpreter or other initial program.

PASSWD Change a password.

- User can change his own password
- Passwords are kept encrypted for security.

NEWGRP Change working group (project). Protects against unauthorized changes to projects.

Terminal Handling

TABS Set tab stops appropriately for specified terminal type.

STTY Set up options for optimal control of a terminal. Insofar as they are deducible from the input, these options are set automatically by LOGIN.

- Half vs. full duplex
- Carriage return + line feed vs. newline
- Interpretation of tabs
- Parity
- Mapping of upper-case to lower-case
- Raw vs. edited input
- Delays for tabs, newlines and carriage returns.

File Manipulation

CAT   Concatenate one or more files onto standard output. Particularly used for unadorned printing, inserting data into a pipeline, and buffering output that comes little by little. Works on any file regardless of contents.

CP   Copy one file to another, or a set of files to a directory. Works on any file regardless of contents.

PR   Print files with title, date, and page number on every page.
- Multi-column output
- Parallel column merge of several files.

LPR   Off-line print. Spools arbitrary files to the line printer.

CMP   Compare two files and report if different.

TAIL   Print last *n* lines of input.
- May print last *n* characters, or from *n* lines or characters to end.

SPLIT   Split a large file into more manageable pieces. Occasionally necessary for editing (ED).

DD   Physical file format translator for exchanging data with foreign systems, especially IBM 370s.

SUM   Sum the words of a file.

Manipulation of Directories and Filenames

RM   Remove a file. Only the name goes away if any other names are linked to the file.
- Step through a directory, deleting files interactively
- Delete entire directory hierarchies.

LN   "Link" another name (alias) to an existing file.

MV   Move a file or files. Used for renaming files.

CHMOD   Change permissions on one or more files. Executable by owner of files.

CHOWN   Change owner of one or more files.

CHGRP   Change group (project) to which a file belongs.

MKDIR   Make a new directory.

RMDIR   Remove a directory.

CD   Change working directory.

FIND   Search the directory hierarchy, finding every file that meets specified criteria.

- Criteria include the following: name matches a given pattern, creation date in a given range, date of last use in a given range, given permissions, given owner, Boolean combinations of above
- Any directory may be considered to be the root
- Perform specified command on each file found.

Running Programs

SH   The shell, or command language interpreter.

- Supply arguments to and run any executable program
- Redirect standard input, standard output, and standard error files
- Pipes: simultaneous execution with output of one process connected to the input of another
- Compose compound commands using the following:
  if ... then ... else; case switches; while loops; for loops over lists; break, continue, and exit; parentheses for grouping
- Initiate background processes
- Perform shell programs, i.e., command scripts with substitutable arguments
- Construct argument lists from all filenames satisfying specified patterns

• Take special action on traps and interrupts
• User-settable search path for finding commands
• Executes user-settable profile upon login
• Optionally announces presence of mail as it arrives
• Provides variables and parameters with default setting.

TEST   Tests for use in shell conditionals.

• String comparison
• File nature and accessibility
• Boolean combinations of the above.

EXPR   String computations for calculating command arguments.

• Integer arithmetic
• Pattern matching.

WAIT   Wait for termination of asychronously running processes.

READ   Read a line from terminal, for interactive shell procedure.

ECHO   Print remainder of command line. Useful for diagnostics or prompts in shell programs, or for inserting data into a pipeline.

SLEEP   Suspend execution for a specified time.

NOHUP   Run a command immune to hanging up the terminal.

NICE   Run a command in low (or high) priority.

KILL   Terminate named processes.

CRON   Schedule regular actions at specified times.

• Actions are arbitrary programs
• Times are conjunctions of month, day of month, day of week, hour, and minute. Ranges may be specified for each.

AT   Schedule a one-shot action for an arbitrary time.

TEE   Pass data between processes and divert a copy into one or more files.

Status Inquiries

LS   List the names of one, several, or all files in one or more directories.
- Alphabetic or temporal sorting, up or down
- Optional information: size, owner, group, date last modified, date last accessed, permissions, i-node number.

FILE   Try to determine what kind of information is in a file by consulting the file system index and by reading the file itself.

DATE   Print today's date and time. Has considerable knowledge of calendric and horological peculiarities.
- May set the UNIX system's idea of date and time.

DF   Report amount of free space on file system devices.

DU   Print a summary of total space occupied by all files in a hierarchy.

QUOT   Print summary of file space usage by user ID.

WHO   Tell who's on the system.
- List of presently logged-in users, ports, and times on
- Optional history of all logins and logouts.

PS   Report on active processes.
- List your own or everybody's processes
- Tell what commands are being executed
- Optional status information: state and scheduling information priority, attached terminal, what it's waiting for, size.

IOSTAT   Print statistics about system I/O activity.

TTY   Print name of your terminal.

PWD   Print name of your working directory.

Backup and Maintenance

MOUNT   Attach a device containing a file system to the tree of directories. Protects against nonsense arrangements.

UMOUNT Remove the file system contained on a device from the tree of directories. Protects against removing a busy device.

MKFS Make a new file system on a device.

MKNOD Make an i-node (file system entry) for a special file. Special files are physical devices, virtual devices, physical memory, etc.

TP, TAR Manage file archives on magnetic tape or DECtape. TAR is newer.

- Collect files into an archive
- Update DECtape archive by date
- Replace or delete DECtape files
- Print table of contents
- Retrieve from archive.

DUMP Dump the file system stored on a specified device, selectively by date, or indiscriminately.

RESTOR Restore a dumped file system, or selectively retrieve parts thereof.

SU Temporarily become the superuser with all the rights and privileges thereof. Requires a password.

DCHECK,
ICHECK,
NCHECK
Check consistency of file system.

- Print gross statistics: number of files, number of directories, number of special files, space used, space free
- Report duplicate use of space
- Retrieve lost space
- Report inaccessible files
- Check consistency of directories
- List names of all files.

CLRI Peremptorily remove a file and its space from a file system. Used to repair damaged file systems.

SYNC Force all outstanding I/O on the system to completion. Used to shut down gracefully.

Accounting

AC   Publish cumulative connect time report.
- Connect time by user or by day
- For all users or for selected users.

SA   Publish shell accounting report. Gives usage information on each command executed.
- Number of times used
- Total system time, user time, and elapsed time
- Optional averages and percentages
- Sorting on various fields.

Communication

MAIL   Mail a message to one or more users. Also used to read and dispose of incoming mail. The presence of mail is announced by LOGIN and optimally by SH.
- Each message can be disposed of individually
- Messages can be saved in files or forwarded.

CALENDAR   Automatic reminder service for events of today and tomorrow.

WRITE   Establish direct terminal communication with another user.

WALL   Write to all users.

MESG   Inhibit receipt of messages from WRITE and WALL.

CU   Call up another time-sharing system.
- Transparent interface to remote machine
- File transmission
- Take remote input from local file or put remote output into local file
- Remote system need not be the UNIX system.

UUCP   UNIX system-to-UNIX system copy.
- Automatic queuing until line becomes available and remote machine is up

- Copy between two remote machines
- Differences, mail, etc., between two machines.

Basic Program Development Tools

Some of these utilities are used as integral parts of the higher-level languages described in the next section.

AR Maintain archives and libraries. Combines several files into one for housekeeping efficiency.

- Create new archive
- Update archive by date
- Replace or delete files
- Print table of contents
- Retrieve from archive.

AS Assembler. Similar to PAL-11, but different in detail.

- Creates object program consisting of the following: code, possibly read-only; initialized data or read-write code; uninitialized data
- Relocatable object code is directly executable without further transformation
- Object code normally includes a symbol table
- Multiple source files
- Local labels
- Conditional assembly
- "Conditional jump" instructions become branches or branches plus jumps, depending on distance.

Library The basic run-time library. These routines are used freely by all software.

- Buffered character-by-character I/O
- Formatted input and output conversion (SCANF and PRINTF) for standard input and output, files, in-memory conversion
- Storage allocator

- Time conversions
- Password encryption
- Quicksort
- Random number generator
- Mathematical function library, including trigonometric functions and inverses, exponential, logarithmic, square root, bessel functions.

ADB   Interactive debugger.

- Post-mortem dumping
- Examination of arbitrary files, with no limit on size
- Interactive breakpoint debugging with the debugger as a separate process
- Symbolic reference to local and global variables
- Stack trace for C programs
- Output formats: 1-, 2-, or 4-byte integers in octal, decimal, or hex; single and double floating point; character and string; disassembled machine instructions
- Patching
- Searching for integer, character, or floating patterns
- Handles separated instruction and data space.

OD   Dump any file. Output options include any combination of octal or decimal by words, octal by bytes, ASCII, opcodes, hexadecimal.

- Range of dumping is controllable.

LD   Link edit. Combine relocatable object files. Insert required routines from specified libraries.

- Resulting code may be shareable
- Resulting code may have separate instruction and data spaces.

LOADER   Place object file names in proper order for loading, so that files depending on others come after them.

NM   Print the namelist (symbol table) of an object program. Provides control over the style and order of names that are printed.

SIZE   Report the core requirements of one or more object files.

STRIP   Remove the relocation and symbol table information from an object file to save space.

TIME   Run a command and report timing information on it.

PROF   Construct a profile of time spent per routine from statistics gathered by time-sampling the execution of a program. Uses floating point.

        • Subroutine call frequency and average times for C programs.

MAKE   Controls creation of large programs. Uses a control file specifying source file dependencies to make new version; uses time last changed to deduce minimum amount of work necessary.

        • Knows about CC, YACC, LEX, etc.

The UNIX System Programmer's Manual

Manual   Machine-readable version of the *UNIX™ Programmer's Manual.*

        • System overview
        • All commands
        • All system calls
        • All subroutines in C and assembler libraries
        • All devices and other special files
        • Formats of file system and kinds of files known to system software
        • Boot and maintenance procedures.

MAN   Print specified manual section on your terminal.

Computer-Aided Instruction (CAI)

LEARN   A program for interpreting CAI scripts, plus scripts for learning about the UNIX system by using it.

        • Scripts for basic files and commands, editor, advanced files and commands, EQN, MS macros, C programming language.

Languages

The C Language

CC Compile and/or link edit programs in the C language. The UNIX operating system, most of the subsystems, and C itself are written in C. For a full description of C, read *The C Programming Language,* by Brian W. Kernighan and Dennis M. Ritchie, Prentice-Hall, 1978.

- General purpose language designed for structured programming
- Data types include character, integer, float, double, points to all types, functions returning above types, arrays of all types, structures and unions of all types
- Operations intended to give machine-independent control of full machine facility, including to-memory operations and pointer arithmetic
- Macro preprocessor for parameterized code and inclusion of standard files
- All procedures recursive, with parameters by value
- Machine-independent pointer manipulation
- Object code uses full addressing capability of the PDP-11
- Runtime library gives access to all system facilities
- Definable data types
- Block structure

LINT Verifier for C programs. Reports questionable or nonportable usage such as the following: mismatched data declarations and procedure interfaces; nonportable type conversions; unused variables, unreachable code, no-effect operations; mistyped pointers; obsolete syntax.

- Full cross-module checking of separately compiled programs.

CB A beautifier for C programs. Does proper indentation and placement of braces.

FORTRAN

F77   A full compiler for ANSI Standard FORTRAN 77.

- Compatible with C and supporting tools at object level
- Optional source compatibility with FORTRAN 66
- Free format source
- Optional subscript-range checking, detection of uninitialized variables
- All widths of arithmetic: 2- and 4-byte integer; 4- and 8-byte real; 8- and 16-byte complex.

RATFOR   Ratfor adds rational control structure similar to that of C to FORTRAN.

- Compound statements
- If-else, do, for, while, repeat-until, break, next statements
- Symbolic constants
- File insertion
- Free format source
- Translation of relationals like >, >=
- Produces genuine FORTRAN to carry away
- May be used with F77.

STRUCT   Converts ordinary ugly FORTRAN in structure FORTRAN (i.e., Ratfor), using statement grouping, if-else, while, for, repeat-until.

Other Algorithmic Languages

BAS   An interactive interpreter, similar in style to BASIC. Interprets unnumbered statements immediately, numbered statements upon "run."

- Statements include comment, dump, for...next, goto, if...else...fi, list, print, prompt, return, run, save
- All calculations double precision
- Recursive function defining and calling

.Built-in functions include log, exp, sin, cos, atn, int, sqr, abs, rnd

. Escape to ED for complex program editing.

DC   Interactive programmable desk calculator. Has named storage locations as well as conventional stack for holding integers or programs.

- Unlimited precision decimal arithmetic
- Appropriate treatment of decimal fractions
- Arbitrary input and output radices, in particular binary, octal, decimal, and hexadecimal
- Reverse Polish operators are $+$, -, $*$, /, remainder, power, square root, load, store, duplicate, clear, print, enter program text, execute.

BC   A C-like interactive interface to the desk calculator DC.

- All the capabilities of DC with a high-level syntax
- Arrays and recursive functions
- Immediate evaluation of expressions and evaluation of functions upon call
- Arbitrary precision elementary functions: exp, sin, cos, atan
- Go-to-less programming.

Macroprocessing

M4   A general purpose macroprocessor.

- Stream-oriented; recognizes macros anywhere in text
- Syntax fits with functional syntax of most higher-level languages
- Can evaluate integer arithmetic expressions.

Compiler-compilers

YACC   An LR(1)-based compiler writing system. During execution of

resulting parsers, arbitrary C functions may be called to do code generation or semantic actions.
- BNF syntax specifications
- Precedence relations
- Accepts formally ambiguous grammars with non-BNF resolution rules.

LEX   Generator of lexical analyzers. Arbitrary C functions may be called upon isolation of each lexical token.

- Full regular expression, plus left and right context dependence
- Resulting lexical analyzers interface cleanly with YACC parsers.

Text Processing

Document Preparation

ED   Interactive context editor. Random access to all lines of a file.

- Find lines by number or pattern. Patterns may include the following: specified characters, don't care characters, choices among characters, repetitions of these constructs, beginning of line, end of line
- Add, delete, change, copy, move or join lines
- Permute or split contents of a line
- Replace one or all instances of a pattern within a line
- Combine or split files
- Escape to shell (command language) during editing
- Do any of above operations on every pattern-selected line in a given range
- Optional encryption for extra security.

PTX   Make a permuted (key word in context) index.

SPELL Look for spelling errors by comparing each word in a document against a word list.

- 25,000-word list includes proper names
- Handles common prefixes and suffixes
- Collects words to help tailor local spelling lists.

LOOK Search for words in dictionary that begin with specified prefix.

TYPO Look for spelling errors by a statistical technique; not limited to English.

CRYPT Encrypt and decrypt files for security.

Document Formatting

ROFF A typesetting program for terminals. Easy for nontechnical people to learn, and good for simple documents. Input consists of data lines intermixed with control lines, such as

```
.sp2    insert two lines of space
.ce     center the next line
```

ROFF is deemed to be obsolete; it is intended only for casual use.

- Justification of either or both margins
- Automatic hyphenation
- Generalized running heads and feet, with even-odd page capability, numbering, etc.
- Definable macros for frequently used control sequences (no substitutable arguments)
- All four margins and page size dynamically adjustable
- Hanging indents and one-line indents
- Absolute and relative parameter settings
- Optional legal-style numbering of output lines
- Multiple file capability
- Not usable as a filter.

TROFF, Advanced typesetting. TROFF drives a Graphic Systems photo-
NROFF typesetter; NROFF drives ASCII terminals of all types. TROFF

and NROFF style is similar to ROFF, but they are capable of much more elaborate feats of formatting when appropriately programmed. TROFF and NROFF accept the same input language.

- All ROFF capabilities available or definable
- Completely definable page format keyed to dynamically planted "interrupts" at specified lines
- Maintains several separately definable typesetting environments (e.g., one for body text, one for footnotes, and one for unusually elaborate headings)
- Arbitrary number of output pools can be combined at will
- Macros with substitutable arguments, and macros that can be invoked in mid-line
- Computation and printing of numerical quantities
- Conditional execution of macros
- Tabular layout facility
- Positions expressible in inches, centimeters, ems, points, machine units, or arithmetic combinations thereof
- Access to character-width computation for unusually difficult layout problems
- Overstrikes, built-up brackets, horizontal and vertical line drawing
- Dynamic relative or absolute positioning and size selection, globally or at the character level
- Can exploit the characteristics of the terminal being used, for approximating special characters, reverse motions, proportional spacing, etc.

The Graphic Systems typesetter has a vocabulary of several 102-character fonts (four simultaneously) in 15 sizes. TROFF provides terminal output for rough sampling of the product.

NROFF will produce multi-column output on terminals capable of reverse line feed, or through the postprocessor COL.

High programming skill is required to exploit formatting capabilities of TROFF and NROFF, although unskilled personnel can easily be trained to enter documents according to canned formats such as those provided by MS, below. TROFF and EQN are essentially identical to NROFF and NEQN, so it is usually possible to define interchangeable formats to produce approximate proof copy on terminals before actual typesetting. The prepocessors MS, TBL, and REFER are fully compatible with TROFF and NROFF.

MS   A standardized manuscript layout package for use with NROFF/TROFF.

- Page numbers and draft dates
- Automatically numbered subheads
- Footnotes
- Single or double column
- Paragraphing, display, and indentation
- Numbered equations.

EQN   A mathematical typesetting preprocessor for TROFF. Translates easily readable formulas, either in-line or displayed, into detailed typesetting instructions. Formulas are written in a style like this:

sigma sup 2 != ! over N sum from i=1 to N (x sub i - x bar)
sup 2 which produces

(*See page 14 of Programmer's Manual for formula and proper symbol to replace !*)

- Automatic calculation of size changes for subscripts, sub-subscripts, etc.
- Full vocabulary of Greek letters and special symbols, such as "gamma", "GAMMA," "integral"
- Vertical "piling" of formulas for matrices, conditional alternatives, etc.
- Integrals, sums, etc., with arbitrarily complex limits
- Diacritics: dots, double dots, hats, bars, etc.
- Easily learned by nonprogrammers and mathematical typists.

NEQN   A version of EQN for NROFF; accepts the same input language. Prepares formulas for display on any terminal that NROFF knows about, for example, those based on Diablo printing mechanism.

- Same facilities as EQN within graphical capability of terminal.

TBL   A preprocessor for NROFF/TROFF that translates simple descriptions of table layouts and contents into detailed typesetting instructions.

- Handles left- and right-justified columns, centered columns, and decimal-point alignment
- Places column titles
- Table entries can be text, which is adjusted to fit
- Can box all or parts of table.

REFER   Fills in bibliographic citations in a document from a data base (not supplied).

- References may be printed in any style, as they occur or collected at the end
- May be numbered sequentially, by name of author, etc.

TC   Simulate Graphic Systems typesetter on Tektronix 4014 scope. Useful for checking TROFF page layout before typesetting.

GREEK   Fancy printing on Diablo-mechanism terminals like DASI-300 and DASI-450, and on Tektronic 4014.

- Gives half-line forward and reverse motions
- Approximates Greek letters and other special characters by overstriking.

COL   Canonicalize files with reverse line feeds for one-pass printing.

DEROFF   Remove all TROFF commands from input.

CHECKEQ   Check document for possible errors in EQN usage.

Information Handling

SORT   Sort or merge ASCII files line by line. No limit on input size.

- Sort up or down

- Sort lexicographically or on numeric key
- Multiple keys located by delimiters or by character position
- May sort upper-case together with lower-case into dictionary order
- Optionally suppress duplicate data.

TSORT   Topological sort. Converts a partial order into a total order.

UNIQ   Collapse successive duplicate lines in a file into one line.

- Publish lines that were originally unique, duplicated, or both
- May give redundancy count for each line.

TR   Do one-to-one character translation according to an arbitrary code.

- May coalesce selected repeated characters
- May delete selected characters.

DIFF   Report line changes, additions, and deletions necessary to bring two files into agreement.

- May produce an editor script to convert one file into another
- A variant compares two new versions against one old one.

COMM   Identify common lines in two sorted files. Output in up to three columns shows lines present in first file only, present in both, and/or present in second only.

JOIN   Combine two files by joining records that have identical keys.

GREP   Print all lines in a file that satisfy a pattern, as used in the editor ED.

- May print all lines that fail to match
- May print count of hits
- May print first hit in each file.

LOOK   Binary search in sorted file for lines with specified prefix.

WC   Count the lines, "words" (strings separated by blanks), and characters in a file.

SED   Stream-oriented version of ED. Can perform a sequence of editing operations on each line of an input stream of unbounded length.
- Lines may be selected by address or range of addresses
- Control flow and conditional testing
- Multiple-output streams
- Multi-line capability.

AWK   Pattern scanning and processing language. Searches input for patterns, and performs actions on each line of input that satisfies the pattern.
- Patterns include regular expressions, arithmetic and lexicographic conditions, Boolean combinations and ranges of these
- Data treated as string or numeric as appropriate
- Can break input into fields; fields are variables
- Variables and arrays (with non-numeric subscripts)
- Full set of arithmetic operators and control flow
- Multiple output streams to files and pipes
- Output can be formatted as desired
- Multi-line capability.

Graphics

The programs in this section are predominately intended for use with Tektronix 4014 storage scopes.

GRAPH   Prepares a graph of a set of input numbers.
- Input scaled to fit standard plotting area
- Abscissae may be supplied automatically
- Control over grid style, line style, graph orientation, etc.

SPLINE   Provides a smooth curve through a set of points intended for GRAPH.

PLOT   A set of filters for printing graphs produced by GRAPH and other programs on various terminals. Filters provided for 4014, DASI terminals, Versatec printer/plotter.

Novelties, Games, and Miscellaneous Features

BACKGAMMON
A player of modest accomplishment.

CHESS   Plays good class D chess.

CHECKERS   Plays class D checkers.

BCD   Converts ASCII to card-image form.

PPT   Converts ASCII to paper tape form.

BJ   A blackjack dealer.

CUBIC   An accomplished player of 4×4×4 tic-tac-toe.

MAZE   Constructs random mazes for you to solve.

MOO   A fascinating number guessing game.

CAL   Print a calendar of specified month and year.

BANNER   Print output in huge letters.

CHING   The *I Ching*. Place your own interpretation on the output.

FORTUNE   Presents a random fortune cookie on each invocation. Limited jar of cookies included.

UNITS   Convert amounts between different scales of measurement. Knows hundreds of units. For example, how many km/sec is a parsec/megayear?

TTT   A tic-tac-toe program that learns. It never makes the same mistake twice.

ARITHMETIC   Speed and accuracy test for number facts.

FACTOR   Factor large integers.

QUIZ   Test your knowledge of Shakespeare, presidents, capitals, etc.

WUMP   Hunt the wumpus, a thrilling search in a dangerous cave.

REVERSI   A two-person board game, isomorphic to Othello®.

HANGMAN   Word-guessing game. Uses the dictionary supplied with SPELL.

FISH   Children's card-guessing game.

OCTAL EQUIVALENTS OF ASCII, FILE SYSTEM HIERARCHY

Appendix C

Octal Equivalents of the ASCII Character Set

This table is included in the UNIX system on-line software. To display the table, enter one of the following command lines:

man 7 ascii <CR>
cat /usr/pub/ascii <CR>

000	nul	001	soh	002	stx	003	etx	004	eot	005	enq	006	ack	007	bel
010	bs	011	ht	012	nl	013	vt	014	np	015	cr	016	so	017	si
020	dle	021	dc1	022	dc2	023	dc3	024	dc4	025	nak	026	syn	027	etb
030	can	031	em	032	sub	033	esc	034	fs	035	gs	036	rs	037	us
040	sp	041	!	042	"	043	#	044	$	045	%	046	&	047	'
050	(	051	)	052	*	053	+	054	,	055	–	056	.	057	/
060	0	061	1	062	2	063	3	064	4	065	5	066	6	067	7
070	8	071	9	072	:	073	;	074	<	075	=	076	>	077	?
100	@	101	A	102	B	103	C	104	D	105	E	106	F	107	G
110	H	111	I	112	J	113	K	114	L	115	M	116	N	117	O
120	P	121	Q	122	R	123	S	124	T	125	U	126	V	127	W
130	X	131	Y	132	Z	133	[	134	\	135	]	136	^	137	_
140	`	141	a	142	b	143	c	144	d	145	e	146	f	147	g
150	h	151	i	152	j	153	k	154	l	155	m	156	n	157	o
160	p	161	q	162	r	163	s	164	t	165	u	166	v	167	w
170	x	171	y	172	z	173	{	174			175	}	176	~	177	del

Reprinted from *UNIX™ Time-Sharing System: UNIX Programmer's Manual,* Seventh Edition, Volume 1, 1979, with permission from Bell Telephone Laboratories, Incorporated.

Hier: File System Hierarchy

The **hier** command is included in the UNIX system on-line documentation. To display **hier**, type "man 7 hier <CR>".

The following outline gives a quick tour through a representative directory hierarchy.

/	root	
/dev/	devices	
	console	main console, *tty*
	tty	terminals, *tty*
	cat	phototypesetter *cat*
	rp	disks, *rp, hp*
	rrp	raw disks, *rp, hp*
	. . .	
/bin/	utility programs, cf /usr/bin/	
	as	assembler first pass, cf /usr/lib/as2
	cc	C compiler executive, cf /usr/lib/c[012]
	. . .	
/lib/	object libraries and other stuff, cf /usr/lib/	
	libc.a	system calls, standard I/O, etc.
	libm.a	math routines
	libplot.a	plotting routines, *plot*
	libF77.a	Fortran runtime support
	libI77.a	Fortran I/O
	. . .	
	as2	second pass of *as*
	c[012]	passes of *cc*
	. . .	
/etc/	essential data and dangerous maintenance utilities	
	passwd	password file, *passwd*
	group	group file, *group*
	motd	message of the day, *login*
	mtab	mounted file table, *mtab*
	ddate	dump history, *dump*
	ttys	properties of terminals, *ttys*
	getty	part of *login, getty*
	init	the father of all processes, *init*
	rc	shell program to bring the system up
	cron	the clock daemon, *cron*
	mount	*mount*
	wall	*wall*
	. . .	
/tmp/	temporary files, usually on a fast device, cf /usr/tmp/	
	e	used by *ed*
	ctm	used by *cc*
	. . .	

/usr/	general-purpose directory, usually a mounted file system		
	adm/	administrative information	
		wtmp	login history, *utmp*
		messages	hardware error messages
	tracct	phototypesetter accounting, *troff*	
	vpacct	line printer accounting, *lpr*	

/usr /bin   utility programs, to keep /bin/ small
      tmp/   temporaries, to keep /tmp/ small

	stm	used by *sort*
	raster	used by *plot*
dict/	word lists, etc.	
	words	principal word list, used by *look*
	spellhist	history file for *spell*
games/		
	bj	blackjack
	hangman	
	quiz.k/	what *quiz* knows

	index	category index
	africa	countries and capitals
	. . .	

    . . .

include/	standard #includes files	
	a.out.h	object file layout, *a.out*
	stdio.h	standard I/O, *stdio*
	math.h	
	. . .	
	sys/	system-defined layouts, cf /usr/sys/h

	acct.h	process accounts, *acct*
	buf.h	internal system buffers
	. . .	

lib/	object libraries and stuff, to keep /lib/ small	
	lint[12]	subprocesses for *lint*
	llib-lc	dummy declarations for /lib/libc.a, used by *lint*
	llib-lm	dummy declarations for /lib/libc.m
	atrun	scheduler for *at*
	struct/	passes for *struct*
	. . .	
	tmac/	macros for *troff*

	tmac.an	macros for *man*
	tmacs	macros for *ms*
	. . .	

	font/	fonts for *troff*

	R	Times Roman
	B	Times Bold
	. . .	

	uucp/	progams and data for *uucp*

	L.sys	remote system names and numbers
	uucico	the real copy program
	. . .	

		suftab	table of suffixes for hyphenation, used by *troff*
		units	conversion tables for *units*
		eign	list of English words to be ignored by *ptx*
/usr/	man/	volume 1 of *UNIX Programmer's Manual, man*
		man0/	general
			intro	introduction to volume 1, *ms* format
			xx	template for manual page
		man1/	chapter 1
			as.1
			mount.1m
			. . .
		cat1/	preprinted pages for man1/
			as.1
			mount.1m
		. . .
	spool/	delayed execution files
		at/	used by *at*
		lpd/	used by *lpr*
			lock	present when line printer is active
			cf	copy of file to be printed, if necessary
			df	daemon control file, *lpd*
			tf	transient control file, while *lpr* is working
		uucp/	work files and staging area for *uucp*
			LOGFILE	summary log
			LOG.	log file for one transaction
	mail/	mailboxes for *mail*
		uid	mail file for user *uid*
		uid.lock	lock file while *uid* is receiving mail
	wd	initial working directory of a user; typically *wd* is the user's login name
		profile	set environment for *sh, environ*
		calendar	user's datebook for *calendar*
	doc	papers, mostly in volume 2 of *UNIX Programmer's Manual,* typically in *ms* format
		as/	assembler manual
		c	C manual
		. . .
	sys/	system source
		dev/	device drivers
			bio.c	common code
			cat.c	*cat*
			dh.c	DH11, *tty*
			tty	*tty*
			. . .
		conf/	hardware-dependent code
			mch.s	assembly language portion
			conf	configuration generator
			. . .

```
        h/              header (include) files
                            acct.h      acct
                            stat.h      stat
                            . . .
        sys/            source for system proper
                            main.c
                            pipe.c
                            sysent.c    system entry points
                            . . .
/usr/  src/     source programs for utilities, etc.
        cmd/            source of commands
                            as/             assembler
                              makefile                      recipe for rebuilding the assembler
                              as1?.s                        source of pass1
                            ar.c            source for ar
                            . . .
                            troff/          source for nroff and troff
                              nmake         makefile for nroff
                              tmake         makefile for troff
                              font          source for font tables, /usr/lib/font/
                                                ftR.c       Roman
                                                . . .
                            term/           terminal characteristics tables,
                                            /usr/lib/term/ tab300.c
                                                            DASI 300

                            . . .
        libc/           source for functions in /lib/libc.a
                            crt/            C runtime support
                              ldiv.s                        division into a long
                              lmul.s                        multiplication to produce long
                                                            . . .
                            csu/            startup and wrapup routines needed with
                                            every C program
                              crt0.s                        regular startup
                              mcrt0.s                       modified startup for cc −p
                            sys/            system calls
                              access.s
                              alarm.s
                              . . .
                            stdio/          standard I/O functions
                              fgets.c
                              fopen.c
                              . . .
                            gen/            other functions in
                              abs.c
                              atof.c
                              . . .
```

	compall	shell procedure to compile libc
	mklib	shell procedure to make /lib/libc.a
libI77/	source for /lib/libI77	
libF77/		
	. . .	
games/	source for /usr/games	

Reprinted from *UNIX^TM Time-Sharing System: UNIX Programmer's Manual,* Seventh Edition, Volume 1, 1979, with permission from Bell Telephone Laboratories, Incorporated.

ANNOTATED BIBLIOGRAPHY

Appendix D

General Information: UNIX System Products Available or on the Way

CBN Comment. "Overcoming the Hurdles in the Path to UNIX." *Computer Business News,* 27 October 1980, p. 8.

Cherlin, E. "The Unix Operating System: Portability a Plus." *Mini-Micro Systems,* April 1981.

Greitzer, John. "UNIX Starts Its Ride to the Top." *Computer Business News,* 13 October 1980, p. 1.

——. "UNIX Proponents Push Products Amid Licensing Policy Confusion." *Computer Business News,* 26 January 1981, p. 1.

Johnson, R. Colin. "Major Firms Join UNIX Parade." *Electronics,* April 1981, pp. 108.

Johnson, Stephen C. "UNIX Time-Sharing System: Language Development Tools." *Bell System Technical Journal* 57 (1978):1971-90.

O'Connor, Rory J. "Users Meet to Voice Support for UNIX Standard." *Computer Business News,* 27 October 1980, p. 1.

Thompson, Kenneth. "The UNIX Command Language." In *Structured Programming — Infotech State of the Art Report,* pp. 375-84. Berkshire, England: Infotech International Ltd., March 1975.

C Language

Anderson, B. "Type Syntax in the Language 'C', an Object Lesson in Syntactic Innovation." *SIGPLAN Notices* 15 (1980).

Strong criticism of C for vague and irregular syntax, especially in data typing.

Bailes, P.A.C. "A Coroutine Package for C." *Australian Computer Science Communications* 1 (1979).

Explains an economical implementation of coroutines for C on UNIX.

Burkowski, F.J.; Mackey, W.F.; and Hamza, M.H. "Micro-C: A Universal High Level Language for Microcomputers." In *IEEE International Symposium on Mini and Micro Computers (Canada/USA)*, 1977/1978.

Describes a subset of C, differing mainly in data precision.

Cain, R. "A Small C Compiler for the 8080s." *Dr. Dobb's*, May 1980.

How and why C was used on 8080 based personal computer.

Hancock, L. "Implementing a Tiny Interpreter with a CP/M-Flavored C." *Dr. Dobb's*, January 1980.

Describes a C subset compiler for the Z80 and 8080 running CP/M.

Johnson, Stephen C. and Kernighan, Brian W. "The Programming Language B." *Computer Science Technical Report No. 8*, Bell Laboratories: January 1973.

Kernighan, Brian W., and Ritchie, Dennis M. *The C Programming Language*. Englewood Cliffs: Prentice-Hall, 1978.

The book that introduced C, with an appendix that is the de facto language standard.

Krieger, M.S. and Plauger, P.J. "C Language's Grip on Hardware Makes Sense for Small Computers." *Electronics*, May 1980, pp. 129-133.

How and why C can help the small-systems programmer.

Reiser, J.F. "Compiling Three-Address Code for C Programs." *The Bell System Technical Journal* 60 (1981):159-166.

Describes a post processor that improves the assembly language code generated by the portable C compiler.

Ritchie, Dennis M.; Johnson, Stephen C.; Lesk, Michael E.; and Kernighan, B.W. "UNIX Time Sharing System: The C Programming Language." *The Bell System Technical Journal* 57 (1978):1991-2019.

An introduction to the language and its development.

———. "The C Programming Language." *Dr. Dobb's,* July 1980.

An overview of C's underlying principles, with consideration of its strengths and weaknesses.

Werner, Loren. "For Many Systems Programs, C Soars Where PASCAL Falters." *EDN,* March 1981, pp. 147-148.

Introduction to UNIX System and Its Concepts _____

Baker, F.T. "Structured Programming in the Production Programming Environment." In *Proceedings International Conference Reliable Software,* IEEE Publications, 1975.

Greenberg, Robert B. "The UNIX Operating System and the XENIX Standard Operating Environment." *Byte,* June 1981, pp. 248-264.

Information and Publication Division. "The UNIX System. An Easier Way to Communicate with Computers." Bell Laboratories, 1979.

Johnson, Stephen C. and Ritchie, Dennis M. "UNIX Time-Sharing System: Portability of C Programs and the UNIX System." *Bell System Technical Journal* 57 (1978):2021-2048.

The theory behind C's portability.

Kernighan, Brian W. and Mashey, John R. "The UNIX Programming Environment." *Software — Practice & Experience* 9 (1979).

———. "The UNIX Programming Environment." *Computer,* April 1981, pp. 12-22.

Lions, J. "Experiences with the UNIX Time-Sharing System." *Software — Practice & Experience* 9 (1979).

An evaluation of the UNIX system as a tool for teaching computer science.

Morgan, S.P. "The UNIX System: Making Computers Easier to Use." *Bell Laboratories Record* 56 (1978).

Popek, G.J. et al. "UCLA Security UNIX." In *AFIPS Conference Proceedings, 1979 NCC,* AFIPS Publishing, 1979.

Ritchie, Dennis M. "The Evolution of the UNIX Time-Sharing System." In *Proceedings Symposium Language Design and Programming Methodology,* Sidney, Australia, 1979.

————. "The UNIX Time-Sharing System." *Communications of the ACM* 17 (1974):365-375.

Ritchie, Dennis M. and Thompson, Kenneth. "The UNIX Time-Sharing System." *The Bell System Technical Journal* 57 (1978).

Rose, G. "An Operating System Case Study." *Operating Systems Review* 12 (1978).

Evaluates the UNIX system as a tool for teaching operating systems theory.

Stiefel, M.L. "UNIX." *Mini-Micro Systems,* April 1978.

Thompson, Kenneth and Ritchie, Dennis M. *UNIX Programmer's Manual,* 6th ed. Murray Hill, New Jersey: Bell Telephone Laboratories, 1979.

"Western Electric Company — UNIX Time-Sharing System." *Auerbach Computer Technology Reports* 610.6898.800, Pennsauken, New Jersey: Auerbach Publishers Inc.

The Purposes, Pros, and Cons Of the UNIX System

Lions, J. "The UNIX Operating System." In *Commentary,* Murray Hill, New Jersey: Bell Telephone Laboratories, 1977.

Ritchie, Dennis M. "UNIX Time-Sharing System: A Retrospective." *The Bell System Technical Journal* 57 (1978):1947-69.

Thompson, Kenneth. "UNIX Implementation." *The Bell System Technical Journal* 57 (1978).

Walker, B.J.; Kemmerer, R.A.; and Popek, G.J. "Specification and Verification of the UCLA UNIX Security Kernel." In *Communications of the ACM* 23 (1980).

Design and implementation of a high-data-security version of the UNIX system.

Operating Systems Like the UNIX System_____

Lycklama, H. and Bayer, D.L. "The Mert Operating System." *The Bell System Technical Journal* 57 (1978).

An operating system that supports both UNIX system operations and real-time processes simultaneously, on PDP-11/45 and PDP-11/70 minicomputers.

Plauger, P.L. and Krieger, M.S. "UNIX-like Software Runs on Mini- and Microcomputers." *Electronics,* March 1981, pp. 125-129.

The rationale of IDRIS is that it is generally compatible with UNIX systems, but with variations aimed at smaller systems.

Implementation_____

Miller, R. "UNIX — A Portable Operating System." *Operating Systems Review* 12 (1978):32-37.

The process of porting the UNIX operating system to the Interdata 7/32.

Weiner, B. and Swartz, D. "Adapting UNIX to a 16-bit Microcomputer" *Electronics,* April 1981.

Bringing up the UNIX system on Z8000.

The Shell_____

Bourne, S.R., "An Introduction to the UNIX Shell." *The Bell System Technical Journal* 57 (1978):2797-2822.

An outline of the inner workings of the Shell.

Ellis, J.R. "A Lisp Shell." *SIGPLAN Notices* 15 (1980).

Proposes a Lisp version of the Shell on UNIX systems.

Mashey, John R. "Using a Command Language as a High-Level Programming Language." In *Proceedings of the 2nd International Conference on Software Engineering,* 1976.

Stabile, L.A. "FP and its Use as a Command Language." In *Proceedings of Distributed Computing — Compcon 80, 21st IEEE Computer Society International Conference,* 1980.

FP is described and proposed as an improved replacement for the Shell in UNIX systems.

Files and Data Bases

Hanson, D.R. "A Portable File Directory System." *Software — Practice and Experience* 10 (1980).

Design and use of a hierarchical directory system similar to the UNIX system directory.

McSkimin, J.R. "Redas — A Relational Data Access System for Real-Time Applications." In *Proceedings of Compsac 78 Computer Software and Applications Conference,* 1978.

An interpreted data-retrieval language written in C.

Stonebraker, M.; Wong, E.; Kreps, P.; and Held, G. "The Design and Implementation of Ingres." In *ACM Transactions on Database Systems* 1 (1976).

Description of a multiuser relational DBMS developed at the University of California at Berkeley.

Networking

Antonelli, C.J.; Hamilton, L.S.; Lu, P.M.; Wallace, J.J.; and Yueh, K. "SDS/Net — An Interactive Distributed Operating System." In *Proceedings of Distributed Computing — Compcon 80, 21st IEEE Computer Society International Conference,* 1980.

A basic approach to networking the UNIX system.

Balocca, R. "Networking and the Process Structure of UNIX: A Case Study." In *Proceedings of Compcon Fall 78,* Computer Communications Networks, 1978.

Theoretical consideration of the UNIX system networking.

Barak, A.B. and Shapir, A. "UNIX with Satellite Processors." *Software — Practice and Experience* 10 (1980).

Guidelines for designing UNIX-based central/satellites networks.

Bennett, C.J. and Frost, D.N. "Network Independent File Transfer at University College London." In *Proceedings of Networks 80 "Data Networks: Development and Uses",* 1980.

An implementation of the Network Independent File Transfer Protocol on a UNIX system-based PDP-11 system is tested against various non-UNIX system implementations.

Chesson, G.L. "The Network UNIX System." *Operating Systems Review* 9 (1975). Also in *Proceedings of the 5th Symposium on Operating Systems Principles,* 1978.

Interfacing UNIX software to the Arpanet.

Holmgren, S.F. "Resource Sharing UNIX." In *Proceedings of Compcon Fall 78,* 1978.

A variant of the UNIX system that supports networking with all nodes of equal status.

Horton, R.E. "Using Personal Computers as Terminals in Computer Networks." In *AEDS Proceedings of the 18th Annual Convention "A Gateway to the Use of Computers in Education",* 1980.

A PDP-11/34 minicomputer running the UNIX system provides facilities, and support to Pet microcomputers.

Lu, P.M. "A System for Resource-Sharing in a Distributed Environment — RIDE." In *Proceedings of COMPSAC, the IEEE Computer Society's Third International Computer Software and Applications Conference,* 1979.

Applications programs moved without changes between single-computer and multi-computer systems.

Lycklama, H. and Christensen, C. "A Minicomputer Satellite Processor System." *The Bell System Technical Journal* 57 (1978):2103-13.

A network of PDP-11 minicomputers and LSI-11 microcomputers off the UNIX system residing in the central PDP-11.

Manning, E.G.; Howard R.; O'Donnell, C.G.; Pammett, K.; and Chang, E. "A UNIX-Based Local Processor and Network Access Machine." *Computer Networks* 1 (1976).

In this network PDP-11 users run the UNIX system and access host computers without interacting with the hosts' command language or operating systems.

Murrel S. and Kowalski, T. "A Real-Time Satellite System Based on UNIX." *Behavioral Research Methods and Instrumentation* 12 (1980).

Development and target computers are networked under the UNIX system.

Nowitz, D.A. and Lesk, Michael E. "Implementation of a Dial-Up Network of UNIX Systems." In *Proceedings of Distributed Computing — Compcon 80, 21st IEEE Computer Society International Conference,* 1980.

A wide-area low-cost network.

Pohm, A.V.; Davis, J.A.; Christiansen, S.; Bridges, G.E.; and Horton, R.E. "A Local Network of Mini and Microcomputers for Experiment Support." *Computer Networks* 3 (1979).

A PDP-11/34 minicomputer running UNIX provides facilities, and support to Pet microcomputers.

Thomas, R.A.C.; DeLobel, C.; and Litwin, W. "Process Structure Alternatives Towards a Distributed Ingres." In *Proceedings of the International Symposium on Distributed Data Bases "Distributed Data Bases",* 1980.

Considerations of a distributed Ingres DBMS and a simulation model for a single computer running under the UNIX operating system.

Tsichritzis, D. "OFS: An Integrated Form Management System." In *Proceedings of the 6th International Conference — Very Large Data Bases,* 1980.

An electronic-office network being developed to link PDP-11 minicomputers and LSI-11 microcomputer.

Software Tools

Cermak, I.A. "An Integrated Approach to Microcomputer Support Tools." In *1977 Electro Conference Record,* 1977.

A software development system, under the UNIX system for the MAC-8 microprocessor.

Dimond, K.R. "Development Aids for Microprogrammable Microprocessors." In *Colloquium on "Development of Bit-Slice Systems" (England),* 1980.

Dolotta, T.A. and Mashey, John R. "An Introduction to the Programmer's Workbench." In *Proceedings of the 2nd International Conference on Software Engineering,* 1976.

———. "An Introduction to the Programmer's Workbench." In *Proceedings 2nd International Conference on Software Engineering,* 1976. Historical review of the UNIX system Programmer's Workbench.

Dolotta, T.A., Haight, R.C., and Mashey, John R. "UNIX Time-Sharing System: The Programmer's Workbench." *Bell System Technical Journal* 57 (1978):2177-2200.

Eanes, R.S.; Hitchon, C.K.; Thall, R.M.; and Brackett, J.W. "An Environment for Producing Well-Engineered Microcomputer Software." In *Proceedings of the 4th International Conference on Sofware Engineering (West Germany/USA),* 1979.

Enslow, P.H., Jr. *Portability of Large Cobol Programs: The Cobol Programmer's Workbench.* Atlanta: Georgia Institute of Technology, 1979.

Feldman, S.I. "Make — A Program for Maintaining Computer Programs." *Software — Practice & Experience* 9 (1979):255-65.

Glasser, A.L. "The Evolution of a Source Code Control System." *SICSOFT* 3 (1978):121-5.

Hall, D. E.; Scherrer, D.K.; and Sventek, J.S. "A Virtual Operating System." In *Communications of the ACM* 23 (1980):495-502.

Hanson, P. Brinch. *Structured Multiprogramming.* Englewood Cliffs, New Jersey: Prentice-Hall, Inc., 1978.

Huck, J. and Neuhauser, C. "I/O Device Emulation in the Stanford Emulation Laboratory." *Sigmicro Newsletter* 10 (1979).

Ivie, E.L. "The Programmer's Workbench — A Machine for Software Development." In *Communications of the ACM,* October 1977.

Johnson, Stephen C. "Language Development Tools on the UNIX System." *Computer,* October 1980, pp. 16-21. Using Yacc, Lex, and other software tools under the UNIX system.

Johnson, Stephen C. and Lesk, Michael E. "Language Development Tools." *The Bell System Technical Journal* 57 (1978).

————. "A Portable Compiler: Theory and Practice." In *Proceedings of the 5th ACM Symposium on Principles of Programming Languages,* Tucson, Arizona, 1978.

Johnstone, I.L.; Taylor, P.; Middleton, M.R. "In House Software Development in the ASGM (Austrialian Graduate School of Management)." In *Proceedings of the National Conference on Library and Bibliographic Applications of Minicomputers, Australia,* 1979.

Book cataloging with a minicomputer running UNIX.

Joy, W.N., Graham, S.L. and Haley, C.B. *UNIX Pascal User's Manual.* Department of Electrical Engineering and Computer Science. Berkeley: University of California, 1977.

Kernighan, Brian W. "Ratfor — A Preprocessor for a Rational Fortran." *Software — Practice and Experience* 5 (1975).

Traces a development language from design criteria through implementation to user experience.

Kernighan, Brian W. and Plauger, P.J. *Software Tools.* Reading, Massachusetts: Addison-Wesley, 1976.

The origin of the Software Tools movement.

————. "Software Tools," In *Proceedings of the 1st National Conference on Software Engineering,* 1975.

Larmouth, J. "Scheduling for a Share of the Machine." *Software — Practice & Experience* 5 (1974):29-49.

Luderer, G.W.R.; Maranzano, J.F.; and Tague, B.A. "The UNIX Operating System as a Base for Applications." *Bell System Technical Journal* 57 (1978).

Mashey, John R. and Smith, D.W. "Documentation Tools and Techniques." In *2nd International Conference on Software Engineering,* 1976.

Developing documentation with Programmer's Workbench.

Morgan, S.P. "Easy Does It (UNIX System)." *Telephony* 196 (1979).

Person, D.J. "The Use and Abuse of a Software Engineering System." In *AFIPS Conference Proceedings, 1979 NCC.*

Rochkind, M.J. "The Source Code Control System." *IEEE Transactions in Software Engineering* SE-1 (1975):364-370.

Roome, W.D. "Programmer's Workbench: New Tools for Software Development." *Bell Laboratories Record* 57 (1979).

Rovegno, H.D. "A Support Environment for MAC-8 Systems." *Bell System Technical Journal* 57 (1978).

Snow, C.R. "The Software Tools Project." *Software — Pratice and Experience* 8 (1978).

Stockenberg, J.E. and Taffs, D. "Software Test Bed Support Under PWB/UNIX." ADA Environment Workshop, DoD High Order Language Working Group, November 1979, pp. 10-26.

Teichroew, D. and Hershey, E.A. III. "PLS/PSA: A Computer-Aided Technique for Structured Documentation and Analysis of Information Processing Systems." *IEEE Transactions in Software Engineering.* SE-3 (1977):42-48.

Teitelman, W. *A Display Oriented Programmer's Assistant,* CSL 77-3, Palo Alto, California: Xerox Corp., Palo Alto Research Center, 1977.

Woodward, J.P.L. "Applications for Multilevel Security Operating Systems." In *AFIPS Conference Proceedings, 1979 NCC.*

Text Formatting

Bisiani, R. and Mauersberg, H. "Software Development for Task-Oriented Multiprocessor Architectures." In *Compcon 79 Proceedings, Using Microprocessors, Extending Our Reach,* 1979.

Gillogly, J.J. "Word Processing with UNIX. In *1978 Midcon Technical Papers,* 1978.
Editing, formatting, and messaging with the UNIX system.

Kernighan, Brian W. and Cherry, L.L. "A System for Typesetting Mathematics." In *Communications of the ACM* 18 (1975):151-7. Also published as "Computer Science Technical Report No. 17." Murray Hill, N.J.: Bell Laboratories, 1977.

Kernighan, Brian W.; Lesk, M.E.; and Ossanna, J.R., Jr. "Document Preparation." *Bell System Technical Journal* 57 (1978).
Using standard UNIX system utilities to edit, format, and send messages.

Lesk, Michael E. "Lex — A Lexical Analyzer Generator." *UNIX Programmer's Manual 2,* Section 20, January 1979.

Lesk, Michael and Kernighan, Brian W. "Computer Typesetting of Technical Journals on UNIX." In *Proceedings of AFIPS National Computer Conference,* 1977.

Theory and practice of equation setting under UNIX system facilities.

McMahon, L.E.; Cherry, L.L.; and Morris, R. "Statistical Text Processing." *Bell System Technical Journal* 57 (1978).

Linguistic analysis for improving word processing under the UNIX system.

Morris, R. and Cherry, L.L. "Computer Detection of Typographical Errors." in *IEEE Transactions on Professional Communication,* March 1975.

Seybold, Patricia B., ed. "Interactive System/One." *The Seybold Report on Word Processing* 3 (1980).

Graphics

McKeown, D.M., Jr. and Reddy, D.R. "A Hierarchical Symbolic Representation for an Image Data Base." In *Proceedings of the Workshop on Picture Data Description and Management,* 1977.

Describes Midas, a system of image data bases under the UNIX system.

Instrumentation and Control

Custead, L.R. and McAlpine, J.L. "Nuclear Physics Data Acquisition with the UNIX TimeSharing System." In *IEEE Transactions on Nuclear Science, 1978 Nuclear Science Symposium and 1978 Symposium on Nuclear Power Systems* 26 (1978/79).

Experiment preparation and data analysis under the UNIX system.

Wonsiewicz, B.C.; Storm, A.R.; and Sieber, J.D. "Microcomputer Control of Apparatus, Machinery, and Experiments." *Bell System Technical Journal* 57 (1978).

In a UNIX system network, microcomputers acts as satellites to perform laboratory jobs.

Communications

Cohen, H. and Kaufeld, J.C. "The Network Operations Center." *The Bell System Technical Journal* 57 (1978).

Enhanced UNIX software supports the monitor system for the Bell toll network.

Other Applications

Bloomfield, P. "An Interactive Statistical Processor for the UNIX Time-Sharing System." In *Computer Science and Statistics — Tenth Annual Symposium on the Interface, 1977/78.*

Fraser, A.G. "Circuit Design Aids." *Bell System Technical Journal* 57 (1978).

Lycklama, H. "UNIX on a Microprocessor." *The Bell System Technical Journal* 57 (1978).

GLOSSARY

Appendix E

A

Address range. For the **ed** text editor, a range of line numbers.

Address. An identifying number (often hexadecimal or binary) that describes a location in computer memory where information is stored.

Allocation (Dynamic). The assignment and reassignment of peripheral devices or memory in a program.

Allocation technique. The method of providing a process with access to a shared resource such as memory or peripherals.

Argument. A variable or constant that is typed with a command to indicate a subset or superset of that command.

ASCII. Abbreviation for "American Standard Code for Information Interchange." This code permits electronic systems to transmit and receive text in a standard format. Each character is assigned a number between 32 and 127. These numbers are then easily transferred electronically between systems, even systems from different manufacturers. Most small computers and terminal products support only a subset of the ASCII character set, typically including upper- and lower-case alphabetic characters, numbers, and special symbols.

Assembly language. The lowest level of computer language, assembly language uses mnemonic names to stand for one or more machine language instructions. Machine language instructions are the most basic instructions in the computer, and assembly language is a "shorthand" method of representing the long strings of ones and zeros found in machine language. The advantage of assembly language over high-level languages is its speed for applications that require frequent and quick data transfer. High-level languages are generally easier to use than assembly language.

B

Backup. A copy of computer programs and data. If the working copy of software is destroyed, the backup copy ensures against total loss of the information.

Batch. A type of operating system which processes one job at a time; each job must be completely executed before the next job begins.

Binary number system. A number system that makes use of only two characters, 0 and 1. The number 2 does not exist in the binary system, just as there is no number beyond 9 in the decimal system. In the binary system the value 2 is written as 10 (1 in the "two's place" and 0 in the "one's place"), just as in the decimal system the number following 9 is 10 (1 in the "ten's place" and 0 in the "one's place"). BIT is the commonly used abbreviation for BInary digiT, and is the basic element of computer data.

Block. A set of consecutive machine instructions, characters, or digits carried by a computer as a unit; used in I/O functions, where blocks of memory are handled consecutively by the CPU.

Bourne Shell. The standard command interpreter which comes with UNIX system Version 7.

Buffering. The process of using areas of memory to isolate I/O devices' activities from each other and from the CPU.

Buffer memory. A part of a computer's memory that is used to store transmitted and/or received data. Buffer memories are used because a peripheral has higher speed requirements than general system memory can support or because additional processing must be performed on the data. Text editing typically uses buffers to move text. Printers contain buffers for text, and the computer must be set to feed text into these buffers at the correct speed, or the buffer will overflow and text will be lost.

Bug. A mistake in the design or implementation of a program which causes in incorrect results.

Bus. A set of parallel connections used to connect the computer's boards together; it allows the transmission of data and information between parts of the computer.

Byte. The basic unit of information in the computer. A byte usually consists of eight binary bits.

C

Capacity. The number of characters or documents that may be stored on a disk drive.

Central processing unit (CPU). The central processing unit controls a computer; it is sometimes referred to as the "brains" of a system. CPUs range from single microprocessor chips to boxes full of boards containing chips and transistors.

Chaining. See also *Linking.* The ability of an executing program to call another program.

Character. A single letter, number, space, or special symbol ($ & ; #). Special characters are often defined for specific applications by programs such as word processing or accounting.

Command. A sequence of letters or numbers that directs the action of the computer. Commands are usually typed at the keyboard of a terminal.

Command interpreter. A program which reads lines typed at the keyboard and interprets them as requests to execute other programs. The command interpreter in the UNIX system is called a shell.

Communication. The ability to pass data and commands from one computer or terminal to another. Communication capability is included in some systems, but requires specialized hardware and software for others. In general, hardware controls the electrical signals connecting systems, while software controls the system so that a document is transferred without errors. In some operating systems, communication facilities are generalized to permit transmission of data across a communication link such as a private branch exchange (PBX), standard telephone line, or microwave link.

Compiler. A language translator that converts a program written in a high-level language (C or COBOL, for example) into machine code form. It usually generates more than one machine instruction for each statement. A cross-compiler can convert a higher-level language program into machine instructions for different CPUs, permitting transportability of programs.

Concatenate. To merge two or more files (or portions of files) together into one file.

Control character. A non-printing character in a document used to specify information to the system. For example, in one text processing program, control-B (^B) requests double strike printing of text until the next ^B appears. Control characters often specify cursor movements and other commands in text editing programs. (Also known as *control code.*)

Copy. The duplication of a document or file, or the movement of text from one file to another.

Crash. Unexpected shutdown or interruption of a working computer.

Create. Start a new file. To create a new file, the operator must specify a unique identifier or name. The system stores this information in its directory, sometimes along with the date and time. After the system finds space on the disk for the new file, the user can enter data into the new file.

CRT. Cathode Ray Tube. A CRT monitor displays the communications of the computer. CRTs are also called terminals or monitors.

Current line. For the **ed** editor, the line in the edit buffer indicated by the line pointer.

Cursor. A special symbol on a CRT that indicates the current screen position for the next entry or file display. The cursor can appear on the CRT in several forms, depending on the program. It is usually displayed as either a blinking or a steady box.

D

Data encryption. A way to scramble information to be transmitted between locations in order to protect proprietary or sensitive data. Another system with a "key" to the encryption method can decipher the data.

Data processing. The electronic manipulation, calculation, reporting, and storage of information. Data processing applications include scientific tasks including telephone system control and satellite operation; office functions including data base management, text editing, and accounting; and financial calculations including income tax preparation, order entry, and budget statement preparation.

Deadly embrace. A computer's state when two processes each unknowingly wait for resources controlled by the other.

Debugger. A system software utility that helps a programmer remove errors from software.

Delete. The ability to remove text from a file, or whole files from the system.

Device. A piece of peripheral equipment, usually for input and/or output of data; includes printers, terminals, and card readers.

Diagnostics. System programs (usually supplied with the operating system) that test the computer's memory, interrupts, timers, and peripheral devices. Diagnostics are often designed to perform automatically whenever the system is turned on.

Direct memory access (DMA). A quick way for peripherals to gain access to memory without going through the computer. It is most often used in CRT terminal displays and disk drives.

Directory. A data file holding names and locations of each file in the data storage system. Each directory entry includes information about the file's name, owner, size, etc. Multiple levels of directories exist in the UNIX system. Directories in the UNIX system are sometimes pointers to subdirectories.

Disk drive. A magnetic storage device in computer systems. Disk drives store files for later recall, modification, and printing.

Diskette. A removable and inexpensive medium for magnetic storage. Two common diskette sizes are "standard"(8 inches in diameter) and "mini" (5¼ inches in diameter).

Display. Another name for a CRT.

Document. A file of text. Documents are stored, retrieved, edited, and printed by computer programs.

Download. To transfer data to a recipient from a donor.

Down time. An interval of time when a computer system is not functional.

Driver. A utility software program that controls the transfer of data to and from I/O devices. Drivers usually have to be written for each new peripheral that is added to a system. Application programs often contain drivers as part of the software. They configure the peripherals to the special functions of the program.

E

Edit. To modify the contents of a document by moving, adding, deleting, or rearranging text.

Editor. A program that creates, concatenates, edits, or deletes files or portions of files. Editors operate on text, program, and data files. In the UNIX system, the standard editor is **ed**.

Electronic mail. A system in a computer to transmit information (memos, letters, data) electronically within a system network or to another local or remote system.

End-of-file. The last element in a file.

End-of-file character. A special character or signal located at the end of a file.

Escape character. Deactivates the special interpretation normally given certain selected characters.

Executable code. A machine language program which can be read and executed.

Execute. A command which instructs the system to perform a previously defined action.

F

Field. A defined space on a terminal display or printout that contains specific information such as a name, address, or telephone number to be filled in by the user; a unit of information.

File. A defined unit of data or text stored on a magnetic tape or disk. Files are named, and information about them may be kept by the system. They can be protected against damage by file commands.

File access permission. Permission to read, write, or execute a file.

File control block (FCB). A data structure in main memory that keeps track of files in use.

File management system. A program or programs within an operating system that controls the organization and allocation of files in directories on disk. This software provides programs to create, delete, or rename files, and facilitates reading and writing of existing files.

Filename. Alphanumeric characters (letters or numbers) used to identify a particular file.

Filter. A program which receives its input from the standard input file, and delivers its output to the standard output file.

Floppy. Another name for a diskette.

Foreground/background. A function in an operating system that gives certain programs priority over other programs. It allows time-critical programs to operate quickly in the "foreground" and to be executed with high priority; "background" programs such as printouts, sorts, etc. are executed simultaneously, but at much lower priority and speed. The UNIX operating system protects the foreground process from influence by background.

Format. A program formats, or initializes, disks to indicate data placement for subsequent read and write functions. It also specifies hard copy appearance for margins, line spacing, tabs, and pitch.

H

Hard copy. Printout of data or text on paper, usually to facilitate dissemination of information or to assure a written record of electronically stored data.

Hard disk. A type of magnetic storage device that has a high storage capacity.

Hardware. The electronic components of a computer system. This includes such items as boards, CRT terminals, and disk drives.

Hashing. An intermixing of elements.

Header. The beginning of a file preceding the content. The header specifies destination, source, priority, etc.

High-level language. Language that uses words as much as possible, rather than symbols that cannot be easily understood by users. It allows a programmer to write software without being concerned with low-level functions of a computer, such as register allocation. Typically, one high-level language command equals many assembly language or machine code commands. Examples of high-level languages include C, FORTRAN, BASIC, COBOL, and Pascal.

I

Index. A number representing the position of a byte in either a file or a record.

Initialize. To set a computer's counters, switches, and addresses to zero or another starting value, or at prescribed points in a computer routine. Initializing also sets the parameters of a disk surface via formatting, so that it can accept data for storage.

Input. To enter data into a system, usually via a keyboard. The system can also read data from a device.

Insert. To add text or data to a file while editing.

Interactive. A computer system that allows the user to type in a command and see an immediate response.

Interface. A connection made by both hardware and software between a system, a peripheral, or another system. Information is transferred via the interface.

Interpreter. A language translator that converts a high-level language such as C or Pascal into a special intermediate code that is simulated (interpreted) by a system program. Usually this intermediate code cannot be directly executed on a computer.

Interrupt. A break in the normal flow of a system. A signal from an external source tells a processor to interrupt execution of the current program. Most operating systems use interrupts to reorder tasks for execution.

I/O device. A piece of hardware that allows the input or output (I/O) of data from or to the computer. Examples are printers, terminals, and modems.

I/O supervisor. The part of an operating system that provides and controls routines for I/O.

J

Job. The collection of program code used to accomplish a task. It often solves a problem.

K

Kernel. The most basic portion of the UNIX operating system, the kernel supports task synchronization, scheduling, communication, and memory allocation activities.

Keyboard. A keyboard is an interface between a computer system and a user. Many keyboards contain more keys than a typewriter keyboard. The additional keys are used to access special functions found in some programs.

Keystroke. A single depression of a key on the keyboard.

L

Library. A collection of programs within a system which may be executed. Libraries eliminate the need for software redesign for each new task.

Line. A single printed line of text. A line usually includes all the characters between carriage returns.

Line editing. An editor program that performs on a line-by-line basis. For example, a line could be deleted by referring to its line number.

Link. A one-bit register in many computers; also an address pointer to the next element of a list or the next record of a file.

Linked list. A list formed by using pointers to tie together several items in a list.

Linker. A system program that connects tasks into a unit that can be moved into memory and executed.

Linking. See also *Chaining.* A technique of joining physically separate instructions or operations into a connected list. The processor starts, and continues to perform, operations which link to the next instruction until the end of the list is reached. This method is used extensively in I/O processors; complex data transfers are accomplished with little user intervention. A file created by linking contains no text; it contains a "map" that lists the component files in the correct order.

Login directory. The root directory associated with an account.

Login name. A one-word name that identifies a user to the UNIX system.

M

Machine language. The lowest level of information that can be directly processed by the computer. It is expressed in binary notation.

Mailbox. A function found in some computer systems that handles message communication. The electronic mail program sends messages to and from personal and departmental boxes of system users.

Mainframe. An adjective that describes large computers.

Main memory. A set of chips or boards in a computer in which data and programs are stored while in use.

Mass storage. Generally, magnetic storage devices capable of holding many pages of data. Examples of mass storage devices are diskettes (100 to 1,000 pages of storage), hard disks (well over 1,000 pages of storage), and tape systems, equivalent in storage to hard disks. Mass storage (also called *bulk storage*) is slower to access than main memory, but holds much larger amounts of data in archive form.

Memory board. A memory board is a flat plastic device containing electronic logic chips that store information in computer-readable form for execution.

Memory protection. A security method for ensuring that the contents of main memory are not altered or inadvertently destroyed by users.

Merge. The capability to concatenate (combine) data or text from several files. The term also refers to the copying of text from one file to another. The copied characters in the original file are not necessarily removed.

Modem. A hardware device that connects a computer or terminal to another device or computer system by transmitting electronic information. These signals are transmitted over telephone lines and are decoded by the device on the other end.

Monitor. At the microprocessor level, a monitor is a small program that permits interaction with the microprocessor to examine and change the contents of registers and memory locations, and to debug programs. In software development it is a common data structure and the set of operations that defines that structure.

Move. The ability to move data or text from one part of a file to another part of the same file or to another file.

Multi-user. A multi-user system allows users to independently access system resources. Multi-user does not necessarily dictate multi-tasking. In a multi-tasking system, several users can access the same programs or data at once, and change the data. The signals from the different users are sorted out and correctly executed by the system.

N

Node. A unit within a communications network. It can be a terminal or a complete computer.

O

Object code. The machine-language commands in a program; an object code program can be loaded directly into memory and executed.

Octal. A numerical system where the base is 8 and the digits are 0, 1, 2, 3, 4, 5, 6, and 7. Many programmers use octal or hexadecimal (base

16), notation; octal is a natural notation of numbers on machines whose "word size" is eight or 16 bits.

Off-line. Equipment or devices not directly controlled by the computer are considered to be off-line.

On-line. Equipment or devices under direct control of the computer; they respond directly and immediately to user commands. When power is turned off, they are considered off-line.

Operating system (OS). An organized collection of procedures and programs for operating the computer. These programs interface users to computers and allow them to interact with the system in an efficient manner.

Overlaying. The method of continuously using the same blocks of storage during consecutive stages of a program; when one program is no longer needed, another program replaces all or part of it in memory.

P

Parameter. An item of information that defines the limits a user supplies when a program is run.

Peripheral. An input/output device that is attached to a computer system. Terminals, printers, and storage devices such as disk drives and tape units are examples of peripheral devices.

Permission. There are three basic permissions in the UNIX system associated with file access: read, write, and execute.

Personal directory. Same as Login directory.

Pipe. Two or more commands connected together so that the output of one command becomes the input of a second command.

Pipe fitting. The process of connecting commands together in a pipeline.

Polling. In electronic mail or data communications, the systematic calling of terminals to determine if messages are waiting to be transmitted or if the terminal is ready to accept messages.

Port. Usually refers to the I/O interface of a computer.

Port Driver. A program which provides a software interface between an I/O port and the computer.

Process. An operating system's basic unit of computation.

Program. A sequence of instructions written in a computer language. The set of instructions tells a computer step by step exactly how to execute a task.

Prompt. A special character displayed by a program when it is waiting for user input.

Protocol. A set of conventions used routinely between equipment such as terminals and computers.

R

RAM. An abbreviation for "Random Access Memory." Changeable main memory. RAM is the location of most programs and data manipulation.

Recursion. The restarting of an active program; a recursive program includes a sequence which calls itself.

Redirection. The shell reassigns the standard input and/or output to other files or devices.

Release. A new set of system programs, numbered by either the vendor or the manufacturer. System releases correct errors and add new features.

Replace. A function of text editing programs that replaces data or text with new input. This feature is sometimes called *global.* For example, it permits a file to be modified to change all incidences of "1980" to "1981."

Resource. Any device or item used by a computer.

ROM. An abbreviation for "Read Only Memory." ROM stores programs that are used repeatedly. It is permanently programmed with one group of frequently used instructions. It does not lose its data when the power is turned off. A program in ROM cannot be changed by the user.

RS-232C. A common type of electrical interface (American National Standards Institute specification) for communication among computers and peripherals such as terminals and printers.

Running. A program is being executed or, more generally, the system is operating.

S

Scrolling. A function of a CRT display that provides a movable display of a document. Scrolling allows the user to edit documents that extend past the length or width of the screen. Horizontal scrolling is controlled by software, and not every terminal or program performs extra wide scrolling past 80 characters.

Search. The ability of a program to find strings of characters. Most systems search either forward or backward from the location of the cursor.

Segmentation. A method of managing different-sized areas of memory segments.

Shell. A term for the UNIX system command interpreter.

Shell prompt. The prompt character displayed by the UNIX system shell program.

Single contiguous allocation. A memory allocation method that assigns all available memory as one block of data.

Subdirectory. A directory within or below another in the file system hierarchy.

Superuser. The privileged user who has unlimited access to all parts of the UNIX system.

Swapping. A technique similar to overlaying; in a multi-user environment, either temporarily bringing a user program into main memory or storing it.

Symbolic debugger. An interactive system debugging tool. The debugging program accesses program symbol tables and a user refers to memory location names rather than absolute addresses in debugging. This is an extremely valuable facility when relocatable code or paged systems may not allow code to be stored at the same memory address each time it is executed.

T

Task. A software instruction that forms the lowest unit of a process.

Terminal. A peripheral device in a system through which data can enter or leave the computer.

Text editor. A computer program used to revise data or text. Text editing is often referred to as "word processing" when advanced, document-oriented commands are included in the system.

Transient area. The space in memory available for user programs and system utilities.

U

Utility. A program often supplied with an operating system, it performs basic system functions such as saving and restoring files, disk handling, and file copying.

W

Word processing. The use of specialized equipment, software, and trained personnel to perform advanced document preparation.

QUICK REFERENCE TO UNIX SYSTEM COMMANDS

Appendix F

How to Read This Appendix

Type **boldface** text literally.

Substitute actual value for *italicized* argument names.

Optional arguments are in square brackets [ ].

Repeatable arguments are followed by ellipses ...

Refer to the page number following the command name for a detailed description of the command.

COMM — Common Lines in Two Files   181

$ **comm** -[123] *file1 file2*
     Display unique and common lines in sorted files
file1 and *file2*. Use the flags **1**, **2**, or **3** to suppress the
display of the corresponding column.

CP — File Copy   186

$ **cp** *file1 file2*
     Make a copy of *file1* and name it *file2*.

$ **cp** *file1 file2... dirname*
     Copy one or more files into the specified
directory.

CRYPT — Encode/Decode Information   332

$ **crypt** *key*
     Encode (or decode) using the *key*.

DATE — Print Current Time and Date   289

$ **date**
     Display the current time and date.

DIFF — Differential File Comparator   190

$ **diff** [-efbh] *file1 file2*
     Find the difference between *file1* and *file2*.
Options:
     -e   **ed** script option
     -b   Ignore spaces and tabs in comparison
     -f   Opposite order script (not for **ed**)
     -h   Use for files of "unlimited" length

DU — Summarize Disk Usage   291

$ **du** [-s] [-a] [*name*]...
     Disk usage for directory or file *name*.
Options:
     -s   Total number of blocks for all files
     -a   Display an entry for each file

ECHO — Echo Arguments   271

$ **echo** [-n] [*arg*]...
     Writes its arguments separated by blanks and
ends in newline unless -n option is used.

FILE — Determine File Type   297

$ **file** *file*...
     Classify the type of *file*.

FIND — Find Files   195

$ **find** *pathname-list... condition...*
     Recursively search each directory in
pathname-list to find files which meet the
specified *conditions*.
Options:
     -name *filename*
          Specify *filename*.

-type *c*
     Specify file type:
          b   Block special file
          c   Character file
          d   Directory
          f   Plain file
-links *n*
     Number of links to file
-user *uname*
     File owner *uname*
-group *gname*
     Group name *gname*
-size *n*
     File size in blocks
-atime *n*
     Last accessed day *n*
-mtime *n*
     Last modified day *n*
-exec *command*
     Execute the *command* for the file meeting
     the above conditions
-ok *command*
     Execute the *command* only on response "y"
-print
     Display the file pathname
-newer *file*
     File modified more recently than *file*

Note: For the conditions above, the argument *n* refers to
a decimal integer. Specify +*n* to mean "more than *n*",
-*n* to mean "less than *n*", or *n* to mean "exactly *n*".
Each option must be preceded with a minus sign, and
can be specified in any order. If more than one option is
specified, files will be selected which fulfill all of the
criteria simultaneously (logical AND condition) unless
the condition follows the OR operator (-o).

GREP — Search a File for a Pattern   339

$ **grep** *-options pattern file ...*
     Find lines in *file* matching *pattern*.

Options:
     -v   Variant: all lines *except* matches
     -c   Count of matching lines
     -l   List of filenames containing *pattern*
     -n   Line number of lines which match
     -h   Header display suppressed
     -y   Lower-case *pattern* will match uppercase
                        letters in the input
     -e *pattern*   Used in case *pattern* begins with "-"

KILL — Terminate a Process   280

$ **kill** *number*...
     Terminate process *number*.

LN — Make Link   206

$ **ln** *name1* [*name2*]

Make link to *name1*, naming it *name2*, or use the last component of *name1* file pathname if *name2* is omitted.

LPR — Line Printer Spooler   213

$ **lpr** *-options file...*

Put *file* in line printer queue.

Options:

-r	Remove *file* after placing in queue
-c	Make copy of *file* for queue
-m	Report by *mail* when printed
-n	Do not report by *mail* (default case)

LS — List Contents of Directory   217

$ **ls** [-ltasdru] *name . . .*

List contents of directory and information on files.

Options:

-l	Long format
-t	Sort by modification time
-a	List all entries
-s	Size in blocks
-d	Directory status information
-r	List in reverse order
-u	Sort by last access time

MAIL — Send or Receive Electronic Mail Among Users   132

$ **mail** *loginname...*

Sends a message to *loginname*.

$ **mail** [-rpq] [-f *file*]

Reads each message in your "mailbox."

Options:

-r	Reverse ordering to first-in, first-out
-q	Exit after an interrupt
-p	Print entire mailbox
-f *file*	Print *file* as if it were a mail file

Disposition of messages:

<CR>	Go to next message
d	Delete the last message
p	Print message again
-	Go back to previous message

s [*file*]...

Saves messages in *file*
(mbox if no *file* named)

w [*file*]...

Same as **s**, only no header is supplied

m [*loginname*] ...

Mails the message to *loginname*

^D	Exit mail
q	Exit mail
x	Exit mail
!*command*	Execute shell *command*
?	Print this command summary

MAN — Print On-Line UNIX Programmer's Manual   149

$ **man** *-options section title ...*

Locates and displays the pages of the *UNIX Programmer's Manual* named *title* in the specified *section*.

Options:

-t	Phototypesets the section using **TROFF**
-n	Prints the section on the standard output using **NROFF**
-e	Use with **-t** or **-n** to preprocess by **neqn** or **eqn**; **-e** alone means **-te**
-w	Pathname to manual section

MESG — Permit or Deny Messages   140

$ **mesg** [-n] [-y]

Report (no option) or set non-user write permission on terminal.

Options:

n	Deny non-user write permission (cannot **write** to you)
y	Enable non-user write permission

MKDIR — Make a Directory   227

$ **mkdir** *dirname ...*

Create directories in your current directory.

MV — Move or Rename Files and Directories   230

$ **mv** *file1 file2.*

Change name of *file1* to *file2*.

$ **mv** *file.. dirname*

Move one or more files to the directory *dirname*.

$ **mv** *dirname newdirname*

Rename the directory *dirname* to *newdirname*.

PASSWD — Change Login Password   129

$ **passwd**

Change your password for logging into the UNIX system.

PR — Print File with Pagination   235

$ **pr** *-options file...*

Formatted printing of *file...*

Options:

-n	Produce *n*-column output
+n	Start printing at page *n*
-**h** *"title line"*	Customized page header *title line*

-w*n*	Page width *n*
-l*n*	Page length *n*
-t	No header printed
-s*c*	Separate column with character c
-m	Print all *files* in multiple columns

PS — Process Status   301

$ ps [-aklx] *process number...*

Print information about active processes.

Options:

-a	For all processes
-k	Used for post-mortem system debugging
-l	Long listing of information
-x	Include info for non-terminal processes

PWD — Print Working Directory   306

$ pwd

Display the full pathname of your current directory.

RM — Remove Files or Directories   242

$ rm [-fri] *file...*

Remove one or more files.

Options:

-f	Force removal of write-protected files
-r	Recursively delete directory
-i	Interactively delete with query

$ rmdir *emptydir*

Remove the empty directory *emptydir*.

SORT — Sort or Merge Files   317

$ sort [-bdfmnrutx] [+*pos1*] [-*pos2*] [-o*fileout*] *filein...*

Sort lines of *filein...* into *fileout*.

Options:

-b	Ignore leading blanks and tabs
-d	Dictionary order
-f	Ignore case distinction
-m	Merge the files
-n	Sort on first numeric field
-r	Reverse order of sort
-u	Eliminate duplicate lines
-c	Check if sorted
-t*x*	Field separator is x

A field is defined as a non-empty, non-blank string separated from other strings by blanks. The notation +*pos1* -*pos2* limits the sort key to a field beginning with *pos1* and ending just before *pos2*. Each *pos1* and *pos2* can be expressed as *m.n* where *m* is the number of fields to skip from the beginning of the line and *n* is the number of characters to skip further. A missing .*n* means .0 and a missing -*pos2* means the end of the line.

SPELL — Find Spelling Errors   345

$ spell -*options* [*file*]...

Display words in *file* not in spelling dictionary.

Options:

-v	Display all non-matches
-b	British spelling checked
-x	Print stem

STTY — Set Terminal Options   308

$ stty [*option...*]

Report setting of options or set options.

Options:

even/-even	Enable/disable even parity
odd/-odd	Enable/disable odd parity
raw/-raw	Enable/disable raw mode
cbreak	Read character at a time
-cbreak	Read line at a time
nl	Accept only newlines to end line
-nl	Accept cr-lf to end line
echo/-echo	Echo/do not echo back characters
lcase	Map upper case to lower case
-lcase	Do not map case
tabs	Preserve tabs
-tabs	Replace tabs by spaces
ek	Reset erase and kill characters
erase c	Set erase character to c
kill c	Set kill character to c
cr0 cr1 cr2 cr3	Carriage return delay
nl0 nl1 nl2 nl3	Newline delay
tab0 tab1 tab2 tab3	Tab delay
ff0 ff1	Form feed delay
bs0 bs1	Backspace delay
tty33	Mode for Teletype 33
tty37	Mode for Teletype 37
vt05	Mode for DEC VT05
tn300	Mode for GE TermiNet 300
ti700	Mode for TI 700
tek	Mode for Tektronix 4014
hup	Hang up dataphone on last close
0	Hang up phone immediately
50 75 110 134 150 200 300 600 1200 1800 2400 4800 9600	Set baud rate

TAIL — Deliver the Last Part of a File   247

$ tail [±*number units*] *file*

Copy the *file* to stdout +*number units* from beginning or -*number units* from end.

Units:
-l	Lines (default)
-b	512-byte blocks
-c	Characters

TEE — Pipe Fitting   285

$ **tee** [**-i**] [**-a**] *file...*
Divert a copy of data to *file*.

Options:
-i	Ignore interrupt signals
-a	Append to *file*

TR — Translate Characters   257

$ **tr** [**-cds**] *string1* [*string2*]
Translate with substitution or deletion of characters.

Options:
-c	Complement of *string1*
-d	Delete characters in *string1*
-s	Squeeze option

TTY — Get Terminal Name   328

$ **tty**
Print pathname of user's terminal.

UNIQ — Remove Repeated Lines in a Sorted File   348

$ **uniq** [**-udc** [+*n*] [-*n*] *input* [*output*]
Remove repeated adjacent lines in *input* file when copying to *output*.

Options:
-u	Display lines not repeated in *input*
-d	Display one copy of repeated lines in *input*
-c	Precede each line by number of times repeated
-*n*	Ignore the first *n* fields
+*n*	Ignore the first *n* characters

A field is defined as a series of non-space, non-tab characters which are separated by spaces and tabs from one another.

WC — Word Count   357

$ **wc** [**-lwc**] *file...*
Count lines, words, and characters in *file*.

Options:
-l	Count lines
-w	Count words
-c	Count characters

WHO — Who is on the System   330

$ **who**
List on-line user's login name, terminal, and login time.

$ **who am I**
Lists your login name.

WRITE — Write to Another User   145

$ **write** *user* [*ttyname*]
Write to *user* on terminal *ttyname*.

INDEX

"The *User Guide to the UNIX System* Team"

Left to right: Denise Penrose, Associate Editor, Osborne/McGraw-Hill; Lynn Grasberg, Word Processing Assistant; Rebecca Thomas, Author; Joanne Clapp, Word Processing Supervisor; Jean Yates, Author.

ABOUT THE AUTHORS

REBECCA THOMAS is cofounder of Yates Ventures, a San Francisco-based firm specializing in UNIX-related market research and documentation. She is Vice President of Research and Development and takes a special interest in communications between CP/M and UNIX-based microcomputers. Rebecca Thomas received her Ph.D. from the University of California at Berkeley and is associated with that facility's Computing Services Department as a consultant on documentation projects. She has extensive experience at program conversion from other environments to UNIX, and specializes in interfacing hardware and software systems.

JEAN YATES is cofounder and President of Yates Ventures. She is a featured speaker at NCC, COMDEX, IEEE, and UNIX User Group meetings, among others, and is regarded in the industry as a top expert on UNIX and small systems. Yates has managed numerous major studies on markets and strategies in the software and small systems areas. She is a frequent contributor to the computer industry press. She was previously manager of Gnostic Concept's UNIX Information Service.

Other OSBORNE/McGraw-Hill Publications

An Introduction to Microcomputers: Volume 0 — The Beginner's Book
An Introduction to Microcomputers: Volume 1 — Basic Concepts, 2nd Edition
An Introduction to Microcomputers: Volume 3 — Some Real Support Devices
Osborne 4 & 8-Bit Microprocessor Handbook
Osborne 16-Bit Microprocessor Handbook
8089 I/O Processor Handbook
CRT Controller Handbook
68000 Microprocessor Handbook
8080A/8085 Assembly Language Programming
6800 Assembly Language Programming
Z80 Assembly Language Programming
6502 Assembly Language Programming
Z8000 Assembly Language Programming
6809 Assembly Language Programming
Running Wild — The Next Industrial Revolution
The 8086 Book
PET™ and the IEEE 488 Bus (GPIB)
PET™/CBM™ Personal Computer Guide, 2nd Edition
Business System Buyer's Guide
Osborne CP/M® User Guide
Apple II® User's Guide
Microprocessors for Measurement and Control
Some Common BASIC Programs
Some Common BASIC Programs — PET™/CBM™ Edition
Some Common BASIC Programs — Atari® Edition
Some Common BASIC Programs — TRS-80™ Level II Edition
Some Common BASIC Programs — Apple II® Edition
Practical BASIC Programs
Practical BASIC Programs — TRS-80™ Level II Edition
Practical BASIC Programs — Apple II® Edition
Payroll with Cost Accounting
Accounts Payable and Accounts Receivable
General Ledger
8080 Programming for Logic Design
6800 Programming for Logic Design
Z80 Programming for Logic Design
CBASIC™ User Guide
Science & Engineering Programs — Apple II® Edition
Interfacing to S-100/IEEE 696 Microcomputer